GUIDE TO PASSING THE EXPERIOR REAL ESTATE Exam

Rick Knowles
Consulting Editor

Dearborn™
Real Estate Education

While a great deal of care has been taken to provide accurate and current information, the ideas, suggestions, general principles and conclusions presented in this book are subject to local, state and federal laws and regulations, court cases and any revisions of same. The reader is thus urged to consult legal counsel regarding any points of law—this publication should not be used as a substitute for competent legal advice.

Senior Vice President and General Manager: Roy Lipner
Publisher: Evan M. Butterfield
Product Acquisitions and Research Analyst: Lisa Stanley
Senior Development Editor: Kristen Short
Production Manager: Bryan Samolinski
Senior Typesetter: Janet Schroeder
Creative Director: Lucy Jenkins

Library of Congress Cataloging-in-Publication Data
   Guide to passing the Experior real estate exam / consulting editor, Rick Knowles.
      p. cm.
   ISBN 0-7931- 4598-8
   1. Real estate agents—Licenses—United States—Examinations, questions, etc.
2. Real estate business—Licenses—United States—Examinations, questions, etc.
3. Real property—United States—Examinations, questions, etc.   I. Knowles, Rick.

HD278.G84 2002
333.33'0973—dc21   2002025971

Table of Contents

Acknowledgments

This work is dedicated to my first and only wife who has made my life complete. To my daughter who has shown me that there is a bright future. To my parents who were part of the "Greatest Generation" who taught me that anything is possible with hard work if you do it honestly and with integrity.

My thanks to my present and former staff members who helped me finish this project: Amy, Annette, Racheal and Linda.

I also thank the following reviewers for their advice, comments and suggestions:

- Ken Trussell, Continuing Education for Licensing, Inc. (CELI) and Texas A&M University: Commerce

- Judy Wolk, Charleston Trident Association of REALTORS®

—Rick Knowles

■ ■ ■ ■ ■

About the
Consulting Editor

The publisher would like to express special appreciation to Consulting Editor, Rick Knowles for his professionalism, expertise and guidance in preparing this textbook. Mr. Knowles is a real estate broker, owner of Capital Real Estate Training Center and operations manager of Texas Tech University's Center for Professional Development HOME STUDY™ Real Estate Education program. Mr. Knowles also is an active member of the Real Estate Educators Association and 2002-2003 president of the Texas Real Estate Teachers Association.

Introduction

So you want to get a real estate license. You have completed your required education classes and now it is time for the last hurdle: *the state exam.*

■ ABOUT THE EXPERIOR REAL ESTATE EXAM

The Experior exam has been designed to test your basic real estate knowledge; none of the material in the exam should be new to you. Your state licensing department has hired Experior to administer the exam in order to identify candidates who have sufficient skills and knowledge to serve the interests of the public. Remember that the point of the exam is to protect the public!

The Experior exam is divided into two parts: (1) general or uniform real estate principles and practices and (2) state-specific law, rules and regulations. The general part of the exam varies from 75 questions to 95 questions, depending on the state. (Every exam will also include several "pretest" questions that will not be graded. These are questions that are being field tested.)

The general part of the exam requires an understanding of basic real estate principles and practices as well as the topics listed in the following outline. This outline is broken into eight content areas and identifies the percentage of questions for each content area. Generally speaking, the percentages are the same for salesperson exam and broker exam. What distinguishes the broker exam is question difficulty.

■ EXPERIOR EXAMINATION CONTENT OUTLINE (GENERAL THEORY/UNIFORM)

I. Business Practices and Ethics (15%)

A. Professional ethics

   1. Public and fiduciary responsibility

   2. Unlawful practice of law

B. Federal requirements for real estate activities

   1. Fair housing and antidiscrimination

   2. Violations of the Sherman Antitrust Act

   3. Advertising

C. Record keeping and document handling

II. Agency and Listing   (15%)

A. Principles of agency

1. Creating agency

2. Liabilities

3. Types and functions of agency

4. Roles and responsibilities of licensees

5. Terminating agency

6. Disclosing agency relationships

B. Types of listings

C. Listing procedures

1. Evaluating property

2. Disclosure of property conditions

3. Fraud and misrepresentations

D. Listing agreement

1. Legal requirements

2. Fiduciary duties and representations

3. Terminating listing

III. Property Characteristics, Descriptions,   (15%)
Ownership, Interests and Restrictions

A. Characteristics of property

1. Legal description of property

2. Interpreting physical and economic characteristics of property

3. Real and personal property

B. Ownership and estates in land

1. Title

2. Types of ownership

3. Types of estates

C. Government restrictions

1. The four governmental powers (police power, eminent domain, escheat, taxation)

2. Environmental regulations and disclosures

3. Water rights

D. Private restrictions

1. Voluntary and involuntary liens

2. Covenants, conditions and restrictions

3. Other encumbrances

IV. Property Valuation and the Appraisal Process   (10%)

A. Principles of valuation

1. Value, price and cost

2. Characteristics of property that affect value

3. Principles of value

B. Determining value

1. Direct sales comparison (market data) approach

2. Cost approach

3. Income approach

C. Appraisal

1. Purpose and use of appraisal

2. Role of appraiser

3. Role of licensee in property valuation

V. Real Estate Sales Contracts   (15%)

A. Purpose, scope and elements of real estate sales contracts

B. Offers and counteroffers

1. Purpose of offer and counteroffer

2. Valid methods of communicating offers

C. Earnest money

D. Completion, termination, breach

VI. Financing Sources   (10%)

A. Essentials of financing

1. Mortgages, deeds of trust and their provisions

B. Qualifying buyer for financing

1. Prequalifying considerations

2. Loan repayment

C. Types of financing

1. Loan programs, their benefits and requirements

2. Financing methods

D. Foreclosure and alternatives (deed in lieu of foreclosure, equitable and statutory rights of redemption)

E. Pertinent laws and regulations

1. Truth-in-Lending Act and Regulation Z

2. Equal Credit Opportunity Act

3. Fair Credit Reporting Act

VII. Closing/Settlement and Transferring Title   **(15%)**

    A. Settlement statement and other critical documents

    B. Closing/settlement

        1. Purpose of closing/settlement

        2. Legal requirements (includes RESPA)

    C. Transferring title

        1. Methods of transfer (includes deeds)

        2. Recording title

    D. Title insurance

        1. Purpose and scope of title insurance

        2. Essentials of title insurance

VIII. Property Management   **(5%)**

    A. Leases, estates, tenancies

    B. Property manager and owner relationships

    C. Laws affecting property management

■ PREPARING FOR THE EXPERIOR EXAM

While everyone has a different philosophy on how to prepare for an exam, it is safe to assume that everyone has the same goal: to pass the exam the first time. Passing the Experior exam requires commitment, focus and, above all, a thorough understanding of real estate principles. Here are some suggestions for preparing the Experior exam:

- PLAN the time in which you will study or prepare. You have a basic idea of how much time you have to study. Pace your study times. For example, establish a timeframe in which you will master the concepts of the first Experior content area, Business Practices and Ethics. Then establish a timeframe for the next content area, Agency and Listing, and so on.

- RE-REVIEW your prelicensing course materials and identify areas that were difficult for you. If you are having trouble with a specific topic, talk to someone who can help you clarify it.

- STUDY KEY TERMS. The content outlines in chapters 2 through 9 and the glossary at the back of the text provide you with brief and concise key term definitions. Review these terms carefully. Flashcards, which you can make yourself, are an excellent study tool to help you remember key term definitions.

- ANSWER QUIZ QUESTIONS. This text has eight Chapters that correspond to the major content areas of the general or uniform part of the Experior exam. Each Chapter contains a quiz that consists of dozens of sample questions. Knowing the definitions will help, but sometimes you will also be asked to *apply* the definitions to a described situation. The questions in each quiz allow you the opportunity to practice, practice and practice some more.

- TAKE A SAMPLE EXAM. This text has four mini-review exams, two sample salesperson exams and two sample broker exams. Set a timer and practice 20 questions to 45 questions at a time. Grade yourself and read the rationales—especially for the ones you answered incorrectly. Again, treat the sample exams as true exams: Set the timer, pace yourself, and don't look at the Answer Key until you are finished!

■ EXAM-TAKING STRATEGIES

On examination day, the most important tip is to read the question that is being asked. This is where many people get into trouble. It sometimes helps to cover the answers while you read the question and think about the concept that you are asked to consider. Many times you can eliminate two of the answers as being obviously wrong; you then are asked to select the *most* correct answer. This is when knowing definitions really helps. You must select the answer that is **MOST** correct.

It is useful to go through the exam at least three times. The first time, you want to read every questions and answer those that you are sure about. You are sharpest during the first hour of the exam, so try to get to the last question during that time. Mark the items about which you are unsure; you can come back to them later. If you are nervous about math, then as soon as you see that it is a math question, mark it and move on.

It is important to NOT "ponder" a question. First, it is possible that your negative self-talk will take over: "you know that you should have studied more, well, you didn't in high school, or grade school, so you will just flunk this as you have other exams in the past..." Negative self-talk is destructive and self-defeating. No matter how long you sit and stare at the question, you will rarely come up with the answer. So mark it and move on.

It is entirely possible that a subsequent question will provide an answer for you, so be on the lookout. Some people take notes.

The second time through the test, read, ponder and answer only those questions that you marked the first time. Now you have plenty of time to do the math questions and to "prove" them.

The third time through, check every question but read only the question with the answer that you have indicated, and ask yourself, "Is this a true statement?" The third time through, you are looking for obvious wrong answers, not to second-guess yourself. You are also looking to see if you "read" too much into the question, or if you tried to "rewrite" the question. Sometimes, you may discover that you answered a question based on how you thought it should read, not on what was actually asked. A correct statement that answers the wrong question is still a wrong answer.

Most people agree that their first response is usually the best one. In other words, don't change an answer just to change an answer.

■ EXPERIOR QUESTION FORMAT

Most Correct

In most of the questions in the Experior exam, you are being asked to select the **MOST** correct answer. For example:

The method of describing land boundaries using terminal points and angles or directions and distances is the

(A) metes-and-bounds.
(B) perimeter.
(C) government survey.
(D) Torrens system.

(A) The correct answer is metes and bounds.

Negative Stem

In "negative" questions, you will find three correct answers, and you must select the answer that is **NOT** correct. In other words, the wrong answer is the right answer. You can identify those questions by the capitalized **NOT, LEAST,** etc. For example:

Which of the following is **NOT** an essential element of a sales contract?

(A) Legality of object
(B) Competent parties
(C) Consideration
(D) Acknowledgment

(D) An acknowledgment is **NOT** an essential element of a sales contract. A valid contract must be signed by competent parties, be for a legal objective and contain consideration. *(Notice that three of the responses are correct; you are being asked to find the incorrect item.)*

Sometimes it helps to treat the multiple-choice format as four True/False questions. If you can find a couple of false, or a couple of true answers, you usually don't have to know all of them to select the correct choice. Take the following question as an example:

A legal action brought by either party to force the other to live up of the terms of a contract is a

(A) lis pendens. *(False: Lis pendens is a pending lawsuit)*
(B) suit to quiet title. *(False: It's used to correct a cloud on the title)*
(C) suit for specific performance. *(Sounds good...)*
(D) suit for nonperformance. *(False: The legal action is FOR performance)*

(C) A suit for specific performance is filed by one of the parties to force the other party to perform.

Another tip: If you find two answers that are exactly the same, then you can eliminate both, because there is only one correct answer (e.g., chattel and personal property). Take the following question as an example:

Which of the following items is real property?

(A) Emblements *(belong to tenant, therefore not real)*
(B) Trade fixtures *(belong to tenant, therefore not real)*
(C) Built-in bookcases *(permanently attached)*
(D) Freestanding bookcases *(key word: freestanding, thus removable)*

(C) Built-in bookcases are real property. Notice that because both emblements and trade fixtures belong to the tenant, they can be eliminated.

Math Questions

The Experior exam will have between 8 percent and 12 percent of the total questions in the general theory exam section. That means there will only be 7 to 11 math questions.

Be careful on how you round the answer in a math problem. Different calculators may give a slightly different answer. As an example: If your calculation is 48.97 and you are sure you did the problem correctly, but the closest answer is 49, then go with 49.

In reviewing your answers for math questions, try to think of what the approximate answer should be. Just because your answer is one of the choices, it still may not be correct. Be sure to read the math question carefully to eliminate the unnecessary distracting information and to also ask, "What exactly am I supposed to calculate?" Sometimes we forget to do the last addition or the last subtraction.

Keep all of your work for one question in one place on your scratch paper. This makes going back later to check your work so much easier.

When you are really stuck on a question, eliminate as many of the choices as possible. Then, make your best guess and choose an answer. Do NOT leave any question unanswered. There is no penalty for guessing. There is always the chance you may "guess" the right answer. You are not given credit for any questions that have been answered incorrectly, left blank or that have more than one answer marked. Remember, also, that you do not receive any credit for answers on the scratch paper.

Calculations

When calculating, remember the following.

- Generally, round off numbers to the nearest whole number.

- Assume that there are 5,280 feet in a mile and 43,560 square feet in an acre.

- Remember the difference between linear and square footage/yardage.

- Base prorations on a banker's year, i.e., 360 days, unless otherwise indicated.

■ EXPERIOR EXAM POLICIES AND PROCEDURES

What To Bring to the Testing Center

For a complete list of required items for examination day, please consult your Candidate Information Brochure or Bulletin or visit Experior at www.experioronline.com. At the very least, you will need a government-issued photo identification (driver's license, passport, military ID, etc. **No one can be admitted without valid photo identification.** Some states also require showing a credit card.

Because the Experior exam is closed book, candidates are not allowed to bring any books or notes into the testing area. No portable or cellular phones, two-way radios or pagers may be brought into the examination room.

The testing center will provide the test, a Question Comment Form and a sheet of scratch paper. If you are taking a paper and pencil test, you will also be given a test booklet and answer sheet. If you are taking the exam on the computer, of course, you will not need these.

Scoring

When you complete your exam, Experior will provide you with a score report, which will indicate your overall score and grade. The score report also will show how well you performed in each content area of the exam.

You must pass each part of the exam independently of the other. In other words, if you pass one portion of the exam, but fail the other portion, you will have to retake and pass the failed portion of the exam within a time period specified by your state licensing department.

Scores will NOT be furnished to anyone other than the candidate, your state real estate commission and Experior. *No examination score will be given over the phone or transmitted by fax to anyone.*

Prohibited Conduct

Candidates discovered engaging in any kind of misconduct may be dismissed and will be reported to the state's real estate commission. Misconduct includes, but is not limited to:

- giving or receiving help on the exam;
- taking part in an act of impersonation, and
- removing exam materials from the testing center.

Here is a true story: An applicant was caught taking the scratch paper from the testing center. He was asked to return from the parking lot to the testing center. The scratch paper with several questions written down was found in the applicant's pocket. The applicant was referred to the state's real estate commission enforcement division. After a full hearing, the person's application for a real estate license was rejected. So, even though the applicant had attended prelicense class and had passed the license exam, the applicant was not eligible to receive a license.

All of the examination questions, each form of the examination and answer sheets are the copyrighted property of Experior. Any distribution of examination content or materials through any form of reproduction or oral or written communication is strictly prohibited and punishable by law.

Last But Not Least

Plan your exam day so you can arrive early. This allows you to complete any required paperwork at a calm and orderly pace. Listen to the instructions carefully and ask questions if you need help with the procedures. Remember, the exam site staff can answer questions about procedures but not about the exam questions themselves. Most states allow applicants to retake the license exam for a small fee, in the event they do not receive a passing score.

■ ■ ■ ■ ■
Real Estate Math

1

In the Experior exam, math questions account for 8 percent to 12 percent of the total questions in the general theory section. Depending on the total number of questions in the general theory section, this means that there will only be 5 to 11 math questions.

■ CONTENT AND QUIZ

To make the math review chapter easier to use, each content area will be followed immediately by one or more quiz questions.

■ THE FORMULA: PART = PERCENT × WHOLE

When dealing with real estate math, the formula **Part = Percent × Whole** will come in handy. You can use this formula to set up and solve several different types of problems on the licensing exam.

PART

The part represents a portion of the whole. In most of the problems, this number will be smaller than the whole. (The exception is appreciation problems.)

Examples: Agent's/broker's share of the commission
               Loan amount
               Annual interest
               Monthly payment
               Net income

PERCENT

The percent is a number usually expressed as a rate or ratio.

Examples: Commission split
               Loan-to-value ratio
               Interest rate
               Qualifying ratio
               Capitalization rates

WHOLE

The whole represents all of the item.

Examples: Total commission
Sales price
Loan amount
Gross monthly income
Gross rent

HELPFUL HINTS!

- To find the Part, **MULTIPLY** the Percent by the Whole.

- To find the Percent, **DIVIDE** the Part by the Whole.

- To find the Whole, **DIVIDE** the Part by the Percent.

Example: The buyer has a lender who charges a 1% loan origination fee. The buyer will put 10% down on a $100,000 home. What is the dollar amount of the origination fee?

Solution: Loan Amount (Part) = LTV (Percent) × Sales Price (Whole)

The problem did not give us the loan amount, but we were given the information to find the loan amount.

Loan Amount (Part) = 90% (Percent) ([100% − 10% Down Payment]) × $100,000 (Whole)
Loan Amount (Part) = $90,000

Now we can find the origination fee.

Origination Fee Amount (Part) = Origination Percentage (Percent) × Loan Amount (Whole)
Origination Fee Amount (Part) = 1% (Percent) × $90,000 (Whole)
Origination Fee (Part) = $900.00

Now let's look at this problem in a different way. What is the sales price if the lender charges a 1% origination fee of $900 and the buyer has a 10% down payment?

Solution: Part = Percent × Whole
$900 (Part) = 1% (Percent) × Loan Amount (Whole)

We need to have all of the known numbers on the same side of the = sign. When we move the percent, the calculation now is reversed.

$900 (Part) ÷ 1% (Percent) = $90,000 (Whole)
$90,000 (Part) = 90% (Percent) × Sales Price (Whole)
$90,000 (Part) ÷ 90% (Percent) = $100,000 (Whole)

■ INTEREST

Interest is the fee lenders charge for the use of their money. It is always expressed as an annual rate.

Annual Interest = Annual Interest Rate × Loan Amount

1. A person borrows $4,400, agreeing to pay back principal and interest in 14 months. If the total payback is $5,170, what annual interest rate was charged?

   (A) 14.8%   (C) 17.5%
   (B) 15.0%   (D) 18.0%

2. A $90,000 30-year fixed-rate loan at 8% interest has monthly principal and interest payments of $835.55. What is the loan balance after the first payment?

   (A) $82,800.00   (C) $89,764.45
   (B) $89,164.45   (D) $89,400.00

3. A lender has agreed to make a $100,000 loan at 11% interest. Calculate the amount of interest if the note is repaid in nine months.

   (A) $ 110.00   (C) $ 8,250.00
   (B) $1,222.22   (D) $11,000.00

■ COMMISSIONS

When you sell or lease a property, your compensation is often paid in the form of a commission expressed as a percentage of the sales price or lease.

Commission = Commission Rate × Sales Price
Share = Commission Split × Commission

4. A salesperson is to receive 60% of all commissions he generates. If the property is listed for $175,000 and the broker charges a 7% commission and the salesperson sells the property for $160,000, what is the salesperson's share?

   (A) $1,120   (C) $6,720
   (B) $1,125   (D) $7,350

5. If a salesperson's commission is 3% and houses are selling for $90,000 each, how many houses must the salesperson sell to earn at least $42,000?

   (A) 8.0   (C) 15.5
   (B) 15.0   (D) 16.0

6. A salesperson receives a commission of $3,125 as half of the total commission. The sales price of the property is $125,000. What rate of commission did the broker charge?

   (A) 2.5%   (C) 5.0%
   (B) 3.0%   (D) 6.0%

■ NET TO OWNER

From time to time, a seller may say he or she wants to "net" a certain amount on the sale of the property after expenses.

Net to Owner + Expenses = 100% − Commission Rate × Sales Price ÷ List Price

7. An owner wishes to net $75,000 on the sale of his property and has agreed to pay the broker a 5% commission. If the owner has allowed $3,125 for closing costs and $1,200 for repairs, at what price must the property sell?

(A) $79,325.00   (C) $83,291.25
(B) $83,075.00   (D) $83,500.00

8. A property listed for $135,000 and sold for $2,000 below that price. The owner has allowed $2,500 for repairs and has agreed to pay the broker a 6.75% commission. How much will the owner net on the sale of the property?

(A) $ 11,477.50   (C) $123,522.50
(B) $121,522.50   (D) $124,022.50

■ TAXES

Taxing entities use the ad valorem system to assess property taxes. *Ad valorem* means according to value.

Annual Taxes = Tax Rate × Assessed Value

9. The assessed value of a property is $80,000. If city taxes are $.80 per hundred, county taxes are $.75 per hundred and school taxes are $1.25 per hundred of assessed value, how much are the annual taxes on the property?

(A) $ 186.67   (C) $2,800.00
(B) $2,240.00   (D) $2,857.00

In some states the property taxes are calculated using a concept called *mills*. As an example: If the tax rate is 48 MILLS, then the tax rate is .048 of the taxable value.

10. A property has a tax value of $100,000 with a mill rate of 50. What are the annual taxes?

(A) $ 500.00   (C) $5,000.00
(B) $1,500.00   (D) $6,500.00

■ PROFIT AND LOSS

Profit or loss is the difference between the cost and the sales price of a property.

Profit = % Profit × Cost

11. An owner originally purchased a property for $25,500 and recently sold it for $54,825. What percentage profit was made on the sale?

   (A) 46.51   (C) 115.00
   (B) 53.49   (D) 215.00

12. A person buys a property for $75,000 and wants to realize an 8% profit on the original investment after paying a 6% commission. The property must sell for at least

   (A) $76,500.   (C) $85,860.
   (B) $85,787.   (D) $86,170.

■ APPRECIATION/DEPRECIATION

Appreciation is the increase in the value or worth of a property while depreciation is a loss in value. (Remember: in appreciation problems the part is larger than the whole.)

Present Value = 100% + Rate of Appreciation × Original Value
Present Value = 100% − Rate of Depreciation × Original Value

13. A property had an average depreciation of 5% each year over the last five years. It recently sold for $85,500. What was the original value?

   (A) $89,775   (C) $106,875
   (B) $90,000   (D) $114,000

14. Four years ago an investor purchased a house and lot for $95,500. Of the total, the value of the lot was $25,000 and the value of the house was $70,500. Using the straight-line method, assuming an average appreciation of 6% on the lot and an average depreciation of 4% on the house, what is the current value of the property?

   (A) $67,280   (C) $ 94,180
   (B) $90,220   (D) $118,420

■ QUALIFYING

Qualifying is the process of determining either the maximum monthly payment or maximum sales price a prospect can afford.

Loan Amount = Loan-to-Value × Sales Price Ratio

Loan Amount ÷ 1,000 × Factor = PI
OR
[PI x 1,000] ÷ Factor = Loan Amount

PI(TI) = Qualifying Ratio × Gross Monthly Income

15. A husband has annual income of $55,000 and his wife has monthly income of $3,300. If a lender is using a 28% ratio, what is the maximum monthly payment these buyers can afford?

(A) $1,632.40   (C) $2,648.80
(B) $2,207.33   (D) $4,583.33

16. A husband and wife have located a lender who is willing to make a 90% loan on a $115,000 home. The loan is a 30-year fixed-rate conventional loan at 8% interest. Monthly payments will be based on a factor of $7.34 per thousand of the loan amount. Taxes are $1,500 annually and the annual hazard insurance is ½ of 1% of the loan amount. How much must the couple earn each month to qualify if the lender is using a 28% ratio?

(A) $2,700   (C) $3,500
(B) $3,314   (D) $5,008

17. A prospective buyer with a gross annual income of $65,000 is planning to use a lender using a 33% ratio. The loan will be a 30-year fixed rate mortgage at 10% and monthly payments will be based on a factor of $8.78 per thousand. Property taxes and hazard insurance will not exceed $350 per month. If the buyer can make a 15% down payment, what is the sales price of the most expensive home he or she can afford? (Round to the nearest $100.)

(A) $109,100   (C) $203,600
(B) $192,600   (D) $239,500

■ CLOSING

The down payment a purchaser must make is the difference between the sales price and the amount the lender is willing to lend (loan-to-value ratio).

$$\text{Down Payment} = \% \text{ Down} \times \text{Sales Price}$$

18. A lending institution has agreed to make an 80% loan on a $125,900 sales price. The prospective buyers have put down $9,500 as earnest money and must pay three discount points and a 1 point loan origination fee. How much in additional funds must the buyers bring to closing?

(A) $19,708.80   (C) $29,208.00
(B) $20,716.00   (D) $30,216.00

■ PRORATIONS

At the closing of a real estate transaction, certain items will be prorated (divided) between the buyer and seller based on the length of time each has owned or will own the property. Generally speaking, the following rules apply:

- Banker's/statutory year = 360 days with 30 days in each month.

- Calendar year = 365 days with actual number days in each month.

- Mortgage payments are due on the first day of the month.

- Assessed value is the taxable value of the property. Until the taxing authority has established the tax value, you would use the sales price to estimate the taxes.

- Some states allow what is called an *equalization factor*. The assessed value is multiplied by the equalization factor to determine the value for tax purposes.

- Taxes are paid annually.

- Seller is charged for the day of closing unless agreed by the parties or specified differently by state law.

- Interest and taxes are paid in arrears.

- Debit the seller and credit the buyer the same amount, and vice versa.

- Rent is paid in advance.

- Credit the buyer for the time he or she will own the property.

19. Using a statutory year, prorate the ad valorem taxes for a property that was purchased on July 13, 2001 for $86,400. The assessed value of the property was $84,600 and the combined tax rate was $1.83 per hundred of assessed value. Taxes for the year 2000 were paid.

    (A) Debit the buyer $830.00; credit the seller $718.18.
    (B) Debit the seller $830.00; credit the buyer the same.
    (C) Debit the buyer $847.66; credit the seller the same.
    (D) Debit the seller $847.66; credit the buyer the same.

20. Using a 365-day year, prorate the interest for a closing on April 13. The buyer is assuming the seller's 9.5% loan with an existing balance of $85,458.27.

    (A) Debit the buyer and credit the seller $289.15.
    (B) Debit the seller and credit the buyer $289.15.
    (C) Debit the buyer and credit the seller $400.32.
    (D) Debit the seller and credit the buyer $400.32.

21. Using a 365-day year, prorate the taxes for a house that sold on October 9 for $112,500 and closed on April 13. The assessed value of the property is $112,000 and the tax rate is $2.18 per hundred.

    (A) Debit the buyer and credit the seller $689.07.
    (B) Debit the seller and credit the buyer $689.07.
    (C) Debit the seller and credit the buyer $752.61.
    (D) Debit the buyer and credit the seller $1,752.61.

22. A buyer is purchasing a duplex that rents for $650 per side per month. All rents have been paid for the month of June. Prorate this item using a 360-day year with 30 days in each month for a closing on June 16, if the buyer and seller have agreed to split rent for the day of closing.

    (A) Credit the buyer and debit the seller $628.29.
    (B) Credit the seller and debit the buyer $628.29.
    (C) Debit the seller and credit the buyer $671.67.
    (D) Debit the buyer and credit the seller $671.67.

■ INVESTMENT AND INCOME

23. A tenant has signed a percentage lease on a 25-foot by 50-foot space in a retail center. The tenant has agreed to pay $.55 per square foot per month, plus 5% of gross monthly sales in excess of $7,500. How much rent would the tenant pay if gross monthly sales are $12,500?

(A) $ 937.50   (C) $1,312.50
(B) $1,062.00   (D) $5,000.00

24. What is the gross rent multiplier if the sales price is $70,000, the gross monthly rent is $525 and the monthly expenses are $125?

(A) .0006   (C) 133.3300
(B) .0008   (D) 175.0000

25. Assume that three rental buildings had sales prices and rents as follows: $107,250 and $16,500; $105,625 and $16,250; and $112,125 and $17,250. What would the value of a similar building be if rents are $16,750?

(A) $107,250   (C) $108,875
(B) $108,300   (D) $112,125

■ APPRAISAL

26. A ten-year-old well-maintained 3,000 square foot house with a 350 square foot garage sits on a lot currently valued at $10,000. The current reproduction cost of the house is $45 per square foot and the current reproduction cost of the garage is $25 per square foot. The house has an economic life of 30 years. What is the current value of the property?

(A) $ 5,833   (C) $135,000
(B) $105,833   (D) $143,750

■ MEASUREMENT PROBLEMS

Common measurement formulas include the following:

Length × Width = Area of rectangle or square
½ Base × Height = Area of a triangle
Length × Width × Height = Volume

Common conversions include:

9 square feet = 1 square yard
27 cubic feet = 1 cubic yard
640 acres = 1 section
5,280 feet = 1 mile
43,560 square feet = 1 acre

27. A rectangular lot 1,000 feet wide contains 5,363 square yards. What is the length?

    (A) 5.36 ft.   (C) 48,267.00 ft.
    (B) 48.27 ft.   (D) 53,630.00 ft.

28. A 1¾ acre rectangular lot was 180 feet deep and sold for $78 per front foot. What was the sales price?

    (A) $14,040.00   (C) $59,459.40
    (B) $33,033.00   (D) $76,230.00

29. An owner wants to build a sidewalk on the front of his lot that is 150 feet long and 65 feet wide. The sidewalk will be four feet wide and three inches thick. What will the total cost be if concrete costs $35 per cubic yard and labor is $12.50 per square foot?

    (A) $1,007.00   (C) $3,334.35
    (B) $1,396.00   (D) $3,503.53

30. An investor purchased a vacant lot with 40 feet of frontage at $2,250 per front foot and arranged with a contractor to erect a structure 40 feet long, 25 feet wide and 15 feet high for $3.25 per cubic foot. What is the total cost of the project?

    (A) $ 1,805.56   (C) $ 91,805.56
    (B) $90,000.00   (D) $138,750.00

31. An owner purchased a lot that was 110′ wide by 160′ long. There was a 20′ easement around the perimeter of the lot and a 20′ wide road that ran lengthwise through the center of the lot. The owner has constructed 8′ high miniwarehouses that generate gross income of $115,000 per year. How much is his or her income per cubic foot per month?

    (A) $ .20   (C) $5.01
    (B) $2.40   (D) $9.57

32. A 6-unit apartment house has two apartments paying monthly rental of $300 each, two paying $350 monthly rental each and two paying $400 monthly rental each. Annual expenses are $7,550. What is the owner's gross annual income on this property?

    (A) $2,100.00   (C) $17,650.00
    (B) $8,650.00   (D) $25,200.00

33. A subdivider has purchased a three-acre parcel. Before dividing the parcel, the subdivider must build a road 30 feet wide and 252 feet long. How many lots will the subdivider be able to create with the remaining land if each lot measures 65 feet by 130 feet?

    (A) 4 lots   (C) 15 lots
    (B) 14 lots   (D) 139 lots

34. A 2.5 acre parcel of land is to be subdivided and sold. If ⅖ of the parcel is too hilly, ¼ of the parcel is taken up by a stream and 15% is reserved for a park, how many acres are left?

    (A) .5 acres   (C) .9 acres
    (B) .7 acres   (D) 1.6 acres

35. How many acres are there in the NW¼ of the NW¼ of the SE¼ of Section T4N?

    (A) 2.5   (C)   10.0
    (B) 5.0   (D) 43,560.0

36. A residential lot 70 frontage feet by 120 feet deep has a 14 foot setback from the street and 10 foot mandatory side yards. What percentage of the lot is usable?

(A) 33   (C) 63
(B) 37   (D) 67

■ ANSWER KEY WITH EXPLANATIONS

Interest

1. (B) The annual interest rate charged was 15%.
   [$5,170 – $4,400] ÷ 14 = $55 interest per month
   $55 × 12 = $660 annual interest
   $660 ÷ $4,400 = .15 or 15 percent

2. (C) The loan balance after the first payment was $89,764.45.
   $90,000 × 8% = $7,200
   $7,200 ÷ 12 = $600 interest
   $835.55 – $600 = $235.55 applied to principal
   $90,000 – $235.55 = $89,764.45

3. (C) The amount of interest is $8,250.00.
   $100,000 × 11% = $11,000 annual interest
   $11,000 ÷ 12 = $916.67 monthly interest
   $916.67 × 9 = $8,250 interest for nine months

Commissions

4. (C) The salesperson's share is $6,720.
   $160,000 × 7% = $11,200 total commission earned by broker
   $11,200 × 60% = $ 6,720 earned by salesperson

5. (D) The salesperson must sell 16 houses.
   $90,000 × 3% = $2,700
   $42,000 ÷ $2,700 = 15.56 or 16 houses

6. (C) The commission rate is 5%.
   [$3,125 × 2] ÷ $125,000 = .05 or 5%

Net to Owner

7. (D) The house must sell for $83,500.00.
   $75,000 + $3,125 + $1,200 = $79,325 total net required
   $79,325 ÷ .95 = $83,500

8. (B) The owner will net $121,522.50.
   [$135,000 – $2,000] = $133,000 actual sale price
   $133,000 × 93.25% – $2,500 = $121,522.50 seller's net after expenses

Taxes

9. (B) The annual taxes are $2,240.00.
   $80,000 × .80 ÷ 100 = $ 640
   $80,000 × .75 ÷ 100 = $ 600
   $80,000 × 1.25 ÷ 100 = $1,000
   Total = $2,240

10. (C) The annual taxes are $5,000.00.
   Move the decimal three spaces to the left before multiplying mills
   $100,000 × .05 = $5,000

Profit and Loss

11. (C) The percentage profit was 115.00.
    $54,825 – $25,500 = $29,325
    $29,325 ÷ $25,500 = 1.15 or 115%

12. (D) The property must sell for at least $86,170.
    $75,000 × 108% = $81,000 (original investment plus 8% profit)
    $81,000 ÷ 94% = $86,170 sale price to realize desired net

Appreciation/Depreciation

13. (D) The original value was $114,000.
    5% × 5 years = 25% depreciation, so today's value is 75% of the original value
    $85,500 ÷ .75 = $114,000

14. (B) The current value is $90,220.
    $25,000 × 124% = $31,000
    70,500 × 84% = $59,220
    31,000 + 59,220 = $90,220

Qualifying

15. (B) The maximum payment they can afford is $2,207.33.
    $55,000 ÷ 12 = $4,583.33
    $4,583.33 + 3,300 = $7,883.33
    $7,883.33 × 28% = $2,207.33

16. (B) The couple must earn $3,314 each month.
    $115,000 × 90% = $103,500 loan amount
    $103,500 × 7.34 ÷ 1,000 = $759.69 monthly P&I payment
    $1,500 ÷ 12 = $125 monthly taxes
    $103,500 × .50% ÷ 12 = $43.125 monthly insurance
    [$759.69 + $125 + $43.125] ÷ 28% = $3,313.64 or $3,314

17. (B) The most expensive house they can afford is $192,600.
    $65,000 ÷ 12 = $5,416.67
    $5,416.67 × 33% = $1,787.50 allowed for PITI
    $1,787.50 – $350 = $1,437.50 PI portion
    $1,437.50 ÷ 8.78 × 1,000 = $163,724.37 loan amount
    $163,724.37 ÷ .85 = $192,616.91 sale price rounded to the nearest $100 = $192,600

Closing

18. (A) They must bring $19,708.80 more to the closing.
    Credits and debits must balance:

CREDIT	DEBIT
$100,720.00 (loan)	$125,900.00
+ 9,500.00 (earnest money)	+ 4,028.80
$110,220.00	$129,928.80
$ 19,708.80 (bring to closing)	
$129,928.80	$129,928.80

Prorations

19. (B) Debit the seller $830.00; credit the buyer the same.
    $84,600 ÷ 100 × 1.83 = $1,548.18
    $1,548.18 ÷ 360 = $4.3005 per day
    $4.3005 × 193 = $830

20. (B) Debit the seller and credit the buyer $289.15.
    $85,458.27 × 9.5% = $8,118.54 ÷ 365 × 13 = $289.15

21. (B) Debit the seller and credit the buyer $689.07.
$112,000 ÷ 100 × 2.18 = $2,441.60
$2,441.60 ÷ 365 = $6.69
6.69 × 103 = $689.07

22. (A) Credit the buyer and debit the seller $628.29.
$650 × 2 = $1,300
$1,300 ÷ 30 = $43.33
$43.33 × 14.5 = $628.29

Investment and Income
23. (A) The rent would be $937.50.
25 × 50 = 1,250
1,250 × $.55 = $687.50
$12,500 − $7,500 = $5,000
$5,000 × 5% = $250
$687.50 + $250 = $937.50

24. (C) The gross rent multiplier is 133.3300.
$70,000 ÷ 525 = 133.3300

25. (C) The value would be $108,875
$16,750 ÷ .15384615384 = $108,875

Appraisal
26. (B) The current value is $105,833.
3,000 × $45 = $135,000
350 × $25 = $8,750
[$135,000 + $8,750] × .66666666 + 10,000 = 105,833.33

Measurement Problems
27. (B) The length is 48.27 feet.
5,363 × 9 = 48,267
48,267 ÷ 1,000 = 48.27

28. (B) The sales price was $33,033.00.
43,560 × 1.75 = 76,230
76,230 ÷ 180 = 423.50
423.50 × $78 = $33,033

29. (C) The total cost will be $3,334.35.
65 × 4 = 260 sq. feet
65 × 4 × [3 ÷ 12] = 65 cubic feet
65 ÷ 27 = 2.41
2.41 × $35 = $84.35
260 × $12.50 = $3,250
$3,250 + $84.35 = $3,334.35

30. (D) The total cost is $138,750.00.
40 × $2,250 = $90,000
40 × 25 × 15 = 15,000 cubic feet
15,000 × $3.25 = $48,750
$90,000 + $48,750 = $138,750

31. (A) The income per cubic foot is $.20.
50 × 120 x 8 = 48,000
115,000 ÷ 48,000 ÷ 12 = .20

32. (D) The owner's gross annual income is $25,200.00. Be careful to note that the question asked for gross, not net, income.
$$[2 \times \$300] + [2 \times \$350] + [2 \times \$400] \times 12 = \$25,200$$

33. (B) The subdivider can create 14 lots.
$$43,560 \times 3 = 130,680$$
$$30 \times 252 = 7,560$$
$$130,680 - 7,560 = 123,120$$
$$123,120 \div [65 \times 130] = 14.57 \text{ or } 14 \text{ lots}$$

34. (A) There remain .5 acres.
$$2.5 \times 43,560 = 108,900$$
$$[2 \div 5] = .40$$
$$.40 + .25 + .15 = .80 \text{ unusable}$$
$$100 - .80 = .20$$
$$108,900 \times .20 = 21,780$$
$$21,780 \div 43,560 = .5$$

35. (C) There are 10 acres.
$$640 \div 4 \div 4 \div 4 = 10$$

36. (C) The usable portion of the lot is 63%.
$$106 \times 50 = 5,300$$
$$120 \times 70 = 8,400$$
$$5,300 \div 8,400 = 63\%$$

Business Practices and Ethics

2

■ ■ ■ ■ ■

■ **CONTENT OUTLINE**

I. Business Practices and Ethics

A. Professional ethics

1. Public and fiduciary responsibility—the purpose for the real estate license is to provide real estate consumers with professional and competent services. It also provides legal recourse to consumers when licensees fail to provide this level of service.

2. Unlawful practice of law—only a licensed attorney can give someone legal advice. A licensee may tell a consumer what he or she knows. However, if there is a legal consequence to the consumer, the agent needs to tell the consumer to contact an attorney before making a decision.

B. Federal requirements for real estate activities

1. Federal housing and antidiscrimination

a. The Civil Rights Act of 1866, as interpreted by *Jones v. Mayer*, prohibits all racial discrimination without exception. If there is a violation based on race that is not covered under the federal Fair Housing Act, the person must file suit in federal court.

b. Federal Fair Housing Act (Civil Rights Act of 1968)—prohibits discrimination on the basis of race, color, religion, national origin, sex, familial status and handicap in the sale or leasing of residential property. For violations not exempted under the federal Fair Housing Act, the person may file a complaint with HUD (the U.S. Department of Housing and Urban Development).

c. Illegal practices

(1) Steering—the channeling or directing of prospective buyers to or away from certain areas based on discriminatory criteria

(2) Blockbusting—inducing homeowners to sell by telling them of the entry or prospective entry of minorities into the neighborhood. Also known as panic selling

(3) Redlining—the illegal practice of a lending institution denying loans or restricting their number for certain areas of a community basing their decisions on race, color or national origin instead of financial reasons

d. Principal parts of the act prohibit:

    (1) Discrimination in the sale or rental of housing
    (2) Discrimination in the financing of housing
    (3) Discrimination in the provision of brokerage services

e. Exemptions (none, if broker is involved)

    (1) For sale by owner, if no discriminatory advertising used
    (2) Religious organizations, offering housing for its own members
    (3) Private clubs, not open to the public, giving preference to its members
    (4) Sale or rental of a single-family home under the following conditions:
        (a) Owner does not use the services of an agent or licensee.
        (b) Owner does not use discriminatory advertising.
        (c) Owner does not own more than three homes at one time and does not sell more than one every two years.
    (5) Rental of rooms or units in an owner-occupied one- to four-family dwelling

f. Enforcement

    (1) By civil action in a U.S. district court
    (2) By HUD administrative law judge with penalties ranging from up to
        (a) $10,000 for first offense
        (b) $25,000 for second offense within five years
        (c) $50,000 for further violations within seven years

2. Violations of Sherman Antitrust Act

    a. Joining competitors to fix prices for real estate services

    b. Joining with other companies to boycott a competitor

    c. Joining brokers in allocating customers

    d. Tying the sale of first product to purchase of a second

    e. Penalties

        (1) Maximum $100,000 fine and three years in prison
        (2) Corporations subjected to up to $1 million in penalties
        (3) In a successful lawsuit, triple damages, plus attorney's fees and court costs

3. Advertising

    a. Agents must maintain high ethics in their advertising.

    b. Agents may not place advertisements that are deceptive or misleading.

    c. No advertising of property for sale or rent may include language indicating a preference or limitation.

    d. Media used to advertise properties for sale or rent cannot target one population to the exclusion of others.

C. Record keeping and document handling—most states require licensees to maintain copies of all documents to all parties affected by them in their transactions.

■ QUIZ

1. The Civil Rights Act of 1866 prohibits discrimination in housing based on

   (A) race.   (C) sex.
   (B) religion.   (D) handicap.

2. The agency responsible for the enforcement of the Fair Housing Act is the

   (A) Department of Justice (DOJ).
   (B) Federal Housing Administration (FHA).
   (C) Department of Housing and Urban Development (HUD).
   (D) Department of Veterans Affairs (DVA).

3. It is illegal for a lending institution to refuse to make a residential real estate loan in a particular area if the sole reason to decline the loan is the

   (A) questionable economic situation of the applicant.
   (B) physical location of the property.
   (C) applicant not being of legal age.
   (D) deteriorated condition of the premises.

4. A discrimination suit may be filed in federal court by the

   (A) aggrieved person because of racial discrimination.
   (B) Department of Housing and Urban Development.
   (C) state or county nondiscrimination officer.
   (D) Federal Housing Administration.

5. The Federal Fair Housing Act does **NOT** prohibit

   (A) blockbusting.
   (B) discriminatory advertising.
   (C) redlining.
   (D) discriminating because of a cocaine addiction.

6. In order to file a complaint with HUD that an act of discrimination has occurred, the complainant must

   (A) be able to prove that discrimination occurred.
   (B) suspect that discrimination occurred.
   (C) be able to prove that the discrimination was intentional.
   (D) be able to produce witnesses to the discrimination.

7. The Fair Housing Act that expanded protection beyond housing receiving federal funds to all residential both public and private housing is contained in which of the following?

   (A) Title VIII of the Civil Rights Act of 1968
   (B) The Civil Rights Act of 1866
   (C) The Civil Rights Act of 1964
   (D) Executive Order No. 11063

8. A prospective homebuyer who is black inquires about the availability of a home in a predominately white residential neighborhood. What should the broker say to this prospect?

   (A) "You wouldn't want to live in this area because the neighbors are trying to protect the integrity of the area."
   (B) "I'd be happy to show you homes in other areas where blacks are welcome."
   (C) "The residents here have expressed a desire to keep the area homogeneous with no blacks."
   (D) "I'll be pleased to show you any houses that you're interested in."

9. Real estate brokers are **NOT** required to

   (A) take affirmative marketing action in advertising.
   (B) take affirmative marketing action in canvassing.
   (C) show all of the properties they have listed.
   (D) prominently display the equal housing opportunity poster.

10. Protection from threats or acts of violence against those who assist and encourage open housing rights is found in the

    (A) Civil Rights Act of 1866.
    (B) Civil Rights Act of 1964.
    (C) Fair Housing Act of 1968.
    (D) Fair Housing Amendments Act of 1988.

11. The provisions of the Fair Housing Act apply

    (A) in all states.
    (B) only in those states that have ratified the act.
    (C) only in those states that do not have substantially equivalent laws.
    (D) only in those states that do not have specific state fair housing laws.

12. The practice of channeling families with children away from other buildings into an apartment building where other families with children reside is

    (A) most practical.   (C) redlining.
    (B) blockbusting.   (D) steering.

13. Which of the following is legal under the fair housing laws?

    (A) Offering advantageous loan terms to encourage the re-segregation of a residential area
    (B) Refusing to show certain residential property to non-English-speaking individuals
    (C) Channeling members of a certain minority group into an area already predominately occupied by members of that minority
    (D) Refusing to show certain residential property to a person who is not financially qualified to purchase it

14. The refusal of a lending institution to make a residential real estate loan strictly because of the racial or ethnic composition of the neighborhood is called

    (A) blockbusting.   (C) steering.
    (B) redlining.   (D) panic peddling.

15. Discrimination based on familial status was prohibited with the passage of the

    (A) Civil Rights Act of 1866.
    (B) Civil Rights Act of 1964.
    (C) Fair Housing Act of 1968.
    (D) Fair Housing Amendments Act of 1988.

16. Which of the following would **NOT** be considered a basis for a discrimination complaint under the federal fair housing laws?

    (A) Ethnic considerations
    (B) Sexual considerations
    (C) Economic considerations
    (D) Religious considerations

17. Federal fair housing laws include certain exemptions. Which of the following is **NOT** exempt from federal fair housing laws?

    (A) Retirement communities
    (B) Private clubs
    (C) Religious organizations
    (D) Racial considerations

18. Steering is **BEST** defined as

    (A) leading prospective homeowners to or away from certain neighborhoods.
    (B) refusing to make loans on properties located in certain areas.
    (C) a requirement for the broker to join MLS.
    (D) a practice of standardizing commission rates.

19. Under the federal Fair Housing Act, it is illegal to discriminate because

    (A) a person has a history of dangerous behavior.
    (B) of a person's political party status.
    (C) a person has AIDS.
    (D) a person has been convicted of distributing a controlled substance.

20. A house for sale was advertised: "Fine executive home in an exclusive neighborhood, suitable for an older couple; near St. Mary's Church." Which of the following is **NOT TRUE?**

    (A) This is descriptive of the property for sale and a good ad.
    (B) An exclusive neighborhood could be interpreted to mean that minorities are not welcome.
    (C) It appears that families with children are not welcome.
    (D) The neighborhood could appear to be undesirable for people who do not follow the same religion as St. Mary's Church.

21. A broker employs several salespeople, one of whom is a member of a minority group. The broker tells this salesperson to work only with minority buyers and solicit listings in only predominately minority neighborhoods. Which of the following is **TRUE?**

    (A) The broker is entitled to direct the activities of this salesperson.
    (B) The fair housing laws do not apply to the broker's practices.
    (C) The salesperson's rights have been violated by the broker.
    (D) The salesperson should be satisfied with the broker's policy.

22. The restrictive covenant in a condominium complex prohibits pets. A prospective buyer with a physical disability relies on an animal to assist him. Which of the following is **TRUE?**

    (A) The condominium has the right to establish this private restriction if it chooses.
    (B) This restriction is unenforceable only if the animal is used to assist people with visual impairments.
    (C) This restriction is unenforceable when any person with a disability uses an animal for assistance.
    (D) The condominium can waive the enforcement of the covenant only if there are suitable accommodations in the complex for an animal.

23. The Americans with Disabilities Act requires that

    (A) all real estate be free of barriers to people with disabilities.
    (B) all employers adopt nondiscriminatory employment practices.
    (C) reasonable accommodations be provided to people with disabilities.
    (D) the existing premises must be remodeled regardless of the cost involved.

24. Under the fair housing laws, which of the following is illegal?

    (A) Refusing to lend money to a minority person who has poor credit
    (B) Refusing to allow families with children to live in a housing development intended exclusively for people over 62
    (C) Refusing to rent to a person in a wheelchair who needs to widen the door to the bathroom
    (D) Refusing to rent to a person who has been convicted of distributing cocaine

25. Under fair housing laws, which of the following would be considered to be legal?

    (A) Charging a family with children a higher security deposit than is charged to adults
    (B) Requiring a person with a disability to establish an escrow account for the costs to restore a property after it has been modified
    (C) Picturing only white people in a brochure as the "happy residents" in a housing development
    (D) Refusing to sell a house to a person who has a history of mental illness

26. When a salesperson makes representations that minorities are moving into the area to get homeowners to sell their properties, this activity is

    (A) blockbusting.
    (B) steering.
    (C) discriminatory advertising.
    (D) legal as long as it is true.

27. The amount of compensation due to a broker is determined by

    (A) state law.
    (B) the local real estate board.
    (C) mutual agreement between the parties.
    (D) court decree.

28. A broker was accused of violating antitrust laws. The broker was probably accused of

    (A) not having an equal housing opportunity sign in his or her office window.
    (B) undisclosed dual agencies.
    (C) a group boycott or price-fixing.
    (D) dealing in unlicensed exchange services.

29. A real estate broker was responsible for a chain of events that resulted in the sale of one of his client's properties. This is referred to as a

    (A) pro forma.   (C) private offering.
    (B) procuring cause.   (D) proffered offer.

30. A salesperson may advertise a property for sale only if he or she

    (A) personally listed the property.
    (B) uses the employing broker's name in the advertisement.
    (C) personally pays for the advertisement.
    (D) is a member of the local real estate board.

31. A parcel of vacant land 80 feet wide and 200 feet deep was sold for $200 per front foot. How much money would a salesperson receive for his or her 60% share in the 10% commission?

    (A) $640   (C) $1,600
    (B) $960   (D) $2,400

32. A real estate salesperson who wishes to be paid as an independent contractor receives

    (A) a monthly salary or hourly wage.
    (B) company-provided health insurance.
    (C) a company-provided automobile.
    (D) negotiated commissions or fees on transactions.

33. In a typical agency relationship between the broker and the client, the broker's compensation is determined by

    (A) state law.
    (B) common charges used by other area brokers.
    (C) mutual agreement between the broker and client.
    (D) minimums based on the property type.

34. A salesperson finally concluded some extremely difficult negotiations that resulted in the sale of a listed parcel of property. For all of her extra efforts, who can the salesperson legally require to pay a performance bonus?

    (A) The seller   (C) Her broker
    (B) The buyer   (D) No one

35. A salesperson working for a broker sells a $150,000 home. The listed commission is 6.5% of the selling price. Out of this amount, 35% goes to the listing broker and 60% belongs to the cooperating broker. The broker and salesperson agreed that the broker would receive 55% of any commission that he generated for the office. For this transaction, the salesperson is entitled to receive

    (A) $2,632.50.   (C) $3,412.50.
    (B) $3,217.50.   (D) $5,850.00.

36. In order to qualify for a commission on a sale of a property, a broker is **NOT** required to

    (A) hold a valid real estate broker's license.
    (B) perform required activities under the employment agreement.
    (C) be employed to perform certain activities.
    (D) belong to a real estate board.

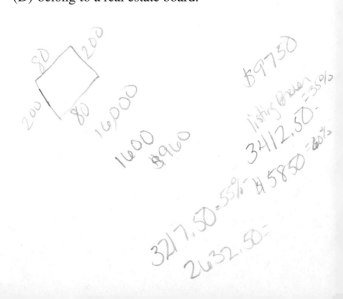

37. A broker lists a property for sale at $100,000 with a 5% commission, and he later obtains an oral offer to purchase the property from a prospective buyer. The seller indicates to the broker that the offer would be acceptable if it were submitted in writing. Before it can be put in writing, the buyer backs out and revokes the oral offer. In this situation, the broker would be entitled to

   (A) a commission of $5,000.
   (B) only a partial commission.
   (C) no commission.
   (D) the normal rate of commission.

38. Which of the following is **NOT** prohibited under the antitrust laws?

   (A) Property management companies standardizing management fees
   (B) Brokers from competing firms allocating markets based on the value of homes
   (C) Real estate companies agreeing to boycott a broker because of the fees that broker charges
   (D) A broker deciding whether to join a MLS

39. A broker's salesperson lists a unit for sale in a condominium building. The salesperson in this transaction

   (A) has a direct contractual relationship with the owners of the unit.
   (B) acts on behalf of the broker.
   (C) acts on behalf of the condominium association.
   (D) must find a buyer for the unit to obtain a share of the commission.

40. There is a spectacular house that a salesperson from Firm A has been trying for several weeks to list for sale. The owners have been interviewing salespeople from different firms. They tell A's salesperson that Firm B will charge 2% less commission for selling the house. What should A's salesperson say to the owner to get the listing?

   (A) Salespeople will not show Firm B's listings because of their commission fees.
   (B) Most brokers in the area charge a standard rate of commission, including Firm A.
   (C) Firm B cannot provide good services because they charge less.
   (D) Firm A provides excellent services to market their sellers' properties.

41. A licensed salesperson may receive compensation or commission from

   (A) only the employing broker.
   (B) the principal.
   (C) any broker.
   (D) a landlord.

42. The listing and selling brokers agree to split a 7% commission 50-50 on a $96,900 sale. The listing broker gives the listing salesperson 30% of his commission and the selling broker gives the selling salesperson 35% of his commission. How much does the selling salesperson earn from the sale?

   (A) $ 971.95   (C) $1,174.78
   (B) $1,139.78   (D) $1,187.03

43. Unless some other written agreement has been made, a broker will usually receive the sales commission when

   (A) the purchaser takes possession of the property.
   (B) the seller lists the property with the broker.
   (C) the transaction is closed.
   (D) an offer is procured from a ready, willing and able buyer.

44. An agent/licensee represents a party in a transaction. What responsibilities, if any, does the licensee have toward the third party?

    (A) The agent/licensee has no responsibility toward the third party.
    (B) The agent/licensee can only interact with their client.
    (C) The agent/licensee must treat the third party fairly and equally.
    (D) The agent/licensee must treat the third party fairly and honestly.

45. A person, licensed as a salesperson, who creates a document for a fee that binds others to perform is

    (A) doing his or her job.
    (B) following his or her principal's instructions.
    (C) practicing law without a license.
    (D) acting according to the law so long as it is notarized.

46. A primary reason for state licensure of real estate agents is to

    (A) provide the state a steady stream of revenue.
    (B) make it easier for people to be sued.
    (C) provide the consumer with professional help.
    (D) provide the real estate trade association a reason to exist.

47. Several brokers meet and agree that they should set their commissions at a level that would make it difficult for new companies to move into their market area. These brokers have

    (A) violated the Sherman Antitrust Act.
    (B) done nothing wrong.
    (C) violated the Realty Members Code of Ethics.
    (D) violated the Grant Price Fixing Act.

48. A broker advertises a listed property. The ad does not reveal the ad was placed by the broker. The broker may have

    (A) done nothing wrong.
    (B) misled the public.
    (C) done nothing wrong if he or she eventually tells the public that he or she is a broker.
    (D) cost the seller a sale.

49. A broker has possession of a document belonging to a client. The broker must

    (A) destroy the document when the relationship ends.
    (B) return the document to its owner when requested.
    (C) keep all documents in a fireproof safe.
    (D) turn all documents over to the state regulators.

50. A salesperson with a brokerage firm takes a listing for the firm. The salesperson leaves the firm before the listing has either expired or the property is sold. The broker should

    (A) do nothing because the salesperson owns the listing.
    (B) have possession of the files on the listing.
    (C) call the salesperson if he or she has a buyer.
    (D) cancel the listing and re-sign with another salesperson.

■ ANSWER KEY WITH EXPLANATIONS

1. (A) The Civil Rights Act of 1866 prohibits racial discrimination. It was reaffirmed by the *Jones v. Mayer* court decision prohibiting all racial discrimination, private as well as public.

2. (C) The Department of Housing and Urban Development (HUD) is the federal agency named in the statute (fair housing laws) to enforce the Fair Housing Act. Persons who suspect a violation of fair housing laws may file a complaint with HUD. HUD will determine if there is a basis for an investigation and if necessary take legal action.

3. (B) The fair housing laws prohibit redlining, when lenders refuse to make loans based on the location of the property instead of the financial qualifications of the borrower.

4. (A) Anyone who suspects a violation can file a complaint with HUD but only the aggrieved party can file a suit in federal court.

5. (D) The federal fair housing laws permit discriminating against a person using illegal drugs. A person who is using an illegal drug is not in the protected class of handicapped.

6. (B) The alleged victim of discrimination does not have to prove the discrimination to file a complaint. The agency that takes the complaint will need to prove that a violation did occur.

7. (A) The Fair Housing Act of 1968 expanded the rights to file a discrimination complaint from government property to all property with only a few exemptions.

8. (D) The agent should show properties that are within the buyer's price range and within the areas defined by the buyer.

9. (C) Brokers and salespeople should show properties that are within the buyer's financial range. They are not required to show a prospective buyer all listed properties.

10. (C) A provision offering protection from threats or acts of violence was added in the Fair Housing Act of 1968.

11. (A) The Fair Housing Act is a federal law that applies in all states. Local and state governments may add additional provisions but cannot create laws that would counteract the federal law.

12. (D) Steering is a practice of channeling or steering a buyer or tenant to a specific property based on the person's race, color, religion, national origin, sex, familial status or handicap.

13. (D) Lack of creditworthiness is **NOT** a protected class. An agent is not required to show property to people who do not have the ability to purchase. For example, if a person is only qualified to buy a home in the range of $100,000, an agent can refuse to show that person $500,000 houses.

14. (B) Redlining is the practice of refusing to make loans in certain neighborhoods (usually because of religious, ethnic or racial composition), rather than basing the decision on the borrower's ability to repay the loan.

15. (D) The protected classes of familial status and handicap were added as part of the Fair Housing Amendments Act of 1988.

16. (C) Federal fair housing laws do not cover economic considerations.

17. (D) Even though there is an exemption for race in the Fair Housing Act of 1968, the Civil Rights Act of 1866 specifically prohibits discrimination in housing based on race.

18. (A) Examples of steering include only showing an Asian couple houses in predominantly Asian neighborhoods or channeling a family with children to only ground-floor apartments.

19. (C) Persons with HIV or AIDS are now in the protected class of the handicapped under the fair housing laws.

20. (A) Running this ad could lead to fair housing advertising complaints because the ad makes reference to several protected categories. It is possible that families with children, minorities or people of another faith might feel unwelcome.

21. (C) While the broker is generally entitled to direct the sales activities of salespeople in the broker's office, the broker may not direct the salesperson to an illegal activity. The salesperson has the right to work with all financially qualified buyers and sellers, not just those in a protected category.

22. (C) Restrictive covenants do not apply to disabled persons who use animals, such as guide dogs, for support.

23. (C) The key phrase is *reasonable accommodations*. The ADA does not force a business or landlord to make major changes that are not economically reasonable.

24. (C) Protection for the handicapped includes allowing the handicapped person to widen doors to accommodate the wheelchair.

25. (B) Under federal fair housing laws, a landlord can take reasonable steps to protect his or her interest, such as requiring that all alterations meet the local building and health codes.

26. (A) Fair housing laws prohibit blockbusting. Blockbusting occurs when agents play on racial, ethnic or religious fears in order to cause widespread selling or renting. It is sometimes referred to as panic selling.

27. (C) A broker's compensation is determined by negotiation between the client and the broker.

28. (C) In real estate transactions, antitrust violations generally refer to group boycotts or to price-fixing.

29. (B) If there is a dispute as to who earned the commission, in order to prove procuring cause, the broker will have to prove that the broker was responsible for a chain of events that resulted in the sale of the property.

30. (B) Generally, state license laws require that the broker's name be on any form of advertising, because the listing contract is between the seller and the broker, not the salesperson sponsored by the broker. This also prevents "blind ads." The public seeing the ad has a right to know who is the responsible party for the advertisement.

31. (B) The salesperson would receive $960.
$80 \times \$200 = \$16,000$
$\$16,000 \times 10\% = \$1,600$
$\$1,600 \times 60\% = \$960$

32. (D) The IRS permits brokers to pay their salespeople as independent contractors for income tax purposes so long as the person holds a real estate license and has an employment contract stating that the compensation is based on sales, not on hours worked.

33. (C) Clients and brokers negotiate the broker's compensation in their listing or employment agreements. Fees are not set by local custom or law.

34. (D) The salesperson may not legally require anyone to pay her a performance bonus. The amount of compensation is determined by the agreement negotiated when the broker was hired to sell the property.

35. (A) The salesperson is entitled to $2,632.50.
$\$150,000 \times 6.5\% = \$9,750$
$\$9,750 \times 60\% = \$5,850$
$\$5,850 \times 45\% = \$2,632.50$

36. (D) Membership in a real estate board is not required to collect a commission. Generally, the broker must hold a valid real estate broker's license and be employed to perform agreed-upon activities.

37. (C) The commission is earned when the buyer and seller agree in writing. The oral offer is not binding on either party. The commission is typically paid at closing.

38. (D) Antitrust laws do **NOT** prohibit brokers joining together to assist in marketing properties. The MLS is a service available in certain markets to help brokers market their properties.

39. (B) The broker is the person hired by the consumer. The sales agent is working under the authority of the broker.

40. (D) Firm *A*'s salesperson should concentrate on the positive aspects of Firm *A*. By not showing Firm *B*'s listing, Firm *A* could be in violation of antitrust laws by boycotting Firm *B*.

41. (A) A salesperson may receive compensation only from his or her employing broker. The client hires and pays the broker.

42. (D) The selling salesperson earns $1,187.03.
$96,900 \times 7\% \times 50\% = \$3,391.50$
$\$3,391.50 \times 35\% = \$1,187.03$

43. (C) The closing is the settlement procedure between the parties when the terms of the agreement are finalized and fees are distributed.

44. (D) The agent/licensee who represents a party in a transaction must treat the other party fairly and honestly. The agent/licensee has a duty to protect the interest of his or her client but cannot take actions that would cause harm to the other side; the agent/licensee will not act equally for both parties. For example, the agent/licensee would need to disclose known defects that have a material effect on the property such as the presence of asbestos or toxic waste but **NOT** the lowest price that the seller will accept.

45. (C) The key word here is "creates" a document that legally binds other people. Salespeople should avoid any situation that could be construed as the unauthorized practice of law. Some states permit real estate agents to fill in blanks of preapproved forms created by an attorney.

46. (C) State licensure was created to provide the public with professional and licensed individuals to assist consumers in their real estate transactions. State licensure also provides the consumer an avenue to resolve specific problems encountered with a real estate agent.

47. (A) The Sherman Antitrust Act makes it illegal for competitors to fix their prices to prevent competition.

48. (B) In order to avoid a "blind ad," any ads published by a broker must be clear that the advertisement is that of a broker and not of a "FOR SALE BY OWNER."

49. (B) When a broker has an item belonging to his or her client, the broker's fiduciary duty is to return the item to the rightful owner when requested by the client.

50. (B) The listing was taken in the name of the broker. The salesperson cannot take the files to another company.

Agency and Listing

3

■ CONTENT OUTLINE

II. Agency and Listing

A. Principles of agency

1. Creating agency

   a. Definitions

      (1) Agent—one who has the authority to represent another person. An agent can be licensed as either a broker or a salesperson.
      (2) Principal—one who hires the agent to represent his or her interests. A principal can be a buyer, seller, landlord or tenant.
      (3) Fiduciary—the relationship of trust, honesty and confidence between agent and principal; the faithful relationship owed by agent to principal.
      (4) Client—the principal
      (5) Customer—third party for whom some level of service is provided

   b. Expressed agency—when parties formally express their intention to establish an agency and state the terms of the agreement. Most states require that the agreement be in writing to be enforceable.

      (1) Listing agreement
      (2) Buyer representation agreement

   c. Implied agency—when parties act as if there is an agreement of representation

2. Liabilities—the law of agency is the body of laws that govern the relationship between an agent and principal. A licensee who represents a consumer is held responsible for his or her actions as a licensee. If a consumer is harmed by the licensee's action or inaction, the licensee can be held responsible.

3. Types and functions of agency

   a. Single agency—the agent or licensee represents only one party in the transaction.

      (1) Seller agency—the agent or licensee represents the seller as his or her client and the buyer is considered a customer.

        (2) Buyer agency—the agent or licensee represents the buyer as his or her client and the seller is considered a customer.

    b. Dual agency—with informed consent of both clients, the broker represents both seller and buyer in the same transaction.

4. Roles and responsibilities of licensees

    a. Care—the agent must exercise a reasonable degree of care.

    b. Obedience—the agent must act in good faith and must obey the principal's lawful instructions.

    c. Accounting—the broker must account for all pertinent funds and documents placed in his or her care.

    d. Loyalty—the principal's interests must come before the agent's.

    e. Disclosure—the agent must keep the principal fully informed of all facts.

5. Terminating agency

    a. Performance by the parties

    b. Expiration of the terms of the agency

    c. Mutual agreement by all parties to the contract

    d. Death or incapacity of either party

    e. Destruction or condemnation of the property

    f. Cancellation by broker; revocation by principal

    g. By operation of law (bankruptcy of owner or broker, eminent domain, etc.)

    h. Breach by one of the parties (in which case the breaching party might be held liable for damages)

6. Disclosing agency relationships

    a. Licensees must explain to both buyers and sellers what agency alternatives exist, how client and customer services differ and how these services affect the interest of each party.

    b. The licensee has an obligation not to take advantage of a consumer by misrepresenting who the licensee represents. Agency disclosure should be made before any confidential information is disclosed as to the consumer's motivation or financial status.

    c. A licensee should inform all parties in the transaction who the licensee represents. Some states require this in writing; some allow a verbal notification.

B. Types of listing

1. Exclusive-right-to-sell—gives the listing broker the right to sell the property and collect compensation if the property is sold by anyone, including the owner, during the listing period.

2. Exclusive-agency—gives the listing broker the right to sell the property for a specified time. The owner reserves the right to sell the property himself or herself and avoid paying the agent compensation.

3. Net listing—a price agreed on by the owner and broker, below which the owner will not sell and above which the broker receives the excess as compensation. Most states do not allow them because net listings can create a conflict of interest between owners and their agents or licensees.

4. Open listing—principal (owner) reserves the right to list with as many brokers as he or she chooses. The broker who brings the owner an acceptable offer receives the compensation.

C. Listing procedures

1. Evaluating property—when the licensee takes a listing, he or she should review the property with the seller. The seller will depend on the licensee to help in establishing the price. Some states do not require an actual inspection of the property.

2. Disclosure of property conditions—if the licensee has knowledge of a material defect in the property he or she is required to disclose this defect.

   a. Fraud and misrepresentation—if the licensee is aware of a fraud or misrepresentation in the transaction, the licensee is required to disclose what he or she knows. If the licensee continues without disclosing these facts, he or she may be held liable.

   b. Negligent representation—a statement that the broker should have known about a material fact was false. If the consumer relies on the broker's statement to the consumer's detriment, the broker may be held liable.

   c. Puffing—exaggerated or superlative comments or opinions.

D. Listing agreement

1. Legal requirements—topics to be included in listing agreement (employment contract)

   a. Broker or firm name

   b. Owner name

   c. Type of agency

   d. Listing price

   e. Authority to offer the property for sale

   f. Acceptable description of the property

   g. Permission to submit the listing to MLS

   h. Permission to place a lockbox on the property when required

   i. Extension beyond termination date with agreement of the parties

   j. Definite termination date not subject to prior notice

   k. Broker's fee

2. Fiduciary duties and representations—the relationship of trust, honesty and confidence between agent and principal; the faithful relationship owed by agent to principal

3. Terminating listing

   a. Performance, fulfillment of the purpose of the listing

   b. Expiration of the time period stated in the agreement

   c. Destruction of the property

   d. A change in property use by outside forces (i.e., a change in zoning)

   e. Transfer of the title to the property by operation of law (such as a bankruptcy)

   f. Mutual consent

   g. Death or incapacity of either party

   h. Breach or cancellation by one of the parties

■ QUIZ

1. The real estate broker's responsibility to keep the principal informed of all of the facts that could affect a transaction is the duty of

   (A) care.   (C) obedience.
   (B) disclosure.   (D) accounting.

2. Which of the following would be considered to be a dual agency?

   (A) The broker acting for both the buyer and the seller in the same transaction
   (B) Brokers cooperating with each other
   (C) The broker representing different principals
   (D) The broker listing and selling the same property

3. The relationship of a broker to his or her client is that of

   (A) a trustee.
   (B) a subagent.
   (C) a fiduciary.
   (D) an attorney-in-fact.

4. A real estate broker acting as the agent of the seller

   (A) is obligated to render faithful service to the principal.
   (B) can disclose the seller's minimum price.
   (C) should present to the seller only the highest offer for the property.
   (D) can accept an offer on behalf of the seller.

5. Statements by a real estate licensee exaggerating the benefits of a property are called

   (A) polishing.   (C) prospecting.
   (B) puffing.   (D) marketing.

6. A broker is permitted to represent both the seller and the buyer in the same transaction when

   (A) the principals are not aware of such action.
   (B) the broker is a subagent rather than the agent of the seller.
   (C) both parties pay the commissions.
   (D) both parties have been informed and agree to the dual representation.

7. Which of the following would **NOT** be considered fraudulent practice?

   (A) Deceitful or dishonest practices
   (B) Exaggerated statements about the property
   (C) Omitted statements of material fact
   (D) Misstatements about the property

8. As an agent for the seller, a real estate broker can

   (A) guarantee a prospective buyer that the seller will accept an offer at the listed price and terms.
   (B) solicit an offer to purchase the property from a prospective buyer.
   (C) advise a prospective buyer of the best manner of taking title to the property.
   (D) change the terms of the listing contract on behalf of the seller.

9. A seller has listed her home with a broker for $90,000, and the broker tells a prospective buyer to submit a low offer because the seller is desperate to sell. The buyer offers $85,000 and the seller accepts it. In this situation, the broker

   (A) has violated the agency relationship between the seller and broker.
   (B) was unethical, but the seller did get to sell her property.
   (C) acted properly to obtain a quick offer on the property.
   (D) is authorized to encourage such bids for the property.

10. When the broker was told by his principal not to advertise her property in the XYZ newspaper, which was out of the area, the broker complied because he

    (A) had never advertised in the XYZ newspaper anyway.
    (B) must obey the lawful instructions of his principal.
    (C) was not intending to advertise the property at all.
    (D) is allowed to advertise only in local newspapers.

11. It is the duty of an agent to disclose to the principal every step taken in the transaction of the principal's business. This is because the

    (A) commission can be adjusted up or down according to the agent's efforts.
    (B) agent has fiduciary obligations to the principal.
    (C) terms of the listing contract require the agent to do so.
    (D) terms of the purchase contract require the agent to do so.

12. The licensee who represents the seller discovers a latent defect in the property. The licensee should discuss the problem with the seller and then

    (A) notify the seller that the defect must be repaired.
    (B) arrange for the repairs to be made.
    (C) inform any prospective buyer of the defect.
    (D) contact the city building inspector about the defect.

13. A landowner subdivides his acreage and offers the lots for sale. A broker tells the landowner that she can sell the lots. After the broker sells some of the lots, the landowner refuses to pay her a commission. The broker can

    (A) report the landowner to the real estate licensing authorities.
    (B) file a lien against the landowner's remaining lots.
    (C) sue the landowner for breach of contract.
    (D) do nothing.

14. Which of the following **BEST** defines the "law of agency"?

    (A) The selling of another's property by an authorized agency
    (B) The rules of law that apply to the responsibilities of a person who acts for another
    (C) The principles that govern one's conduct in business
    (D) The rules and regulations of the state's licensing agency

15. A broker who is the agent of the buyer should

    (A) disclose to the seller that the buyer is a member of a minority group.
    (B) disclose to the seller the maximum price the buyer is willing to pay.
    (C) present to the seller only offers that are acceptable.
    (D) advise the buyer if the listing price of the seller's house is unrealistic.

16. An unrepresented tenant approaches a broker who has listed several properties for rent. Typically, this tenant is the broker's

    (A) client.   (C) customer.
    (B) principal.   (D) fiduciary.

17. A house has been listed for sale for more than one year and the seller is very anxious to move into a retirement condominium. A salesperson from the listing office tells a prospective buyer to make a low offer because the salesperson is sure that the seller will accept it. Regarding this statement, the salesperson

 (A) acted appropriately to get the seller's property sold.
 (B) violated the fiduciary to the seller.
 (C) seems to indicate that he or she is working for the seller.
 (D) is correctly assuming that an anxious seller will accept a lower offer.

18. A salesperson who represents the seller is showing a house to a prospective buyer. The salesperson knows that the house has a wet basement. In this situation,

 (A) withholding the information protects the confidence of the seller.
 (B) disclosing the information could create a fiduciary relationship with the buyer.
 (C) withholding the information prevents the buyer from making an informed decision.
 (D) disclosing the information violates the fiduciary to the seller.

19. When acting for another person in the sale or lease of real estate, generally, who of the following is exempt from licensing requirements?

 (A) One who is personally representing a dealer in real estate
 (B) Anyone acting under a power of attorney
 (C) A relative of the party
 (D) A next-door neighbor

20. A broker may legally collect commissions from both the seller and the buyer when both parties

 (A) are verbally notified after the sale has closed.
 (B) are notified of this fact in writing after the sale has closed.
 (C) sign exclusive-brokerage agreements with the broker.
 (D) have prior knowledge and consent in writing.

21. A broker, in the course of selling a home, told a buyer that the foundation was "solid as a rock" when he knew for a fact that it was slowly sinking into the landfill on which it was built. Which of the following is the broker **NOT** likely to be subjected to?

 (A) Having his real estate license revoked
 (B) Being sued criminally for restitution
 (C) Being sued civilly for damages
 (D) Being sued criminally for fraud

22. Which of the following is **NOT** likely to terminate a listing agreement?

 (A) Sale of the property
 (B) Death of the salesperson
 (C) Agreement of the parties
 (D) Destruction of the premises

23. When executing a listing agreement with a seller, generally, a real estate broker becomes

 (A) a procuring cause.
 (B) obligated to open a special trust account.
 (C) an agent of the seller.
 (D) responsible for sharing commissions.

24. The provision in a listing agreement that obligates the broker to distribute the listing to other brokers is

 (A) a joint-listing clause.
 (B) a multiple-listing clause.
 (C) a net-listing clause.
 (D) an open-listing clause.

25. A building sold for $157,000. The broker charged a 6% commission and divided it as follows: 10% to the salesperson who took the listing; one-half of the balance to the salesperson who made the sale; and the remainder to the broker. What was the listing salesperson's commission?

 (A) $239   (C) $1,570
 (B) $942   (D) $4,239

26. A broker took a listing on a property and shortly thereafter discovered that the court had previously declared the client incompetent. What is the status of the listing?

    (A) Binding as the broker was acting in good faith
    (B) Still valid
    (C) Basis for commission if the broker produces a buyer
    (D) Void

27. What type of listing agreement provides for the payment of a commission to the broker even though the owner makes the sale without the aid of the broker?

    (A) Exclusive-right-to-sell listing
    (B) Open listing
    (C) Exclusive-agency listing
    (D) Option listing

28. A property owner lists his property for sale with a broker. During the negotiations, the owner told the broker that the owner wanted $138,000 for the property, and anything above that amount the broker could keep as his commission. The listing with this type of provision is known as

    (A) a gross listing.
    (B) a net listing.
    (C) an open listing.
    (D) a nonexclusive listing.

29. If the owner of a listed property sells the property on his or her own, under which of the following listing agreements is the owner still obligated to pay the listing broker a commission?

    (A) Option listing
    (B) Exclusive-agency listing
    (C) Open listing
    (D) Exclusive-right-to-sell listing

30. A property owner signed a 90-day listing agreement with a broker. The owner was killed in an accident before the listing expired. Now the listing is

    (A) binding on the owner's heirs for the remainder of the 90 days.
    (B) still in effect as the owner's intention was clearly defined.
    (C) binding only if the broker can produce offers to purchase the property.
    (D) terminated automatically upon the death of the principal.

31. A listing contract in which the broker's commission is contingent on the broker being able to produce a buyer before the property is sold by the owner or another broker is called

    (A) an open listing.
    (B) a net listing.
    (C) an exclusive-right-to-sell listing.
    (D) an exclusive-agency listing.

32. A broker who represents a seller under an exclusive listing receives two offers for the property at the same time, one from one of his salespeople and one from a salesperson of a cooperating broker. The broker should submit

    (A) the offer from his salesperson first.
    (B) the offer from the other salesperson first.
    (C) the higher offer first.
    (D) both offers at the same time.

33. Which of the following is **NOT** a typical provision of a listing agreement?

    (A) Price the seller is asking for the property
    (B) Date the broker will schedule an open house
    (C) Commission rate to be paid to the listing broker
    (D) Responsibilities of the broker

34. The type of listing agreement that provides the **LEAST** protection for the listing broker is the

    (A) exclusive-right-to-sell listing.
    (B) exclusive-agency listing.
    (C) open listing.
    (D) net listing.

35. If a seller needs to net $50,000 after the sale, how much must the real estate sell for if the selling costs include a 7% commission and $1,200 in other expenses?

(A) $54,700.00   (C) $55,053.76
(B) $54,963.44   (D) $55,633.25

36. A seller refused to pay a commission to the broker even though there was a valid listing agreement, and the broker procured a buyer for the property. What can the broker do?

(A) Sue the seller in court for the commission
(B) File a lien on the seller's property for the amount of the commission
(C) Obtain an injunction to stop the transaction until the commission is paid
(D) Collect the commission from the buyer

37. Under an exclusive-agency listing, the listing broker would **NOT** be entitled to a commission if the

(A) broker sells the property herself.
(B) property is sold through another broker.
(C) property is sold through the multiple-listing service.
(D) seller sells the property to a neighbor across the street who has her property listed with another broker.

38. In a brokerage agreement, the protective clause protects

(A) the seller.
(B) the listing broker.
(C) any broker who showed the property.
(D) the buyer.

39. A sales contract may be terminated

(A) when the seller cannot find another property to buy.
(B) when the buyer changes his or her mind.
(C) by mutual agreement of the buyer and seller.
(D) by mutual agreement of the broker and the seller.

40. A seller wants to net $65,000 on the sale of his house after paying the broker a fee of 5%. How much must the gross selling price be?

(A) $66,091   (C) $68,421
(B) $67,035   (D) $68,250

41. A broker enters into a listing agreement with a seller in which the seller will receive $12,000 from the sale of a lot and the broker will receive any sale proceeds over this amount. This is an example of a

(A) gross listing.
(B) legal and ethical way to ensure that the broker is compensated.
(C) good incentive to the broker to get the highest price for the seller.
(D) potential conflict of interest.

42. Which of the following listings is prohibited in some states and discouraged in others?

(A) Exclusive-right-to-sell
(B) Net listing
(C) Buyer-agency agreement
(D) Open listing

43. An owner who is interested in selling his house is usually concerned about how much money he can get when it sells. A competitive market analysis may help the seller determine a realistic listing price. Which of the following is **TRUE?**

(A) A competitive market analysis is the same as an appraisal.
(B) A broker, not a salesperson, is permitted to prepare a competitive market analysis.
(C) A competitive market analysis is prepared by a certified real estate appraiser.
(D) A competitive market analysis contains a compilation of other similar properties that have sold.

44. Two different brokerage companies claimed they were entitled to a commission from the sale of a property that was listed by one of the firms under an open-listing agreement. The broker who is entitled to the commission is the one who

(A) listed the property.
(B) advertised the property.
(C) obtained the first offer.
(D) was the procuring cause of the sale.

45. A broker listed a property for sale under an exclusive-right-to-sell agreement. Today, one of the broker's salespeople obtained an offer to purchase the property along with a certified check for 5% of the purchase price as earnest money. What should the salesperson do with the earnest money check?

(A) Give it to the property owner
(B) Hold it until the closing
(C) Deposit the money in his trust account
(D) Give the money to the broker for deposit in the broker's trust account

46. Which of the following contracts establishes the **MOST** binding employment contract between a buyer and the broker?

(A) Exclusive-right-to-buy agency agreement
(B) Exclusive-agency buyer agency agreement
(C) Open buyer agency agreement
(D) Net buyer agency agreement

47. Before signing a buyer agency agreement a licensee should avoid

(A) explaining forms of agency available.
(B) obtaining financial information from the buyer.
(C) informing the buyer of the charges or compensation for services.
(D) describing specific services to be provided.

48. An owner lists her property for sale with a broker. Another broker, however, finds a buyer for the house. The listing broker did not receive a commission from the sale. The type of listing contract between the owner and the broker could have been

(A) an exclusive-right-to-sell.
(B) an exclusive agency.
(C) an open listing.
(D) a multiple listing.

49. The salesperson received $2,800 commission on her 35% share of the total commission on the sale of a property that sold for $160,000. What was the commission rate?

(A) 4.5%   (C) 7.0%
(B) 5.0%   (D) 10.0%

50. A broker hires sales associates with an agreement to split the commission between the broker—45 percent, the listing salesperson—30 percent, and the selling salesperson. If the broker's share is $2,430, the property sold for $90,000, and the listing salesperson's share was $1,620, what was the selling sales associate's share?

(A) $1,295   (C) $1,800
(B) $1,350   (D) $2,700

ANSWER KEY WITH EXPLANATIONS

1. (B) The broker is required to disclose information known to the broker that might affect the client's position.

2. (A) A broker who represents both the buyer and the seller in the same transaction is considered a dual agent. In some states, dual agency is prohibited.

3. (C) The relationship of a broker to his or her client is that of a fiduciary. A fiduciary relationship is one marked by trust and confidence.

4. (A) A real estate broker must render faithful service to his or her client. As agent for the seller, the broker must present all offers. The broker should not disclose confidential information, such as the seller's minimum price, and may not accept an offer on behalf of the seller.

5. (B) "Puffing" is defined as making exaggerating statements that an ordinary person would recognize as personal opinion, not fact. Thus, stating that "the property has the best view of the river" is puffing. The agent would be misrepresenting if there were no river.

6. (D) A broker may represent both the seller and the buyer in the same transaction only with the informed consent of both parties. In some states, dual agency is illegal. Who does the hiring, not who pays the commission, determines agency representation.

7. (B) Puffing, i.e., exaggerated statements, is not considered fraudulent. Fraudulent practices include deceitful or dishonest practices, omitting material facts, and making misstatements about the property.

8. (B) The agent is hired to offer the property for sale. The broker may not to make statements or actions binding on the seller. The agent should avoid the unauthorized practice of law, such as suggesting how to take title.

9. (A) The seller's position was confidential information. By disclosing the privileged information, the broker violated his or her fiduciary duty of loyalty to the seller.

10. (B) The broker works for the client and must obey the client's lawful instructions.

11. (B) Under the duties of care and accountability, the agent must keep the client fully informed of each step of the transaction.

12. (C) The agent has a duty to be honest and treat the buyer fairly. Failing to disclose a material defect could have negative effects on both the agent and his or her client.

13. (D) In most states, in order to collect a commission, the broker must first have a written agreement in which the seller agrees to pay the broker a commission.

14. (B) The law of agency refers to the rules that apply to the responsibilities of a person who acts for another in a business transaction. Most states have rules to govern these activities and to protect the consumer.

15. (D) A buyer's agent should advise the buyer if the listing price is unrealistic.

16. (C) Since the broker represents the owner, and the tenant has not entered into an agency agreement with the broker, the tenant is the broker's customer. Tenants working **WITH** a broker are customers of the broker, not clients.

17. (B) This agent violated his or her fiduciary duty to the seller to obtain the best price possible.

18. (C) Withholding information that is a material fact, such as a wet basement, prevents a buyer from making an informed decision. The agent should tell the buyer. Such disclosure can also protect a seller from a possible lawsuit.

19. (B) A person who holds a power of attorney is exempt from real estate licensing requirements. A real estate license is required by anyone who is acting on behalf of another in the sale or lease of real estate, whether a dealer, relative or a neighbor.

20. (D) A broker may collect commissions from both buyer and seller only with their prior, informed written consent.

21. (B) Misrepresentation of a material fact is a violation of most license laws and the licensee could be sued in civil court for resolution.

22. (B) The listing agreement is between the seller and the broker. If the salesperson dies, the broker assigns the account to another salesperson. A listing agreement may be terminated by agreement of the parties, performance (sale) or destruction of the property.

23. (C) The listing agreement is the employment agreement that establishes the broker as the seller's agent.

24. (B) A multiple-listing clause is a contractual agreement that requires the broker to list the property in the MLS.

25. (B) The listing salesperson's commission is $942.
$157,000 × 6% = $9,420
$9,420 × 10% = $942

26. (D) The listing is void. When a court rules a person incompetent, he or she would not be allowed to enter into a binding real estate sales contract.

27. (A) An exclusive-right-to-sell listing gives the broker the exclusive rights to sell the property. Therefore, if anyone produces a buyer, the broker has the right to be paid the negotiated commission.

28. (B) This is a net listing. The broker is free to negotiate any price above the $138,000 amount. If the property were sold for less than that amount, the broker would receive no commission. A net listing is illegal in many states and discouraged in others.

29. (D) Under an exclusive-right-to-sell listing, the listing broker is due his or her commission no matter who finds the buyer.

30. (D) The death of either party (broker or seller) terminates the listing agreement.

31. (A) In an open listing, the seller makes the property available to multiple brokers without committing to a specific broker. Whoever produces the buyer earns the commission. If the seller finds the buyer, the seller keeps the commission.

32. (D) The broker is required to present **ALL** offers promptly in order to provide options to the seller. The seller is the only party who has the right to decide which offer to accept.

33. (B) A date for an open house is **NOT** generally included in a listing agreement. Provisions that must be included are asking price, commission rate and the broker's responsibilities.

34. (C) An open listing provides little or no protection to the broker. Only the broker who produces a buyer is entitled to the commission. If the seller finds the buyer, then no broker will receive a commission.

35. (C) The house must sell for at least $55,053.76.
$50,000 + $1,200 ÷ 93% = $55,053.76

36. (A) The broker can sue the seller in court for the commission. The broker should not interfere with the closing because the buyer has no part in the commission dispute. The broker may not file a lien against the property or collect from the buyer.

37. (D) The seller found her own buyer. Under an exclusive-agency agreement, the broker is the only agent involved in the sale. The neighbor's agent was not involved in the sale.

38. (B) A protective clause in a listing agreement protects the broker from a buyer and seller seeking to enter an agreement after the listing expires in order to avoid paying the broker a commission.

39. (C) A sales contract may be terminated by mutual agreement of the buyer and seller. It may not be terminated simply because the seller could not find another property or because the buyer changes his or her mind. The broker is not a party to the sales contract.

40. (C) The gross selling price must be $68,421.
$65,000 ÷ 95% = $68,421

41. (D) In a net listing the broker's commission is the difference between the agreed listing price and the actual selling price.

42. (B) Because of the possibility of a conflict of interest, many states have outlawed a net listing.

43. (D) A real estate licensee may prepare a competitive market analysis (CMA). An appraiser prepares an appraisal. The CMA includes not only sold properties but also properties currently on the market that represent competition to the seller's property.

44. (D) Under an open listing agreement, the broker who is entitled to the commission is the broker who produced the buyer.

45. (D) In this case the broker is the only one who has the authority to hold trust funds. In lieu of an agreement of the parties, the check must be deposited in the appropriate trust account.

46. (A) An exclusive-right-to-buy agency agreement is the most binding between a broker and a buyer. The broker earns a commission no matter who finds the property for the buyer.

47. (B) The buyer's financial information may be considered confidential. A licensee may discuss with a nonrepresented person agency options, charges and compensation for services and a description of specific services to be provided.

48. (C) In an open listing, the only time a broker receives a commission is if he or she procured the buyer.

49. (B) The commission rate is 5%.
$$\$2,800 \div 35\% = \$8,000$$
$$\$8,000 \div 160,000 = .05 \text{ or } 5\%$$

50. (B) The selling sales associate's share is $1,350.
$$[\$2,430 + \$1,620] \div 75\% = \$5,400$$
$$\$5,400 \times 25\% = \$1,350$$

Property Characteristics, Descriptions, Ownership, Interests and Restrictions

4

■ CONTENT OUTLINE

III. Property Characteristics, Descriptions, Ownership, Interests and Restrictions

A. Characteristics of property

1. Legal description of property—an exact way of describing real estate in a contract, deed, mortgage or other document that will be accepted by a court of law

   a. Metes-and-bounds system—describes land boundaries using distances and directions (points and angles)

   b. Rectangular survey system (government survey system)—describes land boundaries using principal meridians and base lines

   c. Lot-and-block (recorded plat) system—requires a survey plat and uses a recorded subdivision plat map

2. Interpreting physical and economic characteristics of property—seven characteristics, four economic and three physical, that define the nature of real estate and affect its use

   a. Economic characteristics

      (1) Scarcity
      (2) Improvements
      (3) Permanence of investment
      (4) Area preference

   b. Physical characteristics

      (1) Immobility
      (2) Indestructibility
      (3) Uniqueness or heterogeneity or nonhomogeneity

3. Real and personal property

   a. Real estate/real property—land and anything permanently attached to it

   b. Personal property—movable items not attached to real estate (study tip: personal property is movable, can be destroyed and duplicated, the opposite of permanent characteristics)

      c. Fixture—item of personal property converted to real property by permanently attaching it to the real estate

      d. Trade fixture—item of tenant-owned personal property used in business that is attached to real estate and that may be removed by the tenant prior to expiration of the lease   *i.e. Farming into*

      e. Tests of a fixture

          (1) Existence of an agreement
          (2) Intention and relationship of the parties
          (3) Method of adaptation
          (4) Method of attachment

B. Ownership and estates in land

    1. Title (the right to ownership of the land; evidence of ownership of land)

      a. Deed—a written document used to convey title to real property

      b. Requirements of valid deed

          (1) Competent grantor
          (2) Grantee
          (3) Consideration
          (4) Words of conveyance
          (5) Legal description
          (6) Signature of the grantor
          (7) Delivery and acceptance by grantee during the grantor's lifetime
              Note: Recording is not a requirement of a valid deed. Recording gives constructive notice of ownership and protects against fraudulent sale.

      c. Types of deeds

          (1) General warranty deed—grantor fully warrants good and clear title to the property extending back to the origins of the property ownership. Offers the most protection to the new owner.
          (2) Special warranty deed—grantor warrants against defects in title only during his or her ownership.
          (3) Quitclaim deed—conveys whatever interest, if any, grantor has but makes no warranties or guarantees; used to convey less than fee simple title or remove clouds on the title.

      d. Exceptions and reservations

          (1) Exception—"subject to" clause in a deed noting exceptions to clear title such as mortgage liens, taxes, easements, etc.
          (2) Reservation—grantor reserves some right or places certain restrictions on grantee's use of the property.

      e. Rights of ownership (bundle of legal rights)

          (1) Possession
          (2) Control
          (3) Enjoyment
          (4) Exclusion
          (5) Disposition

2. Types of ownership

   a. Freehold—an estate in real property that has a potentially indefinite duration

   b. Leasehold—an estate that lasts for a fixed period of time

3. Types of estates (ways title may be held)

   a. Tenancy in severalty—title held by one owner (individual or organization)

   b. Co-ownership—title is held by two or more persons.

      (1) Tenancy in common—two or more owners hold an undivided interest.
          (a) Unity of possession
          (b) Each owner may encumber or convey his or her interest.
          (c) Each interest is inheritable.
      (2) Joint tenancy—two or more owners are named in one conveyance (deed, will, etc.) with right of survivorship.
          (a) Unity of ownership
          (b) Inherent right of survivorship among the owners
          (c) Unities of possession, interest, time and title required

   c. Ownership by married couples

      (1) Tenancy by the entirety—joint ownership of property acquired by husband and wife during marriage
          (a) Husband and wife are considered one legal entity.
          (b) Each has equal, undivided interest with inherent right of survivorship.
          (c) Both husband and wife must sign any documents to convey the property.
          (d) Ways of terminating a tenancy by the entirety include death of either spouse, agreement between both parties, divorce, court-ordered sale.
          (e) On death of one spouse, survivor becomes the sole owner in severalty.
      (2) Community property—consists of all real and personal property acquired during the marriage
          (a) Husband and wife are considered equal partners; both signatures required for conveying or mortgaging.
          (b) Does not have a right of survivorship as joint tenancy does.
          (c) Separate property—consists of real and personal property that was owned solely by either spouse before the marriage. This property may be conveyed without the signature of the nonowning spouse.

   d. Trust—a fiduciary arrangement in which property is conveyed by a trustor (maker) to a person or institution (trustee) to be held and administered on behalf of another person (beneficiary)

   e. Ownership by business organizations

      (1) Partnership—an association of two or more people who operate a business as co-owners and share in the business's profits and losses
          (a) General partnership—the individual partners share the liability.
          (b) Limited partnership—the general partner retains the liability, and the limited partners' liability is limited to their investment.
      (2) Corporation—artificial person or legal entity created by the laws of the state. Disadvantage: Profits are subject to double taxation unless it is a subchapter S corporation. Advantage: The shareholders are not liable for debts of the corporation.

       (3) Syndicate—two or more people or firms make and operate a real estate investment.

       (4) Limited liability companies or LLCs—a form of ownership created by state law. This form of ownership limits the liability for the owners from creditors.

  f. Condominium (form of ownership, not a style of building)

       (1) Unit owner holds a fee simple title to his or her unit plus tenancy in common ownership of specified share of common elements.

       (2) Condominium property is administered by an association of unit owners.

       (3) May require assessments or special payments to address some specific expense, such as a new roof.

  g. Cooperative

       (1) Property is owned by a corporation.

       (2) Residents are stockholders who receive a stock certificate and proprietary lease.

       (3) Burden of any defaulted payment falls on the remaining shareholders, a distinct disadvantage.

  h. Time-share ownership

       (1) Ownership interest that may include an estate interest in property and that allows the use of the property for a fixed or variable time period

       (2) Membership camping is similar to time-share use.

  i. Legal life estates—a form of life estate established by state law that becomes effective automatically when certain events occur

       (1) Dower—life estate that a wife has in the real estate of her deceased husband

       (2) Curtesy—life estate that a husband has in the real estate of his deceased wife

       (3) Homestead—a legal life estate in real estate occupied as the family home; in many states, a portion of the area or value of the property occupied as the family home is exempt from certain judgments for debts such as charge accounts and personal loans.

       (4) Pur autre vie—a life estate based on the life of someone other than the grantee.

C. Government restrictions

  1. The four governmental powers: police, eminent domain, taxation and escheat (study tip: PETE)

    a. Police power—the right of a municipality or county to impose laws, statutes and ordinances to protect public health, safety and welfare

       (1) Zoning—local laws that implement the comprehensive plan and regulate and control the use of land and structures within designated land-use districts

       (2) Buffer zones—landscaped parks and playgrounds to screen residential areas from nonresidential zones

       (3) Nonconforming use—a use of property that is permitted to continue after a zoning ordinance prohibiting it has been established for the area; commonly known as "grandfathering"

      (4) Variance—permission obtained from zoning authorities to build a structure or conduct a use that is expressly prohibited by the current zoning laws; an exception from the zoning ordinances

      (5) Building codes—an ordinance that specifies minimum standards of construction for buildings to protect public safety and health

      (6) Certificate of occupancy—permission to occupy a newly constructed residence; property may be transferred without the certificate but no one can legally occupy.

  b. Eminent domain—the right of a governmental agency or public entity to acquire private property for public use; condemnation is the process of acquiring the property.

  c. Taxation—charge on real estate to raise money to meet the public needs of a government

      (1) Ad valorem—general real estate tax based on the value of the property being taxed. Ad valorem taxes are specific, involuntary, statutory liens.

      (2) Special assessments—taxes levied on real estate to fund public improvements to the property. They are specific and statutory, but they may be voluntary or involuntary.

  d. Escheat—process by which property reverts to the state when the owner dies without a will and with no heirs

2. Environmental regulations and disclosures

  a. While there are no federal regulations that homeowners test for presence of lead-based paint, EPA and HUD regulations require disclosure of any known lead-based paint hazards to potential buyers and renters. Must attach seller's/landlord's/owner's disclosure of information on lead-based paint and lead-based paint hazards to all residential leases and sales contracts along with hazard pamphlet.

      (1) Purchasers have ten days to conduct risk assessment or inspection.

      (2) Purchasers are not bound by real estate contract until 10-day period expires.

  b. Hazardous substances

      (1) Asbestos

         (a) Once used as insulation, asbestos is harmful when disturbed or exposed.

         (b) Removal is costly; encapsulation, or sealing off, of disintegrating asbestos may be preferable method of containment.

      (2) Lead-based paint

         (a) Banned in 1978

         (b) Elevated levels in body cause serious damage to brain, kidneys, nervous system and red blood cells.

      (3) Radon

         (a) Caused by natural decay of radioactive substances

         (b) Colorless/tasteless; impossible to detect without testing

      (4) Urea-formaldehyde (UFFI)

         (a) Banned in 1982

         (b) Used in insulation

      (5) Carbon monoxide

         (a) Colorless, odorless gas, a by-product of burning fuels

         (b) Improper ventilation of equipment, malfunction-created problems

(6) Electromagnetic fields (EMFs)
   (a) Produced by electric currents
   (b) Controversy over claims whether they cause health problems

c. Groundwater contamination

   (1) Contamination from waste disposal sites' run-off, leaking underground storage tanks, use of pesticides and herbicides

d. Underground storage tanks (USTs)

   (1) State and federal regulations govern installation, maintenance, corrosion prevention, overspill prevention, monitoring, record keeping.
   (2) Exemptions include tanks less than 110 gallons, farm/residential tanks of 1,100 gallons or less of motor fuel used for noncommercial purposes, basement tanks (on or above floor of underground area).

e. Waste disposal sites

   (1) Landfill used as disposal site for garbage
   (2) Capping by laying 2-4 feet soil over top and planting grass or other vegetation
   (3) Ventilating with pipe through cap to release accumulation of natural gas

f. Comprehensive Environmental Response, Compensation and Liability Act (CERCLA) and environmental protection

   (1) Created Superfund to clean up uncontrolled hazardous waste sites
   (2) Created process by identifying potentially responsible parties (PRPs)
   (3) Administered by EPA

g. Superfund Amendments and Reauthorization Act (SARA)

   (1) Amended act clarifies obligation of lenders.
   (2) Innocent landowner immunity—establishes criteria to judge if person or business could be exempt from liability.

3. Water rights—each state has different regulation on who owns the water on or beneath a property. Some states allow these rights to be sold and some allow these rights to pass with the property.

a. Riparian rights—common-law rights granted to owners of land along non-navigable waters, i.e., a river or stream

b. Littoral rights—ownership rights for land bordering navigable lakes, seas and oceans

c. Doctrine of prior appropriation—in states where water is scarce, the right to use any water is controlled by the state.

D. Private restrictions

1. Voluntary and involuntary liens

a. Lien—a claim against property that provides for repayment of a debt or obligation of the property owner

   (1) Voluntary—created by property owner's action. For example, with a mortgage the borrower allows the lender to place a mortgage lien against the property.
   (2) Involuntary—created by law, e.g., real estate property taxes.

     (3) General—affect all of a debtor's property (both real and personal); e.g., IRS tax lien, judgment, estate tax lien.

     (4) Specific—secured by a particular parcel of real estate and affects only that property; e.g., mechanic's and materialman's lien, mortgage lien, property tax lien.

2. Covenants, conditions and restrictions—a limitation on the use of real property, generally originated by the owner or developer in a deed. These are private restrictions and must be enforced in court by other property owners. They may not be for illegal purposes, such as excluding certain races, nationalities or religions. If there is a conflict between zoning and deed restrictions, generally, the more restrictive prevails.

3. Other encumbrances—a cloud against clear, free title to property that does not prevent conveyance (e.g., unpaid taxes, easements, deed restrictions, mortgage loans, etc.)

  a. Easement—the right to use another's land for a specific purpose; sometimes referred to as an incorporeal right (a nonpossessory interest) in land

    (1) Easement appurtenant—annexed to the ownership and used for the benefit of another's parcel of land (runs with the land)

    (2) Dominant tenement—parcel that benefits from the easement

    (3) Servient tenement—parcel over which the easement runs

    (4) Party wall easement—a wall located on the boundary line between two adjoining properties for the use of both

    (5) Easement in gross—the limited right of one person to use another's land, often utility companies obtain easements in gross that may be assigned, conveyed and inherited.

    (6) Easement by necessity—created by court order based on the principle that owners have the right to enter and exit their land; they should not be landlocked.

    (7) Easement by prescription—person(s) who has (have) made use of another's land for a certain period of time as defined by state law may acquire the right to continue to use the land.

  b. Terminating easements—no longer needed; merger, release, nonuse, abandonment are some ways to terminate the easement.

  c. License—a personal privilege to enter the land of another for a specific purpose. It may be terminated or revoked.

  d. Encroachment—when some or all of a structure illegally extends beyond the land of its owner or beyond the legal building lines

■ QUIZ

Legal Descriptions

1. How many acres are in a lot that is ¼ of a mile wide by ¼ of a mile long?

   (A) 10
   (B) 40
   (C) 80
   (D) 120

2. A metes-and-bounds legal description

   (A) can be made only in areas excluded from the rectangular survey system.
   (B) is not acceptable in court in most jurisdictions.
   (C) must commence and finish at the same identifiable point.
   (D) is used to complete areas omitted from recorded subdivision plats.

3. How many lots, each measuring 72.5 feet wide by 100 feet deep, could be made from a two-acre parcel of land?

   (A) 6
   (B) 7
   (C) 12
   (D) 14

4. A parcel of land described as "the NW ¼ and the SW ¼ of Section 6, T4N, R8W of the Third Principal Meridian" was sold for $875 per acre. The listing broker will receive a 5% commission on the total sales price. How much will the broker receive?

   (A) $1,750
   (B) $5,040
   (C) $14,000
   (D) $15,040

5. The system of legal description that defines a parcel of land by its perimeter is the

   (A) geodetic survey.
   (B) rectangular survey.
   (C) lot-and-block.
   (D) metes-and-bounds.

6. A section

   (A) is one mile square.
   (B) contains 460 acres.
   (C) has a perimeter of 5,240 square feet.
   (D) can be numbered from one through 50.

7. A lot with a depth of 80 feet and an area of 4,800 square feet was sold for $350 per front foot. What was the total sales price?

   (A) $21,000
   (B) $28,000
   (C) $31,800
   (D) $35,000

8. A recorded subdivision plat is used in the

   (A) geodetic survey system.
   (B) rectangular survey system.
   (C) lot-and-block system.
   (D) metes-and-bounds system.

9. The method of describing land by degrees, feet and monuments is known as the

   (A) angular system.
   (B) metes-and-bounds system.
   (C) rectangular survey system.
   (D) lot-and-block system.

10. Which of the following is the BEST way to ensure that there are no encroachments and verify the boundaries of a parcel of land?

    (A) Write a legal description.
    (B) Get a survey.
    (C) Find the monuments.
    (D) Verify the benchmarks.

11. A farmer owned Section #17 and sold the southern half. He then fenced in the northern half. How many linear feet of fencing did he use if he had two six-foot-wide gates?

    (A) 14,250
    (B) 15,828
    (C) 18,530
    (D) 27,720

12. The owner has a large parcel of land surveyed into lots and streets and files a subdivision plat. Each lot can be legally described by use of which of the following?

    (A) Street address
    (B) Government survey
    (C) Metes and bounds
    (D) Lots and blocks

Physical and Economic Characteristics

13. A buyer is interested in a house that fits most of her needs, but it is located in a busy area where she is not sure that she wants to live. Her concern about the property's location is an example of an economic characteristic called

    (A) physical deterioration.
    (B) situs.
    (C) permanence of investment.
    (D) immobility.

14. Which of the following is an economic characteristic of land, **NOT** a physical characteristic of land?

    (A) Indestructibility   (C) Immobility
    (B) Uniqueness   (D) Scarcity

15. A physical characteristic of land is that it is

    (A) indestructible.
    (B) a wasting asset.
    (C) immune to the forces of supply and demand.
    (D) subordinate to real property rights.

16. Which of the following is a physical characteristic of land?

    (A) Scarcity
    (B) Permanence of investment
    (C) Uniqueness
    (D) Area preference

17. Generally, personal property can be distinguished from real property by its

    (A) greater variety.
    (B) mobility.
    (C) price.
    (D) multiplicity of use.

18. The economic characteristics of land include which of the following?

    (A) Uniqueness
    (B) Immobility
    (C) Homogeneity
    (D) Area preference

19. Which of the following is considered to have the greatest impact on the value of a property?

    (A) Area preference
    (B) Permanence of investment
    (C) Scarcity
    (D) Uniqueness

20. The foremost consideration in the purchase of a home is its affordability. What is the second?

    (A) Construction specifications
    (B) The age of the improvements
    (C) The location of the property
    (D) The landscaping and exterior

Real and Personal Property

21. The phrase "bundle of legal rights" is properly included in

    (A) the definition of real property.
    (B) a legal description.
    (C) real estate transactions.
    (D) leases for less than one year.

22. Which of the following is **NOT** included in one's right to control their property?

    (A) The right to invite people on the property for a political fundraiser
    (B) The right to exclude the utilities' meter reader
    (C) The right to erect "no trespassing" signs
    (D) The right to enjoy pride of ownership

23. Which of the following is considered to be personal property?

    (A) Wood-burning fireplace
    (B) Awnings
    (C) Bathtubs
    (D) Patio furniture

24. Real property can become personal property by

    (A) severance.
    (B) purchase.
    (C) hypothecation.
    (D) attachment.

25. A broker showed an owner-occupied property that had window screens, venetian blinds and a wall bed. The broker secured a buyer whose offer was accepted by the owner, and the transaction was placed in escrow. Before the close of escrow, the seller may remove

    (A) all of the identified items as they are trade fixtures.
    (B) only the venetian blinds as personal property.
    (C) only the wall bed because it is real property.
    (D) none of the identified items.

26. A rancher owns a parcel of land on which oil was discovered. If the rancher has not previously conveyed the subsurface rights, who owns the oil?

    (A) The rancher
    (B) The oil company that discovered the oil
    (C) The state government
    (D) The federal government

27. Certain items on the premises that are installed by the tenant and are related to the tenant's business are called

    (A) fixtures.   (C) trade fixtures.
    (B) emblements.   (D) easements.

28. Which of the following is classified as real property?

    (A) Chattels   (C) Emblements
    (B) Trade fixtures   (D) Fixtures

29. After the construction of a building over a railroad right-of-way, the trains can

    (A) operate as usual.
    (B) no longer use the tracks under the building.
    (C) use the tracks under the building only if they cause no problem for the building's occupants.
    (D) use the tracks under the building as long as they first obtain the building owner's permission.

30. An important characteristic of land is that it may be modified or improved at any given time. Which one of the following would **NOT** be considered to be an improvement?

    (A) Sewers   (C) Crops
    (B) Buildings   (D) Roads

31. A landlord leases store space to a tenant for a restaurant, and the tenant installs his ovens, booths, counters and other equipment. When do these items become real property?

    (A) When they are installed
    (B) When the tenant defaults on his rental payments
    (C) When the lease takes effect
    (D) When they remain on the property after the lease expires

32. Legally, the term *improvements* when referring to real estate would include

    (A) shrubbery.   (C) sidewalks.
    (B) trees.   (D) lawns.

33. Which of the following is **NOT** a test for determining a fixture?

    (A) Intent of the parties
    (B) Size of the item
    (C) Method of attachment of the item
    (D) Adaptation of the item to the real estate

34. The owner of a house wants to fence the yard for her dog. When the fence is erected, the fencing materials are converted to real estate by

    (A) severance.   (C) immobility.
    (B) annexation.   (D) indestructibility.

Title

35. A portion of a building was inadvertently built on another's land. This portion is called an

    (A) accretion.   (C) encroachment.
    (B) avulsion.   (D) easement.

36. A trust is a legal arrangement whereby the title to property is held for the benefit of a third party. The party holding the trust is

    (A) a beneficiary.
    (B) a trustor.
    (C) a trustee.
    (D) an attorney-in-fact.

37. A trust that is established by will after the death of the owner is called a

    (A) trust by will.
    (B) testamentary trust.
    (C) beneficial trust.
    (D) living trust.

38. In a land trust, which of the following is **NOT** a correct statement?

    (A) The beneficial interest can be transferred by assignment.
    (B) The beneficiary is usually the trustor.
    (C) Public records list all the beneficiaries.
    (D) The property can be pledged as security for a loan without recording a mortgage.

39. In a limited partnership

    (A) the number of investors is limited to ten.
    (B) all the partners participate in running the business.
    (C) the general partners run the business.
    (D) investors can participate with a small amount of capital with a minimum risk.

Types of Ownership

40. Two friends bought a store building and took title as joint tenants. One friend died testate. The surviving friend now owns the store

    (A) as a joint tenant with rights of survivorship.
    (B) in severalty.
    (C) as a tenant in common with the deceased friend's heirs.
    (D) in trust.

41. An ownership interest that is limited to the contractual period purchased is the

    (A) fee simple absolute.
    (B) time-share.
    (C) condominium.
    (D) cooperative.

42. In a gift of a parcel of real estate, one of the two owners was given an undivided 60% interest and the other received an undivided 40% interest. The two owners hold their interests as

    (A) cooperative owners.
    (B) joint tenants.
    (C) community property owners.
    (D) tenants in common.

43. In a community property state, separate property is owned

    (A) solely by either spouse before the marriage or acquired by gift or inheritance by either spouse during the marriage.
    (B) by one spouse before the marriage and jointly with the other spouse during the marriage.
    (C) one-half by each living spouse during the marriage and then passes entirely to the survivor.
    (D) jointly by one spouse and his or her deceased spouse's descendants.

44. A person who owns one unit in a multi-unit structure together with a specified undivided interest in the common elements would own a

    (A) cooperative.
    (B) share in a real estate investment trust.
    (C) condominium.
    (D) time-share interest.

45. A joint tenancy with right of survivorship may be created

    (A) automatically if the property is distributed to the surviving children.
    (B) by presumption if another form of ownership is not described.
    (C) by deed or will.
    (D) when a deed is signed by both spouses.

46. The owner of a condominium unit learns that a neighbor has failed to pay his real estate taxes. If this neighbor does not pay the taxes,

    (A) a lien can be filed against the condominium, including all of the units.
    (B) a lien can be filed against the neighbor's unit and his percentage of the common elements.
    (C) a lien can be filed only against the common areas of the condominium.
    (D) the taxing authority can order the condominium to be dissolved.

47. A property held as tenancy by the entirety requires which of the following?

    (A) The cotenants must be husband and wife.
    (B) The property in question must be Torrens property.
    (C) Upon the death of a co-tenant, the decedent's interest passes to his or her heirs.
    (D) In the event of a dispute the property must be partitioned.

48. Because a couple no longer needs their large house, they decide to sell their house and move into a cooperative apartment building. In a cooperative they will

    (A) become stockholders in a corporation.
    (B) own their individual apartment.
    (C) own the common elements.
    (D) receive a 20-year lease to their apartment.

49. Under the condominium form of ownership, the owner's interest in the unit would normally be a

    (A) life estate.
    (B) fee simple estate.
    (C) reversionary estate.
    (D) proprietary leasehold.

50. Two people are joint tenants. One joint tenant sells his interest to another person. What is the relationship of remaining joint tenant and the new owner?

    (A) They are joint tenants.
    (B) They are tenants in common.
    (C) There is no relationship because joint tenants cannot sell their interest.
    (D) The remaining joint tenant owns a ⅔ interest and new owner owns a ⅓ interest.

51. Joint tenancy with *survivorship* means

    (A) the tenancy interest may be inherited.
    (B) the tenancy interest may be held by the remaining tenants upon death.
    (C) the tenant's heirs are survivors.
    (D) this is not a legal tenancy.

52. Acquisition of real estate by a group that includes one or more sponsors (promoters) and several investors is called a

    (A) subdivision.   (C) syndication.
    (B) time-share.   (D) group investment.

53. The owner of a condominium is responsible for paying a monthly maintenance fee. If the owner fails to make this payment, which of the following is **TRUE?**

    (A) The owner is evicted.
    (B) The debt is collected from other owners.
    (C) A lien can be placed against the unit for the debt.
    (D) The debt is added to the mortgage payment.

54. How does a cooperative obtain the funds necessary to cover ongoing operating expenses and mortgage payments?

    (A) Charge rent
    (B) Sell common elements
    (C) Assess shareholders
    (D) Charge special assessments

55. In defining a corporation as a legal entity, which statement is **NOT TRUE?**

    (A) Stockholders have a direct ownership interest in the real estate.
    (B) It is managed by the board of directors.
    (C) It continues to exist until formally dissolved.
    (D) Profits are taxed on two levels: as corporation profit and as dividends top stockholders.

56. The difference between time-share use and a time-share estate is

    (A) the amount of time sold to the buyer.
    (B) that the one limits use to certain months, and the other provides a rotation system for use.
    (C) that time-share use sells only the right of occupancy for a certain number of years; it is not a fee-simple estate.
    (D) none, except in terminology.

Types of Estates

57. In many states, a family may have a legal life estate called

    (A) entirety.   (C) curtesy.
    (B) survivorship.   (D) homestead.

58. A person who has complete control over a parcel of real estate is said to own a

    (A) leasehold estate.
    (B) fee simple estate.
    (C) life estate.
    (D) defeasible fee estate.

59. Which of the following has an indefinite duration?

    (A) Freehold estate
    (B) Less-than-freehold estate
    (C) Estate for years
    (D) License

60. A life estate conveys to the life tenant

    (A) a leasehold for life.
    (B) a reversionary interest.
    (C) a legal life estate.
    (D) ownership for life of the tenant.

61. A vacant lot owned with a fee simple title next to a hospital and was gifted to the hospital. The owner had his attorney prepare a deed that conveyed the ownership of the lot to the hospital "So long as it is used for medical purposes." After the completion of the gift, the hospital will own a

    (A) life estate.
    (B) tenancy for years.
    (C) fee simple determinable.
    (D) periodic tenancy.

62. Creditors suing a homeowner who has obtained a homestead exemption as provided by state law

    (A) can have the court sell the residence and apply the full proceeds of the sale to the outstanding debts.
    (B) have no right to sell the debtor's residence.
    (C) may request a court-ordered sale and have the proceeds in excess of the statutory exemption and exempted liens applied to the debts.
    (D) can force the debtor to sell the residence in order to pay the outstanding debts in full.

63. A deed conveys ownership to the grantee as long as the existing building is not torn down. What type of estate did this deed create?

    (A) A life estate
    (B) A nondestructible estate
    (C) A fee simple estate
    (D) A determinable fee estate

64. An elderly lady conveys a life estate to her grandson and stipulates that upon her death the estate will pass to her son-in-law. The son-in-law has

    (A) an estate in reversion.
    (B) an estate in remainder.
    (C) an estate for years.
    (D) a legal life estate.

65. A daughter conveys the ownership of her apartment building to a nursing home, anticipating that the rental income will help pay for her father's care there. When her father dies, the daughter will recapture the ownership of the apartment building. This is an example of a

    (A) remainder life estate.
    (B) legal life estate.
    (C) life estate pur autre vie.
    (D) leasehold estate.

66. A person wants to ensure that the ownership of real property can be willed to her children. Which of the following forms of ownership would the person want?

(A) A conventional life estate
(B) A fee simple estate
(C) A joint tenancy
(D) A license

67. The severalty owner of a parcel of land sells it to a buyer. The buyer insists that the owner's wife join in signing the deed. The purpose of obtaining the wife's signature is to

(A) terminate any rights the wife may have in the property.
(B) defeat any curtesy rights.
(C) provide evidence that the owner is married.
(D) subordinate the wife's interests to the buyer.

Government Restrictions

68. The major intent of zoning regulations is to

(A) demonstrate the police power of the state.
(B) ensure the health, safety and welfare of the community.
(C) set limits on the amount and kinds of businesses in a given area.
(D) protect residential neighborhoods from encroachment by business and industry.

69. For land to be taken by the government under its right of eminent domain, which of the following must apply?

(A) The taking must be for a public purpose.
(B) There must be a statutory dedication.
(C) This must be an adverse action.
(D) There must be constructive notice.

70. A building is in the middle of the proposed highway. The owner does not want to sell the building. The legal process by which the government can take ownership of a building is

(A) escheat.
(B) eminent domain.
(C) condemnation.
(D) doctrine of public protection.

71. The power by which government can acquire ownership of private land for public use is

(A) escheat.
(B) eminent domain.
(C) condemnation.
(D) doctrine of public acquisition.

72. The current market value of a lot is $35,000. For tax purposes, it is assessed at 40% of market value. The tax rate is $4 per $100 of assessed value. What is the amount of the tax due?

(A) $560   (C) $705
(B) $625   (D) $740

73. The current market value of a property is $255,000 and it is assessed at 35 percent of its current market value with an equalization factor of 1.25. What is the amount of real estate tax due if the tax rate is $3.50 per $100 of assessed value?

(A) $2,756.25   (C) $3,904.69
(B) $3,445.31   (D) $4,880.26

74. A person defaulted in the payment of several of his debts, and the court has ordered his property sold to satisfy them. A title search revealed several outstanding liens against the property. Which of the following liens has first priority?

(A) The outstanding first mortgage lien dated and recorded one year ago
(B) The current year's real estate tax lien
(C) The judgment lien rendered and recorded last month
(D) The mechanic's lien for work started two months before the mortgage was recorded

75. In some states after real estate has been sold by the state or county to satisfy a delinquent tax lien, the defaulted owner usually has a right to

    (A) have the sale canceled by paying the back taxes and penalties.
    (B) pay his or her creditors directly and have their liens removed.
    (C) redeem the property within the time specified by law.
    (D) record a notice of nonresponsibility for the unpaid taxes.

76. Taxes levied on a property owner by the city to pay to install sidewalks or sewers are called

    (A) ad valorem taxes.
    (B) general property taxes.
    (C) special excise taxes.
    (D) special assessments.

77. The purpose of building permits is to

    (A) generate revenue for the municipality.
    (B) control the activities of building inspectors.
    (C) ensure compliance with building codes.
    (D) prevent encroachments.

78. For the past 30 years, a couple has operated a neighborhood grocery store. Last week the city council passed a zoning ordinance that prohibits packaged food sales in the area where the grocery store is located. The store is now an example of

    (A) an illegal enterprise.
    (B) a nonconforming use.
    (C) a violation of the zoning laws.
    (D) a variance of the zoning laws.

79. Which of the following **BEST** describes the purpose of a building permit?

    (A) The method for overriding or substantiating deed restrictions
    (B) The municipal control over the volume of construction
    (C) The evidence of compliance with municipal regulations
    (D) The method of regulating the area and size of buildings

80. The purpose of bulk zoning is to

    (A) ensure that certain kinds of uses are incorporated into developments.
    (B) specify certain types of architecture for new buildings.
    (C) control density and avoid overcrowding.
    (D) set overall development goals for the community.

81. A municipality establishes development goals through its

    (A) subdivision regulations.
    (B) restrictive covenants.
    (C) environmental regulations.
    (D) comprehensive plan.

82. Which of the following is a variance?

    (A) An exception to a zoning ordinance
    (B) A court order prohibiting certain activities
    (C) A reversion of ownership
    (D) A nullification of an easement

Environmental Regulations

83. How much of a partially buried storage tank must be underground to be considered an underground storage tank?

    (A) 10%   (C) 25%
    (B) 15%   (D) 35%

84. Which of the following agencies is responsible for administering the Superfund?

    (A) CERCLA   (C) EPA
    (B) PRP   (D) HUD

85. Asbestos poses a health hazard only when it

    (A) is used in paint, primarily in pre-1978 homes.
    (B) builds up in poorly ventilated areas.
    (C) is released into the air as dust and fibers.
    (D) is released into the groundwater.

86. What are the main sources of lead poisoning?

    (A) Paint and airborne fibers
    (B) Underground storage tanks and landfills
    (C) Paint and plumbing pipes
    (D) Plumbing pipes and airborne fibers

87. An owner is required by federal law to do all the following **EXCEPT**

    (A) disclose the location of known lead paint.
    (B) test for the presence of lead-based hazards.
    (C) give a special pamphlet to buyers and tenants.
    (D) allow a ten-day inspection period.

88. Impaired physical and mental development in children is a symptom of

    (A) exposure to radon.
    (B) lead poisoning.
    (C) sick building syndrome.
    (D) prolonged exposure to EMFs.

89. The Lead-Based Paint Hazard Reduction Act applies to homes built before

    (A) 1974.   (C) 1996.
    (B) 1978.   (D) 1999.

90. A homeowner accepts an offer from a buyer on her vintage Victorian home, which was built in 1892. Based on these facts, all of the following statements are true **EXCEPT** that

    (A) the homeowner must attach a lead-based paint disclosure statement to the sales contract.
    (B) if the homeowner is aware of any lead-based paint on the premises, she must disclose that fact to the buyer.
    (C) if the buyer requests a lead-based paint inspection, the homeowner has ten days in which to obtain one at her own expense.
    (D) the seller is entitled to receive a pamphlet that describes the hazards posed by lead-based paint.

91. In regulations regarding lead-based paints, HUD requires that

    (A) homeowners test for presence.
    (B) paint must be removed from surfaces before selling.
    (C) known paint hazards must be disclosed.
    (D) only licensed contractors may deal with removal.

92. Which of the following is **NOT TRUE** about underground water contamination?

    (A) It is not a major problem in the United States.
    (B) Any contamination can threaten the supply of pure, clean water for private wells and public water systems.
    (C) Protective state and federal laws concerning water supply have been enacted.
    (D) Real estate licensees can assist sellers by conducting an environmental inspection.

Water Rights

93. Many states determine the order of water rights according to which users of the water hold a recorded beneficial use permit. This allocation of water rights is determined by

    (A) accretion.
    (B) riparian theory.
    (C) littoral theory.
    (D) the doctrine of prior appropriation.

94. A homeowner acquired the ownership of land that was deposited by a river running through her property by

    (A) reliction.   (C) avulsion.
    (B) succession.   (D) accretion.

95. The rights of the owner of property located along the banks of a river are called

    (A) littoral rights.
    (B) prior appropriation rights.
    (C) riparian rights.
    (D) hereditaments.

96. Which of the following is **NOT** an ownership right to real estate?

    (A) Buildings located on the property
    (B) Air space above the property
    (C) Easements running with the land
    (D) Navigable rivers running through the property

97. The owner of a secluded area adjacent to the Atlantic Ocean noticed that people from town walked along the shore in front of his property. The owner learned that the local citizens had been walking along this beach for years. The owner went to court to try to stop people from walking along the water's edge in front of his property. The owner is likely to be

    (A) unsuccessful because the local citizens have been doing this for years and thus have an easement.
    (B) unsuccessful because the owner's property extends only to the high-water mark and the public can use the land beyond this point.
    (C) successful because the owner's property extends to the middle of the water bed.
    (D) successful because the owner can control access to his own property.

Voluntary and Involuntary Liens

98. When properly recorded in the county where the real estate of the defendant is located, a judgment becomes

    (A) a voluntary lien.
    (B) an involuntary lien.
    (C) a specific lien.
    (D) an equitable lien.

99. When a company furnishes materials for the construction of a house and is subsequently not paid, it may file

    (A) a deficiency judgment.
    (B) a lis pendens.
    (C) an estoppel certificate.
    (D) a mechanic's lien.

100. Which of the following liens does NOT need to be recorded to establish who is first in line to be paid in the event of a forclosure?

    (A) Mortgage lien
    (B) Real estate tax lien
    (C) Judgment lien
    (D) Mechanic's lien

101. When a lien against a parcel of real estate may result from a lawsuit currently before the court, one examining the public records would look for

    (A) the chain of title.
    (B) a lis pendens.
    (C) a suit to quiet title.
    (D) a judgment lien.

102. A mechanic's lien would be properly classified as

    (A) an equitable lien.
    (B) a voluntary lien.
    (C) a general lien.
    (D) a statutory lien.

103. Which of the following is a voluntary lien?

    (A) Mortgage lien
    (B) Estate tax lien
    (C) Real estate tax lien
    (D) Judgment lien

104. The filing requirements for mechanics' liens are found in

    (A) federal law.
    (B) state law.
    (C) common law.
    (D) case law.

105. A court orders real estate to be sold to satisfy an unpaid lien in an action known as

    (A) an encumbrance.
    (B) an attachment.
    (C) a seizure.
    (D) a foreclosure.

106. A mechanic's lien can be filed against an owner's real estate by

   (A) a real estate salesperson claiming part of the broker's commission.
   (B) a lumber company furnishing materials ordered by the property owner.
   (C) a real estate broker claiming a commission under a rejected offer.
   (D) an individual who obtained a judgment against the property owner.

107. Judgment liens are

   (A) specific liens.   (C) statutory liens.
   (B) voluntary liens.   (D) equitable liens.

108. Normally, the priority of general liens is determined by

   (A) the order in which they are filed or recorded.
   (B) the order in which the cause of action arose.
   (C) the size of the claim.
   (D) the court.

109. Which of the following is a general lien?

   (A) Real estate taxes
   (B) IRS lien
   (C) Mortgages
   (D) Mechanics' liens

110. When establishing priorities for liens,

   (A) a mechanic's lien is always first in priority.
   (B) the date on which the lien was recorded determines priority.
   (C) the date on which the debt was incurred determines priority.
   (D) a broker's lien is automatically first in priority.

111. What is the difference between a general and a specific lien?

   (A) A general lien cannot be enforced in court, while a specific lien can be enforced.
   (B) A specific lien is held by one person, while a general lien is held by at least two persons.
   (C) A general lien covers all of the debtor's property, while a specific lien covers only a certain piece of real property.
   (D) A specific lien covers real estate, while a general lien covers personal property.

112. Debts that are incurred by an individual and that become liens against the real property owned by that person are

   (A) general liens.
   (B) specific liens.
   (C) fiduciary encumbrances.
   (D) special assessments.

Private Restrictions

113. Restrictive covenants may **NOT** be created by

   (A) deed.
   (B) statute.
   (C) written agreement.
   (D) general plan of a subdivision.

114. Restrictive covenants that run with the land

   (A) are no longer effective when the title is transferred.
   (B) apply only until the developer has conveyed the title.
   (C) can be removed by a court of competent jurisdiction.
   (D) apply to and bind all successive owners of the property.

115. Which of the following deed restrictions are illegal?

   (A) Sizes and types of structures to be built
   (B) Potential future uses of the properties
   (C) The race of future owners and occupants of the properties
   (D) Exterior finish and decoration of the structures

116. A residential developer's deed restrictions would **NOT** include

   (A) easements in gross for the installation of public utilities.
   (B) the consent of the neighbors to sell.
   (C) the minimum square-footage for any home to be built in the subdivision.
   (D) a reference to the use of community facilities by residents only.

117. If the buyer of a vacant lot builds a house that violates the restrictions in his or her deed, the buyer may

   (A) forfeit the title to the property.
   (B) be sued and required to alter the structure to conform with the restrictions.
   (C) be sued and required to pay damages to the other residents in the neighborhood.
   (D) do so without any fear of reprisal by the residents in the area.

118. Which of the following is **NOT** an example of police power?

   (A) Zoning ordinances
   (B) Building codes
   (C) Restrictive covenants
   (D) City planning requirements

119. Deed restrictions are a means by which

   (A) local zoning laws are enforced.
   (B) the planning commission controls developers.
   (C) municipalities enforce building restrictions.
   (D) grantors control the future use of the property.

120. The purchase of a ticket for a professional sporting event gives the bearer

   (A) an easement right to park his car.
   (B) a license to enter and claim a seat for the duration of the game.
   (C) an easement in gross interest in the professional sporting team.
   (D) a license to sell goods and beverages at the sporting event.

121. If the owner of the dominant tenement becomes the owner of the servient tenement and merges the two properties,

   (A) the easement becomes dormant.
   (B) the easement is unaffected.
   (C) the easement is terminated.
   (D) the properties retain their former status.

122. A decedent left a will giving his neighbor the right to use a well on the decedent's land as long as the neighbor was alive. The neighbor's interest in the property is properly called

   (A) a license.
   (B) an easement in gross.
   (C) an easement appurtenant.
   (D) a life estate.

123. Your neighbors use your driveway to reach their garage on their property. Your attorney explains that the ownership of the neighbors' real estate includes an easement appurtenant giving them the driveway right. Your property is the

   (A) leasehold interest.
   (B) dominant tenement.
   (C) servient tenement.
   (D) license property.

124. The developer grants the gas company the right to install transmission lines. This right is called

   (A) a license.
   (B) an easement in gross.
   (C) an easement by prescription.
   (D) a conditional use permit.

125. A lot is encumbered by a sewer easement that runs where the foundation of a building would be. How will this affect the owner who wants to build a house?

   (A) It will have no effect because the sewer line is deeper than the foundation would be.
   (B) The house must be constructed to avoid the easement.
   (C) The municipality must move the sewer line prior to construction.
   (D) Any easement through the buildable part of the lot will prevent construction.

126. The owner divides a parcel into two lots, one of which is surrounded by other lots and has no street access. Which of the following is **TRUE?**

(A) The municipality must construct a street to create access.
(B) The owner must create an easement by condemnation to provide access.
(C) An easement by prescription should be granted.
(D) An easement by necessity should be created for the landlocked parcel.

■ ANSWER KEY WITH EXPLANATIONS

Legal Descriptions

1. (B) There are 40 acres in a lot that is ¼ mile by ¼ mile.
$5,280 \div 4 = 1,320$
$1,320 \times 1,320 = 1,742,400 \div 43,560 = 40.$

2. (C) A metes-and-bounds description begins at a point and describes the perimeter and must end at the same identifiable point.

3. (C) The two-acre parcel may be divided into 12 lots.
$43,560 \times 2 = 87,120$
$87,120 \div [72.5 \times 100] = 12.$

4. (A) The listing broker will receive $1,750.
$640 \div 4 \div 4 = 40$ acres sold
$40 \times \$875 = \$35,000$
$\$35,000 \times 5\% = \$1,750$

5. (D) A metes-and-bounds description begins at a point, describes the perimeter and ends at the same point. It is the oldest method of describing property.

6. (A) A section is a mile on each side.

7. (A) The lot sold for $21,000.
$4,800 \div 80 = 60$ front feet
$60 \div \$350 = \$21,000$

8. (C) Under the most modern form of property identification, the lot-and-block system requires that the recorded subdivision plat be recorded in the courthouse.

9. (B) A metes-and-bounds description utilizes degrees, feet and monuments to describe the perimeter of the property. It must begin and end at the same identifiable point.

10. (B) A survey will identify boundaries and show encroachments. It is best to have the survey done prior to closing, not after.

11. (B) The farmer used 15,828 feet of fencing for this parcel.
$2,640 + 2,640 + 5,280 + 5,280 - [6 + 6] = 15,828$

12. (D) Each lot is defined by a lot and block in the recorded plat.

Physical and Economic Characteristics

13. (B) Concern over a property's location is an example of situs, or area preference, the economic principle in which a person has a personal preference for one area over another, not necessarily based on objective facts and knowledge.

14. (D) Scarcity is a function of supply and demand, in other words, an economic characteristic. Physical characteristics include immobility, nonhomogeneity and indestructibility.

15. (A) Physical characteristics of land include indestructibility, immobility, and nonhomogeneity (uniqueness).

16. (C) Physical characteristics of land include uniqueness (nonhomogeneity), indestructibility and immobility.

17. (B) Personal property is identified by its mobility, destructibility and duplicatability.

18. (A) Area preference is an economic characteristic of real estate. Economic characteristics also include scarcity, permanence of investment and adaptation.

19. (A) Area preference, or situs, is the personal preference of people for one area over another, not necessarily based on objective facts and knowledge. This preference may lead to demand and higher prices. Lack of preference will lead to lower demand and lower prices.

20. (C) Buyers must have the financial capability to purchase a home in the area that they desire. Demand for a location can drive up prices. Lack of preference will lead to lower demand and lower prices.

Real and Personal Property

21. (A) "Bundle of rights" is the concept of land ownership that includes ownership of all legal rights to the land, including control, possession, use and disposition.

22. (B) The property owner does not have the right to exclude certain government employees, such as a utilities meter reader, from entering the private property. Under the "bundle of rights," the owner may include or exclude people on the property and has the right to take pride in ownership.

23. (D) Patio furniture is considered personal property. Real property physical characteristics include immobility, nonhomogeneity and indestructibility. Personal property is exactly the opposite: movable, easily duplicated, and can be destroyed.

24. (A) Real property becomes personal property when it is severed from the real property. An example of severance is when a hurricane uproots a large old tree. Prior to the storm, the tree was part of the real estate; after the storm, the tree is considered personal property and can be cut up and carried away.

25. (D) The seller may not remove any of the built-in items. The window screens, venetian blinds and wall bed all meet the test of attachment for real property. As this is not a "trade" property, the trade fixture rule would not apply.

26. (A) The rights to the oil are considered a part of the bundle of rights the rancher originally purchased.

27. (C) Items installed by the business tenant for the tenant's trade are called trade fixtures and remain the personal property of the tenant.

28. (D) A fixture is an item that was once personal property but now, by the way in which it is installed, has become real property. Examples include light fixtures, sinks and tubs. Personal property includes chattels, emblements and trade fixtures.

29. (A) The building owner purchased the rights to use the air space above the railroad tracks. The railroad retained the rights to the surface to operate its trains.

30. (C) Crops are not considered an improvement. In real estate terminology, an improvement is a human-made, permanent attachment to the land. Examples of improvements include sewers, buildings and roads. By the way, the word "improvement" is neutral; it does not necessarily mean better.

31. (D) If the business tenant installs trade fixtures and does not remove them prior to lease termination, the trade fixtures become the property of the landlord by accession.

32. (C) A sidewalk is an example of an improvement. In real estate terminology, an improvement is a human-made, artificial and permanent attachment to the land. The word "improvement" is neutral; it does not necessarily mean better.

33. (B) Size of the item is not one of the four basic tests used by courts to determine whether an item is a fixture (real property) or personal property. The four basic tests include intent, method of annexation, adaptation to real estate and agreement between the parties.

34. (B) The fence is real property. Annexation is the process by which personal property (lumber, nails, cement, etc.) may be changed to real property (a permanently installed fence).

Title

35. (C) An example of an encroachment is a building or some portion of it that extends beyond the land of the owner and illegally intrudes on some land of an adjacent landowner or a street or an alley.

36. (C) The trustee is the person who holds the title for the trust.

37. (B) A testamentary trust is established by will after the death of the owner. A living trust is established within the person's lifetime.

38. (C) Land trusts usually do **NOT** list the names of the beneficiaries to the trust in the public records.

39. (C) In a limited partnership, the general partners run the business and the limited partners supply the investment.

Types of Ownership

40. (B) As a joint tenant, the surviving friend became the owner at the time of the other's death. The surviving owner owns "in severalty." Property owned jointly is conveyed to the surviving owner, not to people named in the will.

41. (B) A time-share ownership interest is limited to the amount of time purchased.

42. (D) Tenancy in common is a type of ownership in which two or more people have an undivided interest in property, without the right of survivorship. Upon death of one of the owners, his or her interest passes to his or her heirs or devisees.

43. (A) In the states that recognize community property, separate property is that which was owned by either spouse before the marriage or acquired by gift or inheritance during the marriage.

44. (C) Condominium is a form of ownership, not a style of building. Condo owners own the unit together with a specified undivided interest in the common elements. Examples of condo ownership may be found in residential and commercial properties, even docks and parking spaces.

45. (C) The parties must create joint tenancy by deed or will. It must be done in writing, and it is never presumed.

46. (B) If a condo owner fails to pay his or her real estate taxes, the taxing authority may file a lien against the unit and the owner's percentage of the common elements.

47. (A) Only married couples may hold title as tenants by the entireties.

48. (A) The couple becomes stockholders in the corporation that owns the property. Their share of stock is inseparable from the proprietary lease.

49. (B) The owner's interest in a condominium unit is generally a fee simple estate. This estate may be held in severalty, as tenants in common or as joint tenants with right of survivorship.

50. (B) The remaining tenant (owner) is now a tenant in common with the new owner. They have to make a new determination if they should want to own jointly.

51. (B) In joint tenancy with survivorship, survivorship indicates that upon the death of one of the owners, his or her property interest transfers to the surviving owner(s).

52. (C) A syndication is not a legal entity; rather it is a combination of people or firms formed to accomplish a business venture of mutual interest by pooling resources.

53. (C) If the owner does not pay the monthly maintenance fee, the condo association may place a lien against the unit.

54. (C) In the event the association needs to do repairs, debt reduction, maintenance, etc., that are above the funds available, the cooperative association has the right to assess the owners for their share of the debt.

55. (A) Shareholders in a corporation own shares (personal property), and the corporation owns the real estate.

56. (C) A time-share use sells only the right of occupancy for a certain number of years; the developer retains ownership of the property. A time-share estate is a fee simple interest limited to the contractual period purchased.

Types of Estates

57. (D) Many states have created a legal life estate called homestead, which protects the family home from certain unsecured creditors.

58. (B) A fee simple estate is the highest form of ownership in a property. This type of ownership is said to run forever because it passes to the owners' heirs.

59. (A) A freehold estate can run for an indeterminable amount of time, or forever.

60. (D) The ownership of life estate is limited to lifetime of the recipient. An example of this could be a parent selling the homestead to the children and the children granting a life estate back to the parents so long as the parents live.

61. (C) The hospital will own a fee simple determinable, an estate that may be lost by the occurrence or nonoccurrence of a specified event. In this illustration, as long as the hospital uses the land for "medical purposes," the hospital retains ownership.

62. (C) The "homestead" protection according to state law protects the person's homestead from forced sale. In some states, the protection is limited to a monetary amount protected from creditors.

63. (D) A determinable fee estate rests on the occurrence or nonoccurrence of an event. In this situation, the grantee retains ownership as long as the existing building is not torn down.

64. (B) The son-in-law has a remainder estate. He will receive the remaining part of the estate upon his mother's death. The grandson holds a life estate.

65. (C) Pur autre vie is a life estate based on the life of someone other than the grantee of the property. In this case, the nursing home hold a life estate based on the life of the father; when he dies, the property reverts to the daughter.

66. (B) A fee simple estate is the highest form of ownership recognized by law. It may be willed to the next generation or sold outright.

67. (A) Getting the wife's signature on the deed terminates any rights that the wife may have in the property. These rights vary from state to state, depending on community property laws, dower and curtesy rights, and division of marital assets.

Government Restrictions

68. (B) The broad intent of zoning is to protect the entire community by regulating and controlling the character and use of property. Zoning is an example of the use of police power, and it may set limits and protect areas for certain uses.

69. (A) The government cannot take a person's property under its police power abilities; the government must prove there is a public need or purpose and pay a fair price to the owner.

70. (C) Condemnation is the legal process by which the government can force the sale of a building in the middle of a proposed highway. The government has the right the acquire private property for public use under eminent domain.

71. (B) Eminent domain is one of the government's police powers. The government must establish that the taking is for the good of the public, offer fair and just compensation, and permit an appeal.

72. (A) The taxes on the lot are $560.
$[\$35,000 \times 40\%] \div 100 \times 4 = \$560$

73. (C) The current real estate taxes on this property are $3,904.69.
$\$255,000 \times 35\% = \$89,250$
$\$89,250 \times 1.25 = \$111,562.50$
$\$111,562.50 \div 100 \times 3.5 = \$3,904.69$

74. (B) Tax liens would be paid first, then the other liens as filed by earliest date and time.

75. (C) Each state has different rules for a tax foreclosure. After the property is sold, the defaulting owner may have a specific amount of time to redeem the property. This is called the statutory right of redemption.

76. (D) A special assessment is a tax or levy customarily imposed against only those specific parcels of real estate that will benefit from a proposed public improvement like a street or a sewer.

77. (C) The purpose of building permits is to ensure compliance with building codes.

78. (B) When zoning is imposed on an area, generally, a nonconforming use is granted to existing properties that do not meet the current zoning standards. This is sometimes called "grandfathering in." Local laws vary as to the conditions for this property's use.

79. (C) Building permits are issued to ensure compliance with municipal regulations.

80. (C) Bulk zoning is a special land-use objective to control density and to avoid overcrowding by imposing restrictions such as setbacks, building heights and percentage of open area, or by restricting new construction projects.

81. (D) Local governments establish development goals by creating a comprehensive plan, sometimes called a master plan. These plans are an effort to control growth and development.

82. (A) A variance, if granted, permits the landowner the right to use his or her property in a manner that is strictly prohibited by the existing zoning.

Environmental Regulations

83. (A) The official definition of an underground storage tank is that at least 10% of it be underground.

84. (C) The Superfund was established by CERCLA and is administered and monitored by the EPA.

85. (C) Asbestos is hazardous as dust and fibers.

86. (C) Paint and pipes are the main sources of lead poisoning.

87. (B) Owners are not required to test for lead.

88. (B) When ingested, lead can cause serious damage to the brain, kidneys, nervous system and red blood cells.

89. (B) The Lead-Based Paint Hazard Reduction Act targets homes built before 1978 because that was the year lead was banned from most paints.

90. (C) While no one is required to test for lead, the federal law gives the prospective buyer ten days (or any time agreed to or the buyer may waive the right) to have the home tested for lead at the buyer's expense.

91. (C) HUD requires the known presence of paint hazards in the property to be disclosed.

92. (D) Real estate licensees are required to disclose what they know but are not qualified by having a real estate license to do environmental inspections.

Water Rights

93. (D) Prior appropriation is a concept of water ownership in which the landowner's right to use available water is based on a government-administered permit system. This is primarily used in western states where water is scarce.

94. (D) Accretion is the addition of land through deposits left by the actions of a river flowing through the property.

95. (C) Riparian rights are an owner's rights in land that borders on or includes a stream, river or lake. Generally, these rights include access to and use of the water.

96. (D) Navigable rivers are not owned by a nearby property owner. They are considered public highways in which the public has an easement or right to travel. Ownership rights may include buildings, air space above the property and easements running with the land.

97. (B) Generally, a beach is public land and the owner's right of exclusion extends only to the highest water line.

Voluntary and Involuntary Liens

98. (B) Judgments, when recorded, are regarded as involuntary liens against the property.

99. (D) A mechanic's lien is filed by people who supply or do the work on the property. In some states, the mechanic's lien is effective as the date the materials were delivered or the work done. If this happened just prior to a sale, the mechanic's lien would be effective prior the new mortgage lien even if the mechanic's lien was filed after closing.

100. (B) Real estate tax liens have priority over other liens whether or not they are actually filed against the property.

101. (B) The phrase "lis pendens" means that a suit or a possibility of a suit is pending.

102. (D) The rights of this type of lien are established by statute.

103. (A) The mortgage lien is considered voluntary. Involuntary liens include an estate tax, real estate tax and judgment lien.

104. (B) State law provides the requirements for a mechanic's lien.

105. (D) When a court orders a property to be sold to satisfy unpaid debts, the property goes through a foreclosure procedure.

106. (B) A supplier of materials used by a person who actually does the work has a right to file a mechanic's lien to protect his or her interest. Brokers and salespeople may go to court with a commission dispute, and they may be awarded a judgment which they could file against the property. However, this is **NOT** a mechanic's lien.

107. (D) Judgment liens are general, involuntary, equitable liens on real and personal property owned by the debtor.

108. (A) Lienholders are paid in the order in which the liens were filed or recorded.

109. (B) An IRS lien is a general lien against the person and is, thus, a lien against all the real and personal property owned by the debtor.

110. (B) Generally, a lien filed first has highest priority. However, in some states, a mechanic's lien may take precedence over earlier recorded liens when the state allows the mechanic's lien to take effect when the work was done or the materials supplied.

111. (C) A general lien covers all of the debtor's property, while a specific lien covers only a certain piece of real property.

112. (B) A specific lien affects or attaches only to a certain, specific parcel of land or piece of property.

Private Restrictions

113. (B) Since deed restrictions are private, created by the property owners, they cannot be created by statute. Also known as restrictive covenants, they may be created by deed, written agreement and in a general plan of a subdivision.

114. (D) Deed restrictions are attached to land, not the owners. Thus, a restrictive covenant is binding on all successive owners of the property.

115. (C) Deed restrictions based on race or religion are illegal. Deed restrictions are legal so long as they do not violate current law. Thus, they may limit the size and types of structures, future uses, and the exterior finish of the structures.

116. (B) Generally, deed restrictions will not limit the owner's right to sell. However, many condominium communities do reserve the "right of first refusal." Deed restrictions may include an easement in gross to the utility companies, establish a minimum square footage and restrict the use of community facilities to residents only.

117. (B) A property owner who builds in defiance of the deed restrictions may be sued and forced to alter the property to conform to the restrictions.

118. (C) Restrictive covenants are private and must be privately enforced. Government restrictions include zoning ordinances, building codes and other city planning requirements.

119. (D) Deed restrictions permit the grantor control over the future use of the property.

120. (B) The purchase of a ticket gives the bearer a license to enter and claim a seat. Licenses are personal and may be revoked.

121. (C) The easement is created to service one of the properties. When the property is merged under one owner, there is no need to provide this specific right.

122. (B) An easement in gross is a personal easement given to the neighbor and terminates with the neighbor's death.

123. (C) The servient tenement or property will "serve" the neighbors' property, allowing them to have access to the property. The property that benefits from the easement is the dominant tenement.

124. (B) Developers often grant an easement in gross to utility companies. This is a personal right and may be revoked. There is no dominant tract of land that benefits from this easement, although there are many servient tenements.

125. (D) Any easement through the buildable part of the lot will prevent construction.

126. (D) The owner must have legal access. An easement by necessity should be created for any landlocked parcel.

Property Valuation and the Appraisal Process

5

■ CONTENT OUTLINE

IV. Property Valuation and the Appraisal Process

A. Principles of valuation—an estimate of value

1. Value, price and cost

   a. Value—what the property is worth

      (1) Market value—the most probable price at which a willing seller would sell and a willing buyer would buy, neither being under abnormal pressure

   b. Price—what the owner is asking for the property

   c. Cost—the price to replace the property

2. Characteristics of property that affect value (study tip: DUST)

   a. Demand

   b. Utility

   c. Scarcity

   d. Transferability

3. Principles of value

   a. Anticipation—value can increase or decrease if one anticipates some future benefit or detriment from the property.

   b. Change—no physical or economic condition remains constant.

   c. Competition—excess profits tend to attract competition.

   d. Conformity—maximum value is realized when the use of land conforms to existing neighborhood standards (homogeneity).

   e. Contribution—the value of any component is what its addition contributes to the whole or what its absence detracts from the whole.

   f. Highest and best use—the possible use of land that would produce the greatest net income and develop the highest land value.

g. Increasing returns—money spent on improvements produces an increase in income or value.

h. Diminishing returns—additional improvements do not produce a proportionate increase in income or value.

i. Plottage—the merging of adjacent lots into one may produce a higher total value than the sum of the two lots valued separately; the process of merging two separately owned lots under one owner is known as assemblage.

j. Regression and progression—between dissimilar properties, the worth of the better property is affected adversely by the presence of the lesser-quality property; usually, the higher valued property decreases significantly, while the lesser-valued property increases slightly.

k. Substitution—maximum value of a property tends to be set by the cost of purchasing an equally valuable and desirable substitute property (basis of sales comparison approach to value).

l. Supply and demand—value will increase if the supply decreases and demand either increases or remains constant, and vice versa.

B. Determining value

1. Sales comparison (market data) approach—value is based on comparison of subject property with recently sold comparable properties. Based on the principle of substitution.

2. Cost approach—value is based on current construction costs, less depreciation, plus land value.

3. Income approach—value is based on the monetary returns a property can be expected to generate; capitalization of net income.

   a. Gross rent multiplier—method used to appraise single-family homes not purchased primarily for the income they can produce

   b. Capitalization rate—a mathematical process used for estimating the value of a property using a proper rate of return on the investment and the expected annual net operating income. The lower the cap rate, the greater the value (less risk); and vice versa.

4. Types of depreciation (loss of value due to any source)

   a. Physical deterioration—loss of value due to ordinary wear and tear (may be curable or incurable)

   b. Functional obsolescence—loss of value due to changes in building arts or styles (may be curable or incurable)

   c. Economic obsolescence a.k.a. external obsolescence—loss of value caused by factors not on the subject property such as environmental, social or economic (always incurable)

5. Reconciliation—the process in which the validity and reliability of each approach are weighed to arrive at the single best and most supportable conclusion of value

C. Appraisal

1. Purpose and use of appraisal—to help establish a reasonable value of a specific property or properties

    a. State the problem—purpose of the appraisal.

    b. List data needed and the sources.

    c. Gather, record and verify data.

    d. Analyze and interpret data.

    e. Reconcile data for final value estimate.

    f. Prepare a report.

2. Role of the appraiser—provides his or her opinion of the value of a specific property or properties.

3. Role of the licensee in property valuation—a licensee may provide an opinion of value but not the details as a certified appraiser. The licensee can assist the appraiser by providing up to date market conditions. The licensee can assist the consumer by preparing a competitive market analysis (CMA) to arrive at a good listing price or offering price.

■ QUIZ

1. The income approach to value would be **MOST** important in the appraisal of

    (A) a condominium.
    (B) an office building.
    (C) a single-family residence.
    (D) a vacant residential lot.

2. In an old retail building, which of the following would **MOST** likely be a cause of incurable functional obsolescence?

    (A) Deficient and inadequate lighting
    (B) Closely spaced internal support columns
    (C) An unattractive store front
    (D) A decrease in the area's population

3. Which of the following is NOT a characteristic of value?

    (A) Scarcity   (C) Obsolescence
    (B) Transferability   (D) Utility

4. The expression "more buildings are torn down than fall down" refers to

    (A) curable physical deterioration.
    (B) incurable physical deterioration.
    (C) the enforcement of building codes.
    (D) functional and external depreciation.

5. The value of real estate is **NOT** affected by

    (A) depreciation.
    (B) supply and demand.
    (C) prices of similar properties.
    (D) the seller's asking price.

6. The term *depreciation* refers to the

    (A) value of real estate after the expiration of its useful life.
    (B) loss of value in real estate from any cause.
    (C) costs incurred to renovate or modernize a building.
    (D) capitalized value of lost rental income.

7. When appraising real estate, the first consideration of the appraiser should be the

    (A) asking price of the property.
    (B) highest and best use of the property.
    (C) original cost of the property.
    (D) selling prices of similar properties.

8. Which of the following would be classified as a cause of external obsolescence?

   (A) A leaking roof that needs to be completely replaced
   (B) Poorly maintained properties in the neighborhood
   (C) A poorly designed floor plan that could be modified
   (D) Convenient access to schools and recreational facilities

9. It is necessary to calculate a dollar value for depreciation when using

   (A) the sales comparison approach to value.
   (B) the cost approach to value.
   (C) the income approach to value.
   (D) gross rent multipliers.

10. When using the income approach, the appraiser will use

   (A) the equalization factor.
   (B) depreciation.
   (C) appreciation.
   (D) the capitalization rate.

11. In the valuation of a large apartment complex, the **MOST** weight would be given to which of the following approaches to value?

   (A) The cost approach
   (B) The income approach
   (C) The sales comparison or market data approach
   (D) All approaches would be equally weighted.

12. In the cost approach to value, the appraiser makes use of the

   (A) owner's original cost of the building.
   (B) estimated replacement cost of the building.
   (C) sales prices of similar buildings in the area.
   (D) assessed value of the building.

13. The sales comparison approach to value would be **MOST** important when estimating the value of

   (A) an existing residence.
   (B) an apartment building.
   (C) a retail location.
   (D) a new residence.

14. The construction cost of exactly duplicating the slate shingles on a Victorian building is called the

   (A) depreciation schedules.
   (B) capitalization rate.
   (C) reproduction cost.
   (D) replacement cost.

15. An appraiser is using the sales comparison approach to value. Which of the following homes will **NOT** be used as a comparable property?

   (A) Sold over six months ago
   (B) Sold recently but is located in another similar neighborhood
   (C) Sold by the owners who were undergoing a foreclosure
   (D) Sold recently but is located on a much larger lot

16. Using which of the following approaches will require the value of the land to be calculated separately from the value of the improvements?

   (A) The income approach
   (B) The cost approach
   (C) The sales comparison approach
   (D) The gross rent multiplier

17. Reconciliation is **BEST** described as

   (A) selecting the highest value given by the three approaches to value.
   (B) comparing comparable properties and identifying their amenities.
   (C) determining the final value by selecting one value from those given.
   (D) analyzing the results obtained from the three approaches to value.

18. A building is valued at $215,000 and contains four apartments that rent for $470 each per month. The owner estimates that the net operating income is 65% of the gross rental receipts. What is the capitalization rate?

   (A) 3.7 percent   (C) 10.5 percent
   (B) 6.8 percent   (D) 14.2 percent

19. The steps in the appraisal process do **NOT** include

    (A) gathering specific data on the subject property.
    (B) gathering general data for the area of the subject property.
    (C) considering the seller's estimate of the property's value.
    (D) applying the three approaches to value to the collected data.

20. The gross rent multiplier is used as a guideline for estimating value based on the

    (A) ratio of the gross rents to the net rents after expenses.
    (B) proportion of rents due to the actual rents collected.
    (C) capitalization of the annual gross rental income.
    (D) relationship of the sales price to the rental income.

21. The loss of value due to the normal wear and tear on a property is called

    (A) external depreciation.
    (B) physical depreciation.
    (C) functional obsolescence.
    (D) economic deterioration.

22. To find the value of a property using the income approach to value, if the net operating income and the capitalization rate were known, the appraiser would

    (A) multiply the net operating income by the capitalization rate.
    (B) multiply the effective gross income by the capitalization rate.
    (C) divide the net operating income by the capitalization rate.
    (D) divide the capitalization rate by the net operating income.

23. An appraiser has been employed to estimate the market value of a parcel of vacant land. The resulting appraisal report would **NOT** include reference to the

    (A) highest and best use of the parcel.
    (B) listed price of the parcel.
    (C) most probable price the parcel will bring.
    (D) physical dimensions of the parcel.

24. When appraising a commercial property, the appraiser is **MOST** concerned with the

    (A) accrued depreciation on the property.
    (B) net income generated by the property.
    (C) gross income generated by the property.
    (D) total debt service on the property.

25. In the appraisal of an office building, which of the following would be classified as external depreciation?

    (A) Termite damage to the structural components of the building
    (B) A poor architectural design resulting in a cluttered floor plan
    (C) An inadequate number of elevators and antiquated restroom facilities
    (D) Proximity to a factory under EPA investigation

26. The period of time over which an improvement to the property will contribute to its value is known as its

    (A) amortized life.
    (B) chronological life.
    (C) actual life.
    (D) economic life.

27. Of the following, specific data includes the

    (A) dimensions of the subject property.
    (B) employment opportunities in the area.
    (C) regional comprehensive plan.
    (D) environmental impact statement.

28. When estimating the value of property using the cost approach, which of the following would **NOT** be considered by the appraiser?

    (A) Loss of value due to uncollected delinquent rent
    (B) Estimated loss attributable to an outdated heating system
    (C) Quality of materials and workmanship in the original structure
    (D) Excessive amount of traffic noise outside the property

29. The market price of real estate is generally the same as the

    (A) sales price.
    (B) market value.
    (C) highest and best use.
    (D) assessed value.

30. Under the cost approach, which of the following may **NOT** be depreciated?

    (A) Location   (C) Gross income
    (B) Buildings   (D) Land

31. An appraiser has been hired to prepare an appraisal on a property that includes an elegant old mansion that is now used as an insurance company office. Which approach to value would the appraiser rely on **MOST?**

    (A) Income approach
    (B) Gross rent multiplier approach
    (C) Sales comparison approach
    (D) Replacement cost approach

32. A house with outmoded plumbing is suffering from

    (A) functional obsolescence.
    (B) curable physical deterioration.
    (C) incurable physical deterioration.
    (D) external depreciation.

33. A four-bedroom house with one bathroom for today's standards would be considered to be

    (A) physically obsolete.
    (B) functionally obsolete.
    (C) economically obsolete.
    (D) diminished.

34. In the cost approach, an appraiser uses which of the following?

    (A) Sales prices of similar properies
    (B) The owner's original cost of construction
    (C) An estimate of the building's replacement cost
    (D) The property's depreciated value as used for income tax purposes

35. The purpose of an appraisal is to

    (A) estimate the value of a property.
    (B) set the market price of a property.
    (C) determine the projected income of a property.
    (D) set the amount of consideration the seller should accept from a purchaser.

36. In the income approach, which of the following is NOT considered when calculating the net operating income?

    (A) Real estate taxes
    (B) Management fees
    (C) Debt service
    (D) Utilities

37. May a broker prepare an appraisal for a client?

    (A) Yes, because a broker can prepare an appraisal
    (B) No, because a broker is not an appraiser
    (C) Only if the client pays for the appraisal
    (D) Only if the broker has taken an appraisal class

38. A developer just purchased six different properties and combined them into one property. This larger property has a greater value than the individual properties added together. This resulting larger value is a result of

    (A) substitution.   (C) change.
    (B) contribution.   (D) plottage.

39. What effect does the capitalization rate have when determining the value of the property?

    (A) No effect
    (B) Lower the rate, higher the value
    (C) Higher the rate, lower the value
    (D) Depends on the situation

40. The first step in the appraisal process is to

    (A) determine the highest and best use.
    (B) list the data needed and the sources.
    (C) state the problem.
    (D) gather, record and verify the necessary data.

41. For residential properties, most government agencies require the

 (A) Uniform Residential Appraisal Report (URAR).
 (B) Certificate of Reasonable Value (CRV).
 (C) Uniform Standards of Professional Appraisal Practice (USPAP).
 (D) Letter of Conditional Commitment (LCC).

42. In the sales or market approach to value, adjustments are made to the price of the

 (A) comparable properties.
 (B) subject property.
 (C) replacement cost.
 (D) reproduction cost.

43. Who actually determines fair market value?

 (A) Appraiser and seller
 (B) Seller only
 (C) Buyer only
 (D) Buyer and seller

44. A real estate salesperson is **MOST** likely to complete and deliver to a seller

 (A) an appraisal.
 (B) a competitive market analysis.
 (C) a real estate analysis.
 (D) a certificate of reasonable value.

45. An appraiser must assign a value to a brand new home, never lived in before. The appraiser will assign the **MOST** weight to the value determined by the

 (A) market approach.
 (B) cost approach.
 (C) income approach.
 (D) quantity-survey method.

■ ANSWER KEY WITH EXPLANATIONS

1. (B) Of the four, the only property that generates income would be an office building.

2. (B) Closely spaced internal support columns are a cause of incurable functional obsolescence because the expense to relocate them would be prohibitive. Functional obsolescence is incurable when the work to correct outmoded or unacceptable physical or design features is not economically feasible.

3. (C) Obsolescence is an estimation of loss of value due to depreciation. Four characteristics of value include demand, utility, scarcity and transferability (remembered easily by the acronym DUST).

4. (D) The expression "more buildings are torn down than fall down" refers to structurally sound buildings being torn down for reasons unrelated to their quality and more because of a change in highest and best use.

5. (D) The value of real estate is **NOT** generally affected by the seller's asking price. It **IS** affected by supply and demand, comparable sales and depreciation.

6. (B) Depreciation is a loss of value for any cause. For example, a home with kitchen appliances from the 1950s would suffer from depreciation or have less value than a home with new kitchen appliances.

7. (B) The property's value is first based on the highest and best use of the property in that area.

8. (B) Poorly maintained neighborhood properties are a cause for external obsolescence. External obsolescence is a result of negative factors outside of the subject property—for example, a deteriorating neighborhood or proximity to a polluting factory.

9. (B) Depreciation is a key element in the cost approach to establishing value. The appraiser must deduct the accrued depreciation from the cost to construct the building to determine the estimated land value.

10. (D) In the income approach, the net income is divided by the capitalization rate to establish the value of the property.

11. (B) When dealing with investment property, the value is in the return on investment. For this reason, the income approach is used for income-producing properties.

12. (B) The appraiser must estimate the cost to replace this building minus depreciation in the cost approach. A **NEW** building would be of more value than an older building of the same construction; therefore the appraiser must depreciate the value of the new construction to equal the value of the existing property.

13. (A) The sales comparison approach is the most reliable in appraising existing, single-family homes in established neighborhoods.

14. (C) Reproduction cost consists of the expenses in making an exact duplicate of the subject property, in this case slate shingles. Replacement cost is the cost to use current construction methods and materials; an example would be fiberglass shingles. Generally speaking, reproduction is more expensive.

15. (C) Because foreclosure sales are generally conducted under duress and do not reflect a true market-value sale, an appraiser would not consider a property in which the owners are undergoing foreclosure. However, an appraiser would consider properties sold less than a year ago, those located in similar neighborhoods, and homes that are similar to the subject property but situated on a larger lot.

16. (B) When using the cost approach, the appraiser must determine the value of the land, as if it were vacant, by using the sales comparison approach. Then the appraiser will add the adjusted value of the building(s) to the value of the land in order to arrive at the fair market value.

17. (D) Reconciliation is the process of analyzing and effectively weighing the findings from the three approaches. That is, the appraiser must reconcile or bring to a conclusion all the different data he or she has obtained about the property. Reconciliation is **NOT** an averaging of the prices.

18. (B) The capitalization rate is 6.8 percent.
Capitalization Rate = Net Income ÷ Value
[470 × 4] × 12 × 65% ÷ $215,000 = .0682 or 6.8%.

19. (C) The appraiser may not consider what the seller wants for the property. The appraiser must gather specific and general data on the subject property and apply all three approaches.

20. (D) The gross rent multiplier and gross income multiplier are used for estimating value based on the relationship of the gross rental income to the selling price. The gross rent multiplier (GRM) is generally used with single family rentals and the gross income multiplier (GIM) is used for larger apartment complexes.

21. (B) Physical depreciation is the loss of value due to physical wear and tear on the property. It may be curable or incurable.

22. (C) To estimate the value of a property using the income approach, the appraiser divides the Net Income by the Cap Rate.

23. (B) The appraiser does not utilize what the owner wants for the property. The appraiser estimates the value by examining the highest and best use of the parcel and its physical dimensions.

24. (B) Under the income approach, the appraiser is most interested in the net income of the property, not the gross income or total debt service. Accrued depreciation is important when using the cost method.

25. (D) The property owner has **NO** control over laws affecting the property or of uses inconsistent for the owner's property. Proximity to a waste site is out of the property owner's control. External depreciation is always incurable.

26. (D) The economic life of a property is the number of years during which an improvement will add value to the land.

27. (A) Specific data includes details of the subject property, such as the dimensions of the subject property and those of the comparable properties. General data cover the nation, region, city and neighborhood. Examples of general data include area employment opportunities, a comprehensive plan and environmental impact statements.

28. (A) Uncollected rents affect the income when using the income approach, **NOT** the cost approach. Value as determined by the cost approach will be affected by an outdated heating system, quality of materials and workmanship in the original structure and excessive traffic noise.

29. (A) The market price is set by what buyers are willing to pay for property in the area and for what sellers are willing to sell. These values will vary from location to location.

30. (D) Land may never be depreciated under the cost approach. It does not "wear out."

31. (A) The appraiser should use the income approach because the old mansion is now generating income through rents received.

32. (A) Outmoded plumbing is an excellent example of functional obsolescence, that is, a loss of value to a real estate improvement because of functional problems that may be caused by age or poor design.

33. (B) Functional obsolescence is a characteristic of a property that does not conform to current standards. Today, a four-bedroom house with only one bath is definitely functionally obsolete.

34. (C) Using the cost approach, the appraiser must determine the cost to replace a similar building today. Unless the property is brand new, the appraiser will have to subtract an estimate of the depreciation due to its age.

35. (A) The appraiser estimates value; the appraiser does not set or determine value.

36. (C) When determining net income, the appraiser will not consider the debt service. It may be helpful to remember that not all owners carry debt; it is **NOT** an expense of the property.

37. (B) For most federally related loans, only a licensed or certified appraiser may prepare an appraisal. A broker may only prepare a broker's opinion of value or a competitive market analysis.

38. (D) The principle of plottage holds that merging or consolidating several lots into one larger one produces a greater total value than each separately. Assemblage is the process of bringing the lots together.

39. (B) The lower the cap rate, the higher the value. For example, when using net income of $10,000: divided by 8%, value is indicated as $125,000. When divided by 10%, value is indicated as $100,000. The higher cap rate indicates a greater risk and thus a lower value.

40. (C) The first step in the appraisal process is to state the problem. That is followed by listing the data needed followed by gathering, recording and verifying the necessary data. Using this information allows the appraiser to then determine highest and best use.

41. (A) For residential properties, most government agencies require the URAR, Uniform Residential Appraisal Report.

42. (A) In the sales or market approach, adjustments are made to the sale prices of the comparable properties. It is not possible to adjust the value of the subject property, because that value has not yet been determined.

43. (D) The agreement between the buyer and seller actually determines market value.

44. (B) A real estate salesperson is most likely to prepare a **CMA,** competitive market analysis, to assist the seller in determining a fair asking price. Buyers also consider **CMAs** when preparing to make an offer. The sold properties tell the price that other buyers have paid (substitution), asking prices of those currently on the market (competition) and those prices which have expired (more than other buyers are willing to pay).

45. (B) The cost approach is most useful in determining the value of a newly constructed home. No depreciation is applied.

Real Estate Sales Contracts

6

■ CONTENT OUTLINE

V. Real Estate Sales Contracts

A. Purpose, scope and elements of real estate sales contracts

1. Contracts and contract law

   a. Types of contracts

      (1) Express—oral or written contract in which the parties state the contract's terms and express their intentions in words
      (2) Implied—agreement demonstrated by acts and conduct
      (3) Unilateral—only one party makes a promise to perform so as to induce a second party to do something, e.g., option
      (4) Bilateral—both parties make a promise to perform, e.g., sales contract.

   b. Legal effect of contracts

      (1) Valid—binding and enforceable on both parties
      (2) Void—lacks the essential elements to be valid, has no legal effect or force.
      (3) Voidable—seems on the surface to be valid but may be rescinded or disaffirmed by the party who might be harmed if the contract were enforced (study tip: able to void; e.g., subject to financing; minor who enters a contract).
      (4) Unenforceable—has all elements of a valid contract; however, neither party can sue the other for specific performance. Usually oral contracts are unenforceable.

   c. Essential elements of a valid contract

      (1) Competent parties
      (2) Offer and acceptance
      (3) Consideration
      (4) Legal purpose, legality of object
      (5) Reality of consent
      (6) In writing—the statute of frauds requires that a contract for sale of a real property must be in writing to be enforceable. Most states allow enforcement of oral leases if the term is less than one year.

       d. Option—contract by which an optionor (usually owner) gives the optionee (prospective purchaser or lessee) the right to buy or lease the owner's property at a fixed price within a stated period of time

       e. Contract for deed (a.k.a. land contract, installment contract)—contract by which owner finances the sale and retains title until the terms of the contract are met, then conveys title

B. Offers and counteroffers

   1. Purpose of offer and counteroffer—this allows the buyer to express his or her desire to purchase a specific property. The counteroffer is the method the parties negotiate their differences.

       a. Offer—promise made by one party (offeror) with the request for something in exchange for that promise

       b. Counteroffer—a new offer that rejects the original offer

   2. Valid methods of communicating offers—the statute of frauds provides that for a contract on real property to be enforceable it must be in writing and signed.

C. Earnest money (liquidated damages)

   1. Earnest money is evidence of the buyer's intention to carry out the terms of the contract, a good-faith deposit from the buyer to the seller.

   2. Should be held by the broker, escrow agent or attorney in a trust or escrow account.

   3. A licensee may not commingle earnest money with his or her own personal funds.

   4. Not required for valid contract.

D. Completion, termination, breach

   1. Completion—in most cases the completion of the contract is performance (occurs at closing and funding of the transaction).

   2. Termination

       a. Partial performance

       b. Substantial performance

       c. Impossibility of performance

       d. Mutual agreement by the parties to cancel the contract

       e. Operation of law, i.e., the voiding of a contract by a minor

       f. Rescission

   3. Breach—occurs when one party breaks the contract. An example of this would be the buyer or seller changes his or her mind and refuses to close.

■ QUIZ

1. A void contract is one that

   (A) has no legal force or effect.
   (B) is not legally enforceable.
   (C) may be rescinded by agreement.
   (D) is voidable by only one of the parties.

2. The legal proceeding or legal action brought by either the buyer or the seller under a purchase contract to enforce the terms of the contract is known as

   (A) an injunction.
   (B) a lis pendens.
   (C) an attachment.
   (D) specific performance.

3. Of the following, which is required to form a binding contract?

   (A) Offer and counteroffer
   (B) Notarized signatures
   (C) Offer and acceptance
   (D) Earnest money

4. If, upon the receipt of an offer to purchase his or her property under certain conditions, the seller makes a counteroffer, the prospective buyer is

   (A) bound by his or her original offer.
   (B) bound to accept the counteroffer.
   (C) bound by whichever offer is lower.
   (D) relieved of his or her original offer.

5. The amount of earnest money deposit is determined by

   (A) the real estate licensing statutes.
   (B) an agreement between the parties.
   (C) the broker's office policy on such matters.
   (D) the acceptable minimum of 5% of the purchase price.

6. A written real estate contract is assumed to be the complete agreement of the parties because of the

   (A) statute of frauds.
   (B) parol evidence rule.
   (C) statute of limitations.
   (D) rule of contracts.

7. Which of the following gives the **BEST** evidence of the buyer's intention to carry out the terms of the real estate purchase contract?

   (A) The "subject to" clause
   (B) The agreement to seek mortgage financing
   (C) The earnest money deposit
   (D) The provision that "time is of the essence"

8. The term "rescind" **MOST** nearly means

   (A) change.
   (B) cancel.
   (C) substitute.
   (D) subordinate.

9. Which of the following signatures are necessary to create a binding, enforceable contract for the sale of real estate?

   (A) Signatures by a seller who is 35 and a buyer who is 16
   (B) Signatures by a seller who is 17 and a buyer who is 35
   (C) Signatures by the guardian of a minor seller and a buyer who is 35
   (D) Signatures of the daughter of a seller age 98 and a buyer who is 35

10. What is the effect of an option?

    (A) Requires the optionee to complete the purchase
    (B) Gives the optionee an easement on the property
    (C) Keeps the offer open for a specified time
    (D) Makes the seller liable for a commission

11. At the point that a seller accepts a written purchase offer from a prospective buyer, then the

    (A) seller conveys possession of the real estate to the buyer.
    (B) seller grants the buyer ownership rights.
    (C) buyer receives legal title to the property.
    (D) buyer receives equitable title to the property.

12. A buyer agrees to purchase a property for $230,000 and deposits a $6,900 earnest money check with the broker. However, the seller is unable to clear the title to the property, and the buyer demands the return of the earnest money as provided in the purchase contract. The broker should

   (A) deduct his commission and return the balance to the buyer.
   (B) deduct his commission and give the balance to the seller.
   (C) return the entire amount to the buyer.
   (D) give the entire amount to the seller as damages for the unfulfilled contract.

13. Every real estate contract must have

   (A) a grantor and a grantee.
   (B) a legal purpose.
   (C) an acknowledgment by a notary.
   (D) a legal description.

14. A bilateral contract is one in which

   (A) only one of the parties is obligated to act.
   (B) the promise of one party is given in exchange for the promise of the other party.
   (C) something is to be done by one party only.
   (D) a restriction is placed in the contract by one party to limit the performance by the other.

15. A buyer makes an earnest money deposit of $1,500 on a $15,000 property and then withdraws her offer before the seller can accept it. The broker is responsible for disposing of the earnest money by

   (A) turning it over to the seller.
   (B) deducting the commission and giving the balance to the seller.
   (C) returning it to the buyer.
   (D) depositing it in the broker's trust account.

16. A broker arrives to present a purchase offer to the seller, an invalid, and finds the seller's son and daughter-in-law also present. In the presence of the broker, both individuals persistently urge the seller to accept the offer, even though it is much lower than the price she has been asking for her home. If the seller accepts the offer, she may later claim that

   (A) the broker should not have brought her such a low offer for her property.
   (B) she was under undue duress from her son and daughter-in-law and, therefore, the contract is void.
   (C) the broker defrauded her by allowing her son and his wife to see the purchase offer he brought to her.
   (D) her consumer protection rights have been usurped by her son and daughter-in-law.

17. The law that requires real estate contracts to be in writing to be enforceable is the

   (A) law of descent and distribution.
   (B) statute of frauds.
   (C) parol evidence rule.
   (D) statute of limitations.

18. An owner takes his property off the market for a definite period of time in exchange for some consideration, while granting the right to purchase the property within that period for a stated price. This is an example of

   (A) an option.
   (B) a contract of sale.
   (C) a right of first refusal.
   (D) an installment agreement.

19. Which of the following **BEST** describes earnest money?

   (A) The consideration for the sale of the property
   (B) The money to be used as damages if the buyer defaults
   (C) The commission to be paid to the broker
   (D) The money to be used for paying for some of the closing costs

20. To assign a contract for the sale of real estate means to

    (A) record the contract with the county recorder's office.
    (B) permit another broker to act as agent for the principal.
    (C) transfer one's rights under the contract.
    (D) allow the seller and the buyer to exchange positions.

21. The seller accepted the buyer's low offer, and the buyer was notified of the acceptance. A few days later, the seller received a higher offer for the property. The seller may not accept the second higher offer because the first buyer already holds

    (A) reversionary rights.
    (B) equitable title.
    (C) legal title.
    (D) possessory rights.

22. If a broker deposits the buyer's earnest money in a trust account, at what time is the seller entitled to receive it?

    (A) When the offer is presented to the seller
    (B) At the time of settlement
    (C) After the settlement
    (D) When the seller accepts the offer made by the buyer

23. An offeree has the right to

    (A) reject an offer.
    (B) revoke an offer.
    (C) rescind an offer.
    (D) release an offer.

24. Which of the following **BEST** describes a contract that is voidable?

    (A) The contract has no legal effect.
    (B) The contract is oral.
    (C) The contract may be voided by one of the parties.
    (D) The contract has not been signed.

25. Two salespeople working for the same broker obtained offers on a property listed with their firm. The first offer was obtained early in the day. A second offer for a higher purchase price was obtained later in the afternoon. The broker presented the first offer to the seller that evening. The broker did not inform the seller about the second offer so that the seller could make a decision about the first offer. Which of the following is **TRUE?**

    (A) The broker's actions are permissible provided the commission is split between the two salespeople.
    (B) After the first offer was received, the broker should have told the salespeople that no additional offers would be accepted until the seller decided on the offer.
    (C) The broker has no authority to withhold any offers from the seller.
    (D) The broker was smart to protect the seller from getting into a negotiating battle over two offers.

26. A broker has an exclusive-right-to-sell listing on a building. The owner is out of town when the broker gets an offer from a buyer to purchase the building providing the seller agrees to take a purchase money mortgage. The buyer must have a commitment from the seller before the seller is scheduled to return to the city. Under these circumstances

    (A) the broker may enter into a binding agreement on behalf of the seller.
    (B) the broker may collect a commission even if the transaction falls through because of the seller's absence from the city.
    (C) the buyer is obligated to keep the offer open until the seller returns.
    (D) the broker must obtain the signature of the seller to effect a contract.

27. A broker took a listing and later discovered that the client was previously declared legally incompetent. The listing is now

    (A) binding because the broker was acting as the owner's agent in good faith.
    (B) of no value to the broker because it is void.
    (C) the basis for the recovery of a commission if the broker produces a buyer.
    (D) renegotiable.

28. On Monday, the seller offers to sell his vacant lot to the buyer for $12,000. On Tuesday, the buyer counteroffers to buy for $10,500. On Friday, the buyer withdraws the counteroffer and accepts the original offer of $12,000. Under these conditions

    (A) there is a valid agreement because the buyer accepted the seller's offer exactly as it was made.
    (B) there is not a valid agreement because the buyer's counteroffer was a rejection of the seller's offer and, once it was rejected, it cannot be accepted later.
    (C) there is a valid agreement because the buyer accepted before the seller advised the buyer that the offer is withdrawn.
    (D) there is not a valid agreement because the seller's offer was not accepted within 72 hours.

29. In a option to purchase real estate, the optionee

    (A) must purchase the property, but may do so at any time within the option period.
    (B) has no obligation to purchase the property.
    (C) is limited to a refund of the option consideration if the option is exercised.
    (D) is the prospective seller of the property.

30. The broker receives an earnest money deposit with a written offer to purchase that includes a clause stating that the offer is void after ten days. On the fifth day, before the offer is accepted, the buyer notifies the broker that she is withdrawing the offer and demands the return of the earnest money deposit. In this situation

    (A) the buyer cannot withdraw the offer because it must be held open for the full ten days.
    (B) the buyer has the right to revoke the offer at any time until it is accepted and recover the earnest money.
    (C) the seller and the broker have the right to each retain ½ of the deposit.
    (D) the broker declares the deposit forfeited and retains it for his services.

31. At the time a buyer was negotiating the purchase of a lot on which to build a new home, the seller represented that the soil is firm enough to support the construction of a building when, in fact, the seller knew it is not. This contract is

    (A) void.
    (B) voidable by the buyer because of fraud.
    (C) voidable by the seller because of the misrepresentation.
    (D) voidable by neither party because no harm was done yet.

32. The concept that requires that an injured party bring an action within a specific period of time after the injury is

    (A) a variance.
    (B) the statute of limitations.
    (C) the statute of fraud.
    (D) a waiver.

33. Before an offer to purchase becomes a purchase contract, the parties must accept the offer prior to

    (A) the payment of any money.
    (B) the death of the offeror.
    (C) the close of the tenth business day following the offer.
    (D) a similar offer being made to a third party.

34. A real estate sales contract becomes valid or in effect when it has been signed by

    (A) only the buyer.
    (B) the buyer and seller.
    (C) only the seller.
    (D) the broker and the buyer.

35. Which of the following would **NOT** terminate an offer?

    (A) Revocation of the offer before acceptance
    (B) Death of the offeror before acceptance
    (C) A counteroffer by the offeree
    (D) An offer from a third party

36. An essential element of a valid contract is consideration. For a bilateral contract such as a lease or agreement of sale, which of the following **BEST** describes consideration?

    (A) Earnest money
    (B) Promise of sales price
    (C) Agent's commission
    (D) Option money

37. A broker meets a seller at a restaurant to present an offer. The broker buys the seller several alcoholic drinks. The seller signs the offer and then calls a cab to drive him home. The contract is

    (A) valid and enforceable.
    (B) void.
    (C) voidable.
    (D) executed.

38. A broker receives a $5,000 check as earnest money. All parties accept the offer. The broker must

    (A) place the earnest money in the broker's business account.
    (B) place the money in an interest-bearing trust account.
    (C) hold the check until closing.
    (D) place the money in a special account or deposit it with an escrow agent.

39. To have an enforceable contract it must be conveyed to the parties

    (A) orally in person.
    (B) in writing and signed by all parties.
    (C) orally by phone or in person.
    (D) by certified mail.

40. A buyer submitted an offer to a seller. The buyer dies before the seller can accept the offer. The offer

    (A) dies with the buyer.
    (B) is enforceable against the buyer's estate.
    (C) is enforceable against the seller but not the buyer.
    (D) is not affected by the death of the buyer.

41. A buyer changes her mind after signing the contract with a seller. She notifies the seller after the contract has been delivered that she does not wish to buy the property. Which of the following statements is **TRUE**?

    (A) The buyer has no problem because a buyer can always change his or her mind.
    (B) The buyer is subject to legal consequences for breach of contract.
    (C) The seller must lower the price to convince the buyer to continue.
    (D) The buyer's broker is liable for the buyer's breach.

42. A property is sold under an option contract. During the option period, who can terminate the contract?

    (A) Either buyer or seller
    (B) Buyer only
    (C) Seller only
    (D) Neither buyer or seller

43. A corporation contracts to sell a property it owns. Before the sale can take place, the president of the corporation dies. The contract

    (A) dies with the president.
    (B) is valid but closing must wait until the president's will is probated.
    (C) continues despite the death of the president.
    (D) is voidable by the corporation.

44. A contract whose terms have been fully performed is called

    (A) a bilateral contract.
    (B) a unilateral contract.
    (C) an implied contract.
    (D) an executed contract.

45. A buyer and seller agree on the sale of a property. They made this agreement and sealed the deal with a handshake. The transaction

   (A) cannot close because an oral agreement is not valid.
   (B) can close if they sign a contract at closing.
   (C) can close, but neither party can enforce the terms of the agreement.
   (D) is illegal.

■ ANSWER KEY WITH EXPLANATIONS

1. (A) A contract is void if it lacks some or all of the essential elements of a contract. A void contract has no legal effect.

2. (D) Specific performance is a suit that requires a party to the contract to comply with the terms of the contract—in other words, to perform to the specifics of the contract.

3. (C) An offer that has been accepted in its totality is required to make a binding contract. A counteroffer is a rejection of the offer. Signatures do not have to be notarized. An exchange of promises is required, but not earnest money (liquidated damages).

4. (D) Once the seller makes a counteroffer, the buyer is relieved of his or her offer and now must agree to any of seller's changes before the buyer is bound to the terms of the seller's offer.

5. (B) The buyer and seller will agree on what amount of earnest money that will be deposited once the contract is signed. Earnest money is a form of liquidated damages and is not required to make a valid contract.

6. (B) The parol evidence rule provides that a written agreement is the final expression of the agreement of the parties.

7. (C) Earnest money is the best evidence of those listed as to the buyer's sincerity in making the offer because the buyer's funds can be lost if the buyer fails to comply with the terms of the contract. A large earnest money deposit is considered an act of good faith.

8. (B) The term "rescind" most nearly means to cancel or to take back.

9. (C) A minor cannot enter into a legally binding contract; however, a guardian for the minor can. Just because the seller is 98 years old does not mean that this elderly person cannot enter into a contract. The seller's daughter can sign for the seller only if the daughter holds a power of attorney or guardianship for the seller.

10. (C) The optionee has the ability to complete the transaction under prescribed terms or may cancel the agreement. The optionor may not terminate the option. The option contract will specify under what conditions, if any, the seller is liable for a commission.

11. (D) At the time that the buyer and seller agree in a contract, equitable title passes to the buyer. Equitable title is an intangible encumbrance on the property. This allows buyers to protect their interest in the property before they actually close on the property.

12. (C) The seller contracts with the buyer to deliver good and clear title. If the seller is unable to do this, the contract is void, and the earnest money is returned to the buyer. The broker may not deduct the commission. If the broker feels that he has earned a commission, the broker will have to sue the seller in court.

13. (B) In order to be valid and enforceable, a contract must be for a legal purpose. You cannot bind a party to perform an illegal act.

14. (B) A bilateral contract is a promise for a promise. Examples of bilateral contracts include a purchase agreement and a lease.

15. (C) The buyer may revoke the offer at any time up to notification of acceptance, and the earnest money must be returned promptly. The earnest money is a good-faith deposit to show the buyer's good intentions.

16. (B) Just because the woman is an invalid does not mean that she is mentally incompetent. If she alleges that she was "pressured" into accepting an offer, she may have the legal right to void the contract.

17. (B) According to the statute of frauds, contracts must be in writing to be enforceable in a court of law. To prevent confusion, many states have found it best to require real property contracts to be reduced to writing and signed by all parties.

18. (A) An option is defined as the right to purchase property within a definite time at a specified price. There is no obligation to purchase, but the seller is obligated to sell if the option holder exercises the right to purchase.

19. (B) Earnest money is best described as liquidated damages, to be used if the buyer does not perform as the buyer promised he or she would.

20. (C) Assignment occurs when one party transfers its rights to another. The person who receives the rights must comply with the terms of the contract. A person cannot assign his or her responsibilities under the contract.

21. (B) Equitable title is an intangible encumbrance on the property. This allows buyers to protect their interest in the property before they actually close on the property.

22. (B) Typically, the buyer uses the earnest money as part of the buyer's closing costs. Therefore, the seller receives the funds at closing (settlement). If the transaction does not close, the money may be required to be returned to the buyer.

23. (B) Offers are revoked; contracts are rescinded. There is no contract until the offer is accepted and delivered. Prior to that event, the offeree (person receiving the offer) may revoke the offer.

24. (C) A voidable contract is one that can be voided by at least one of the parties, however, the parties may decide to perform on the contract.

25. (C) Only the seller has the right to reject an offer. The broker exceeded his or her authority as the seller's agent by not presenting both offers.

26. (D) The broker is not authorized to sign on behalf of the seller. The buyer is not obligated to keep the offer open.

27. (B) When a court rules a person incompetent, he or she may not enter into a binding contract. Anything signed by the person ruled incompetent is void.

28. (B) When the buyer changed the price on the $12,000 offer, the seller's offer had been rejected. The buyer would need to have the seller accept the second offer of $12,000.

29. (B) The purpose of the option is to allow the optionee an "out" to terminate the agreement. Therefore, if the buyer is the optionee the buyer can force the seller to sell but the seller cannot force the buyer to buy. A unilateral agreement is a promise for performance.

30. (B) The buyer may revoke her offer at any time prior to notification of acceptance. If the seller does not accept the offer within the ten-day period, the earnest money must be returned to the buyer. If the seller never accepts an offer, they have **NO** right to the earnest money.

31. (B) Because the owner made an intentional misstatement of fact, the buyer has the ability to terminate. However, the buyer may decide to continue with the purchase. The seller may not use his or her misrepresentation as an "out" for nonperformance.

32. (B) The statute of limitations is designed to limit the amount of time a injured person can bring legal action.

33. (B) The offer must be accepted during the lifetime of both parties. If either party dies before the offer is accepted, the offer is void. In many cases at the moment of death, the ownership changes and the new owners may not want to sell. Plus, they may not be able to sell because of clouds on title created by the death of the offeror.

34. (B) Both parties must accept the agreement in order for a contract to become valid. They do so by signing the contract after they agree to all the changes.

35. (D) Receiving an offer from a third party does not terminate the first offer. An offer may be terminated by a revocation or by the death of either party before acceptance. A counteroffer is a rejection of the offer.

36. (B) Consideration in a purchase agreement is the mutual exchange of promises between the buyer and the seller. The buyer promises to buy at a certain sales price; the seller promises to sell and to deliver title.

37. (C) The seller may declare incompetence due to the alcohol. In the event the agent is responsible for intoxicating a person who signs a contact, the person may no longer be competent at the time the contract was signed.

38. (D) The broker must place the money in a special escrow or trust account, and the money cannot be mixed with the broker's own funds. The broker may deposit the money with another escrow agent who can legally hold trust funds.

39. (B) The statute of frauds requires an enforceable contract on real property to be in writing and signed by the parties.

40. (A) Because the seller did not accept the offer before the buyer died, the offer is automatically voided at the time of the buyer's death.

41. (B) As a party to a binding contract, the buyer cannot simply change her mind; she is subject to legal consequences for breach of contract.

42. (B) The buyer is the party who purchases the option from the seller. During the option period, the buyer is the only one who can terminate.

43. (C) The corporation is considered an artificial person so when the president dies, the corporation survives. Contracts signed on behalf of the corporation are binding even if the president dies.

44. (D) When all the terms of a contract have been completed and the transaction closes, the contract terms have been executed.

45. (C) The statute of frauds requires that contracts on real property be in writing and signed to be enforceable. This does not prohibit an oral contract from closing if the parties agree.

Financing Sources

7

       (3) Acceleration—to provide for default, a clause in a mortgage or deed of trust that can be enforced to make the loan balance due and payable immediately if the borrower defaults on a payment or other covenant

       (4) Assignment of the mortgage

       (5) Release of the mortgage lien

       (6) Tax and insurance reserves

       (7) Assignment of rents

       (8) Buying subject to or assuming a seller's mortgage or deed of trust

       (9) Alienation clause (due on sale)—a clause in a mortgage or deed of trust that enables the lender to call the loan balance due and payable immediately if the borrower sells the property

      (10) Recording mortgages and deeds of trust

      (11) Priority of mortgages and deeds of trust

B. Qualifying buyer for financing

   1. Prequalifying considerations

      a. Loan application—includes information on

         (1) Purpose of the loan

         (2) Amount

         (3) Rate of interest

         (4) Terms of repayment

      b. Information about borrower

         (1) Employment

         (2) Earnings

         (3) Assets

         (4) Financial obligations

      c. Information about the real estate

         (1) Legal description

         (2) Improvements

         (3) Title, survey and taxes

   2. Loan repayment

      a. Financing terms

         (1) Interest—a charge for using money, may be due at either the end (in arrears) or at the beginning (in advance)

         (2) Usury—charging a rate of interest above that allowed by state law

         (3) Origination fee—a fee charged by lenders in connection with making a loan, not prepaid interest

         (4) Point—one percent of the loan amount

         (5) Discount point—a fee charged by lenders to increase the yield on lower than market value loans

C. Types of financing

   1. Loan programs, their benefits and requirements

      a. Primary lenders—those who deal directly with the consumer

         (1) Savings banks

         (2) Commercial banks

         (3) Mutual savings banks

(4) Life insurance companies
(5) Mortgage bankers
(6) Mortgage brokers
(7) Credit unions

b. Secondary lenders—those who provide the capital to primary lenders

(1) Fannie Mae (formerly Federal National Mortgage Association or FNMA) organized as privately owned corporation that deals in conventional and FHA and VA loans

(2) Ginnie Mae (also known as Government National Mortgage Association or GNMA), government agency that works with Fannie Mae in the secondary market; with tandem plan allows Fannie Mae to buy risky loans and Ginnie Mae gurantees payment and absorbing differences between low yield and current market prices.

(3) Freddie Mac (also known as Federal Home Loan Mortgage Corporation or FHLMC) provides a secondary market for mortgage loans, primarily conventional; does not guarantee payment of Freddie Mac mortgages.

c. Loan programs

(1) Conventional loan—neither insured nor guaranteed by federal government
  (a) Loan-to-value ratio lowest; borrower makes significant down payment.
  (b) Security for the loan is provided solely by the mortgage.

(2) Private mortgage insurance
  (a) Provides additional security for the loan for the lender, insuring 20% to 25% of the loan
  (b) PMI to drop automatically when loan-to-value is 22%

(3) FHA-insured loan—insured by the federal government
  (a) Most common program: Title II, Section 203(b)
  (b) For owner-occupied one- to four-family residences
  (c) Borrower or someone else pays mortgage insurance premium (MIP) in cash or it may be financed.
  (d) The property must be appraised by an FHA-approved appraiser.
  (e) Loan amount that can be insured generally is 97% of the first $25,000 of appraised value or contract price, whichever is less, 95% up to $125,000, and 90% of the remainder up to the prescribed limit in your area including allowable closing costs, or 97.75% of sales price or assessed value, whichever is less.

(4) VA-guaranteed loans—guaranteed by the Department of Veterans Affairs (VA)
  (a) Authorizes the guarantee of owner-occupied one- to-four family home loans for eligible veterans.
  (b) Sets the minimum service times of 90 days, 181 days or two years, depending on the calendar dates of service.
  (c) Generally, no down payment is required.
  (d) Typically, lenders will loan up to four times the veteran's available guarantee amount ($4 \times \$50,750 = \$203,000$).

2. Financing methods

a. Straight loans

(1) Periodic payments of interest only with the entire principal balance due at the end of the loan term

      (2) Generally used for home improvement and second mortgages, not for residential first mortgage loans

  b. Amortized loans

      (1) Each payment is the same dollar amount.
      (2) The amount applied to the interest decreases with each payment.
      (3) The amount applied to the principal increases with each payment.

  c. Adjustable-rate mortgages (ARMs)

      (1) Interest rates fluctuate, and therefore, so do the payments.
      (2) Interest rate tied to the movement of an index, which fluctuates.
      (3) Margin represents the lender's cost of doing business and it does **NOT** fluctuate for the life of the loan.
      (4) Rate caps that limit the amount the rate can increase both periodically and over the life of the loan.

  d. Balloon payment loans

      (1) Partially-amortized loans
      (2) Periodic payments are not sufficient to fully repay the principal loan balance, so final payment is larger than others.

  e. Growing-equity mortgages (GEMs) (used when borrower's income is expected to rise to keep pace with increasing loan payments)

      (1) Increase in payments during the term of the loan reduces the principal amount more rapidly.
      (2) Fixed interest rate

  f. Reverse-annuity mortgages (RAMs) (usually elderly owner is land rich, cash poor)

      (1) Regular monthly payments are made to the borrower.
      (2) Accrued debt (principal and interest) becomes payable at some specified future event, such as the sale of the property or by the estate upon the death of the owner.

  g. Purchase-money mortgages

      (1) Generally the seller extends to the buyer credit that enables the buyer to purchase the property.
      (2) Buyer receives title to property, gives note and mortgage to seller.

  h. Package mortgages

      (1) A loan on the value of land and improvements plus equipment
      (2) Used in conveying furnished condominium units, home builders

  i. Blanket mortgages

      (1) Security for loan provided by more than one parcel or lot
      (2) Often used to finance subdivision developments, to consolidate loans, or even to finance the purchase of improved properties

  j. Wraparound mortgages

      (1) A method of refinancing in which the new mortgage includes both the unpaid principal balance of the first mortgage plus any additional amount the lender loans

       (2) May be used to refinance real property or to finance the purchase of real property when an existing mortgage cannot be prepaid

    k. Sale and leaseback arrangements

       (1) Transaction in which an owner sells improved property and signs a long-term lease to remain in possession

       (2) Enables a business that has built to suit its own needs to free money tied up in real estate to be used as working capital

D. Foreclosure and alternatives

1. Foreclosure—the legal procedure whereby the property pledged as collateral is sold to satisfy the debt

2. Methods of foreclosure

    a. Judicial—property pledged as security may be sold by court order after the mortgagee gives sufficient public notice.

    b. Nonjudicial—when a power of sale clause is found in the deed of trust, the trustee can sell the property without going through court proceedings.

    c. Strict foreclosure—after proper notice is given and the defaulted debt remains unpaid, the court awards legal title to the lender.

3. Alternatives

    a. Deed in lieu of foreclosure—the borrower forfeits any equity in the property and deeds it to the lender.

    b. Redemption

       (1) Equitable right of redemption—any time before the foreclosure sale, the defaulted borrower can bring the debt current and have it reinstated.

       (2) Statutory right of redemption—the specific period allowed for redemption after the foreclosure sale; state laws vary widely.

E. Pertinent laws and regulations

1. Truth in Lending (Regulation Z)—requires lending institutions to inform borrowers of the true cost of borrowing.

    a. The most common method is providing an APR (annual percentage rate) calculated using certain closing fees and interest costs.

    b. Commercial and agriculture loans are not subject to Regulation Z.

    c. Personal property credit transactions over $25,000 are exempt.

2. Equal Credit Opportunity Act—federal law that prevents creditors from discriminating against credit applicants.

    a. May not discriminate on the basis of race, color, religion, national origin, sex, marital status, age (provided the applicant is of legal age) or dependency on public assistance.

    b. Lenders must inform rejected credit applicants the reason for denial of credit in writing within 30 days.

    c. Borrowers are entitled to a copy of the appraisal if the borrower paid for the appraisal.

3. Fair Credit Reporting Act—federal law that requires credit reporting agencies to provide up to date accurate information. It also limits who has access to a person's credit history.

■ QUIZ

1. Under an installment contract, the legal title to the property is held by the

   (A) vendor.
   (B) vendee.
   (C) trustor.
   (D) trustee.

2. Charging more interest than is legally allowed is known as

   (A) escheat.
   (B) usury.
   (C) deficiency.
   (D) estoppel.

3. A mortgagor is the one who

   (A) grants the mortgage to another.
   (B) holds the mortgage.
   (C) provides the mortgage funds.
   (D) forecloses on the mortgage.

4. A promissory note

   (A) may not be executed in connection with a real estate loan.
   (B) is an agreement to perform or not to perform certain acts.
   (C) is the primary evidence of a debt.
   (D) is a guarantee by a government agency.

5. A land contract provides for the

   (A) sale of unimproved land only.
   (B) sale of real property under an option agreement.
   (C) conveyance of legal title at a future date.
   (D) immediate transfer of reversionary rights.

6. The finance fee charged by the lender to make the loan is

   (A) a prepayment penalty.
   (B) an advance interest payment.
   (C) a loan origination fee.
   (D) a prepayment of mortgage insurance.

7. If the amount realized at a sheriff's sale as part of a mortgage foreclosure is more than the amount of the indebtedness and expenses, then the excess belongs to the

   (A) mortgagor.
   (B) mortgagee.
   (C) sheriff's office.
   (D) county.

8. A person has just made the final payment on her home mortgage to her lender. There will still be a lien on her property until the lender records

   (A) a satisfaction of mortgage.
   (B) a reconveyance of mortgage.
   (C) an alienation of mortgage.
   (D) a reversion of mortgage.

9. An existing mortgage loan can have its lien priority lowered through the use of a

   (A) hypothecation agreement.
   (B) satisfaction of mortgage.
   (C) subordination agreement.
   (D) reconveyance of mortgage.

10. The right a mortgagor has to regain the property by paying the debt after a foreclosure sale is called

    (A) acceleration.
    (B) redemption.
    (C) reversion.
    (D) recapture.

11. The clause in a trust deed or mortgage that permits the lender to declare the entire unpaid balance immediately due and payable upon default is the

    (A) judgment clause.
    (B) escalator clause.
    (C) forfeiture clause.
    (D) acceleration clause.

12. A building was sold for $115,000. Earnest money in the amount of $15,000 was deposited in escrow, and the buyer obtained a new loan for the balance of the purchase price. The lender charged two discount points on the loan. What was the total amount of cash used by the buyer for this purchase?

    (A) $ 2,300   (C) $17,000
    (B) $15,000   (D) $17,300

13. When a mortgage loan has been paid in full, it is important for the borrower to be sure that

    (A) the paid note is placed in a safe deposit box.
    (B) he or she obtains a deed of partial reconveyance.
    (C) the paid mortgage is returned to the lender.
    (D) a satisfaction of mortgage is recorded.

14. In what way does a deed of trust differ from a mortgage?

    (A) In the number of parties involved in the loan
    (B) In the obligation of the borrower to repay the funds
    (C) In the redemption rights allowed after foreclosure
    (D) In the time period permitted to cure a default

15. A person who assumes an existing mortgage loan is

    (A) not personally liable for the repayment of the debt.
    (B) not in danger of losing the property by default.
    (C) personally responsible for paying the principal balance.
    (D) generally released from liability, but not always.

16. The interest in a property held by the owner in excess of any liens against it is called

    (A) hypothecation.   (C) leverage.
    (B) subordination.   (D) equity.

17. The mortgagee foreclosed on a property after the borrower defaulted on the loan payments. At the foreclosure sale, however, the house sold for only $29,000. The unpaid balance of the loan at the time of the sale was $40,000. What must the lender do to recover the $11,000 the borrower still owes?

    (A) Sue for damages
    (B) Sue for specific performance
    (C) Seek a judgment by default
    (D) Seek a deficiency judgment

18. The clause in a mortgage instrument that would prevent the assumption of the mortgage by new purchaser is a

    (A) due-on-sale or alienation clause.
    (B) power of sale clause.
    (C) defeasance clause.
    (D) certificate of sale clause.

19. The defeasance clause in a mortgage requires the mortgagee to execute

    (A) an assignment of mortgage.
    (B) a satisfaction of mortgage.
    (C) a subordination agreement.
    (D) a partial release agreement.

20. The seller agrees to sell the house to the buyer for $100,000. The buyer was unable to qualify for a mortgage loan for this amount so the seller and buyer enter into a contract for deed. The interest the buyer has in the property under a contract for deed is

    (A) legal title.
    (B) equitable title.
    (C) joint title.
    (D) mortgagee in possession.

21. A "friendly foreclosure" enables a mortgagor to prevent the mortgagee from taking the property by statutory means. This can be accomplished by

    (A) a deed in lieu of foreclosure.
    (B) a reconveyance deed.
    (C) an assumption.
    (D) an escrow deed.

22. Mortgage lenders want assurance that future real estate taxes will be paid. The **MOST** common way to do this is to require the borrower to

   (A) obtain title insurance.
   (B) sign a note.
   (C) pay into an impound account.
   (D) submit paid tax receipts.

23. The pledging of property as security for payment of a loan is

   (A) disintermediation.   (C) hypothecation.
   (B) equity.   (D) subordination.

24. When real estate is sold under an installment land contract and the buyer takes possession of the property, the legal title

   (A) is subject to a purchase-money mortgage.
   (B) must be transferred to a land trust.
   (C) is kept by the seller until the purchase price is paid according to the contract.
   (D) is transferred to the buyer.

25. Which of the following is **TRUE** about an option contract?

   (A) The buyer must purchase the property.
   (B) The seller receives a fee for the option.
   (C) The buyer may or may not pay a fee for the option.
   (D) The seller has a right to terminate.

26. If a buyer obtains a $50,000 mortgage with four points, how much will the lender charge at closing?

   (A) $ 200   (C) $ 6,000
   (B) $2,000   (D) $40,000

27. In absence of an agreement to the contrary, the mortgage having priority will be the one

   (A) for the highest amount.
   (B) that was recorded first.
   (C) which was the first mortgage.
   (D) that is a construction loan.

28. The purpose of a mortgage is to

   (A) provide security for the loan.
   (B) convey title of the property to the lender.
   (C) restrict the borrower's use of the property.
   (D) create a lien on the property.

29. If a property sold at a mortgage foreclosure does not sell for an amount sufficient to satisfy the outstanding mortgage debt, the mortgagor may be responsible for

   (A) a default judgment.
   (B) a deficiency judgment.
   (C) liquidated damages.
   (D) punitive damages.

30. Under a fixed-rate loan, the interest the borrower will pay over the life of the loan is

   (A) simple interest.
   (B) compound interest.
   (C) prepaid interest.
   (D) discounted interest.

31. The amount of a loan expressed as a percentage of the value of the real estate offered as collateral is the

   (A) amortization ratio.
   (B) loan-to-value ratio.
   (C) debt-to-equity ratio.
   (D) capital-use ratio.

32. The purpose of the Real Estate Settlement Procedures Act (RESPA) is to

   (A) see that buyers do not borrow more money than they can repay.
   (B) make real estate brokers more responsive to the needs of buyers.
   (C) help sellers know how much money is required to purchase the property.
   (D) see that buyers and sellers know all of their settlement costs.

33. If the quarterly interest at 10½ percent is $3,150, the principal amount of the loan is

   (A) $30,000.   (C) $ 90,000.
   (B) $60,000.   (D) $120,000.

34. Fannie Mae

    (A) makes FHA loans.
    (B) buys FHA loans.
    (C) services FHA loans.
    (D) insures FHA loans.

35. The grantor becomes the lessee and the grantee becomes the lessor under which of the following financing arrangements?

    (A) Partial sale
    (B) Wraparound mortgage
    (C) Sale and leaseback
    (D) Assumption of mortgage

36. Which of the following pairs of terms is considered synonymous?

    (A) Interim financing and construction loan
    (B) Construction loan and pass-through loan
    (C) Pass-through loan and take-out loan
    (D) Take-out loan and construction loan

37. The type of real estate loan that allows the lender to increase the outstanding balance of a loan up to the original sum in the note while advancing additional funds is the

    (A) wraparound mortgage.
    (B) open-end mortgage.
    (C) growing-equity mortgage.
    (D) graduated-payment mortgage.

38. Which of the following statements is **TRUE** regarding a VA loan?

    (A) The borrower can use the guarantee to purchase a six-unit apartment building.
    (B) The veteran must pay for private mortgage insurance if he or she puts no money down.
    (C) A deed of trust is typically conveyed to the VA borrower.
    (D) A buyer does not have to be a veteran to assume a VA loan.

39. The Truth-in-Lending Act does **NOT** apply to loans for which of the following?

    (A) Household use
    (B) Business use
    (C) Room additions
    (D) Swimming pools

40. An FHA-insured mortgage loan would be obtained from

    (A) the Federal Housing Administration (FHA).
    (B) the Department of Housing and Urban Development (HUD).
    (C) any qualified lending institution.
    (D) any qualified insuring institution.

41. Fannie Mae, Ginnie Mae, and Freddie Mac have in common the purpose of

    (A) originating residential mortgage loans.
    (B) purchasing existing mortgage loans.
    (C) insuring residential mortgage loans.
    (D) guaranteeing existing mortgage loans.

42. A mortgage broker generally offers which of the following services?

    (A) Handling the escrow procedures
    (B) Bringing the borrower and the lender together
    (C) Providing credit qualification and evaluation reports
    (D) Granting real estate loans using investor funds

43. An eligible veteran made a purchase offer of $80,000 on a home he wants to finance with a VA-guaranteed loan. Four weeks after the offer was accepted, a certificate of reasonable value (CRV) for $77,000 was issued for the property. In this situation, the veteran could **NOT** do which of the following?

    (A) Withdraw from the transaction without penalty
    (B) Purchase the property with a $3,000 cash down payment
    (C) Negotiate with the seller to reduce the price $3,000
    (D) Borrow the $3,000 for the cash down payment

44. A borrower obtained a $7,000 second mortgage loan for 5 years at 6% interest per annum. Monthly payments were $50. The final payment included the remaining outstanding principal balance. What type of loan is this?

    (A) A fully amortized loan
    (B) A straight loan
    (C) A partially amortized loan
    (D) An accelerated loan

45. The discount points charged on a VA-guaranteed mortgage loan used to purchase a home cannot be paid by which of the following?

    (A) The buyer
    (B) The seller
    (C) The buyer and seller
    (D) Financing the points into the loan

46. The principal distinction between the primary mortgage market and the secondary mortgage market is in the

    (A) insuring versus the guaranteeing of mortgage loans.
    (B) origination versus the purchase of mortgage loans.
    (C) use of mortgages versus the use of deeds of trust.
    (D) use of discount points versus the use of origination fees.

47. A real estate loan payable in periodic installments that are sufficient to pay the principal in full during the term of the loan is called

    (A) a conventional loan.
    (B) a straight loan.
    (C) a participation loan.
    (D) an amortized loan.

48. An extension of credit from a seller to a buyer to allow the buyer to complete the transaction is called a

    (A) growing-equity mortgage.
    (B) purchase-money mortgage.
    (C) package mortgage.
    (D) blanket mortgage.

49. When compared with a 30-year payment period, taking out a loan with a 20-year payment period would **NOT** result in

    (A) faster amortization.
    (B) higher monthly payments.
    (C) quicker equity buildup.
    (D) greater impound amounts.

50. If the interest rate on an FHA-insured mortgage loan is 11½ percent and the monthly interest payment is $1,412, the principal sum would be

    (A) $ 12,278.   (C) $162,383.
    (B) $147,339.   (D) $194,561.

51. PMI is the acronym for private mortgage insurance often used by borrowers whose LTV (loan-to-value) ratio is less than 20 percent. Lenders must cease charging PMI when the LTV is

    (A) 22%.   (C) 29%.
    (B) 27%.   (D) 35%.

52. From which of the following would a borrower **MOST LIKELY** obtain a residential real estate mortgage loan?

    (A) An insurance company
    (B) A pension fund
    (C) A commercial bank
    (D) A savings association

53. Regulation Z applies to

    (A) business loans.
    (B) real estate sales agreements.
    (C) commercial loans under $10,000.
    (D) personal credit transactions under $25,000.

54. FNMA's activities do **NOT** include

    (A) buying and selling FHA and VA mortgages.
    (B) buying and selling conventional mortgages.
    (C) buying and selling mortgages only at full face value.
    (D) buying and selling mortgages at discounted values.

55. As an entity operating in the secondary mortgage market, the Federal Home Loan Mortgage Corporation was established to assist the

    (A) Federal Housing Administration.
    (B) Federal National Mortgage Association.
    (C) federal savings and loans.
    (D) federal banks.

56. A graduated payment loan is one in which

    (A) mortgage payments decrease.
    (B) mortgage payments balloon in five years.
    (C) mortgage payments increase.
    (D) the interest rate on the loan adjusts annually.

57 If the amount of a loan is $13,500 and the interest rate is 7½%, what is the amount of the semiannual interest payment?

    (A) $457.14   (C) $596.55
    (B) $506.25   (D) $602.62

58. The type of mortgage loan that uses both real and personal property as security is a

    (A) blanket mortgage.
    (B) package mortgage.
    (C) purchase-money mortgage.
    (D) wraparound mortgage.

59. The supply of mortgage money for single-family homes is regulated by the Federal Reserve System through which of the following?

    (A) Reserve requirements and discount rates
    (B) Federal National Mortgage Association
    (C) Federal Housing Administration
    (D) Resolution Trust Corporation

60. Lenders who make home loans to the public are called

    (A) secondary lenders.
    (B) primary lenders.
    (C) federal lenders.
    (D) friendly lenders.

61. If a house sold for $80,000 and the buyer obtained a loan for $72,000, how much money would the buyer pay if the lender charged three points?

    (A) $ 240   (C) $2,328
    (B) $2,160   (D) $2,400

62. A mortgage loan requires monthly payments of $175.75 for 20 years and a final payment of $5,095. This type of a mortgage loan is

    (A) a wraparound mortgage.
    (B) an accelerated mortgage.
    (C) a balloon mortgage.
    (D) a variable mortgage.

63. In a sale-and-leaseback arrangement the

    (A) seller retains legal title to the real estate.
    (B) buyer becomes the lessee.
    (C) broker will not earn a commission.
    (D) buyer becomes the lessor.

64. Last month's loan payment included $412.50 interest on a $60,000 loan balance. What is the annual rate of interest?

    (A) 7½%   (C) 8¼%
    (B) 7¾%   (D) 8½%

65. A person owned her house for over 50 years. It has fallen into disrepair but, because she lives on a fixed income, she does not have the money to make the needed repairs. She has a considerable amount of equity in the house. What type of loan **BEST** suits her needs?

    (A) A home equity loan
    (B) A reverse-annuity mortgage
    (C) A blanket loan
    (D) An open-ended loan

66. The type of loan that will **MOST** likely have the lowest loan-to-value ratio is a

    (A) VA loan.
    (B) FHA loan.
    (C) PMI loan.
    (D) conventional loan.

67. A lender may protect its interest in a mortgage loan by obtaining additional security from

    (A) private mortgage insurance.
    (B) title insurance.
    (C) the borrower's note.
    (D) impound accounts.

68. A lender will take certain factors into consideration when deciding whether to grant a borrower a mortgage loan. Which of the following is **NOT** a legitimate factor?

    (A) The marital status of the borrower
    (B) The creditworthiness of the borrower
    (C) The amount of the borrower's income
    (D) The ability of the borrower to make the payments

69. One of the ways lenders increase their revenue is by servicing loans. Which of the following is **NOT** an activity of servicing loans?

    (A) Collecting payments
    (B) Paying real estate taxes from escrow accounts
    (C) Renegotiating interest rates
    (D) Sending overdue notices

70. A developer had a mortgage loan on his entire housing development. When he sold a lot to a buyer, he was able to deliver title to that lot free of the mortgage lien by obtaining a partial release. What type of loan did the developer have?

    (A) Blanket mortgage
    (B) Purchase-money mortgage
    (C) Package mortgage
    (D) Open-end mortgage

■ ANSWER KEY WITH EXPLANATIONS

1. (A) Under an installment sale (a.k.a. contract for deed), the vendor (seller) retains legal title to the property and the vendee (buyer) takes possession and receives equitable title. When the buyer has made all the payments, legal title passes.

2. (B) If the interest rates exceed the amount allowed by law, any rate charged over that amount is considered usury.

3. (A) The mortgagor is the borrower who gives the mortgage to the mortgagee (lender) as security for the note. The mortgagee records the mortgage.

4. (C) A promissory note is the primary evidence of a debt. The borrower promises to repay the note.

5. (C) A land contract is also referred to as a contract for deed. It provides for the conveyance of legal title at a future date.

6. (C) The loan origination fee helps compensate the lender for the work in processing the loan.

7. (A) A mortgage foreclosure is a sale, and any proceeds that exceed the liens on the property go to owner/mortgagor.

8. (A) The lender must record a satisfaction of mortgage, that is, the lender must release its claim before the property is free and clear. In some states, this is called a release.

9. (C) In a subordination agreement, a lender agrees to take a lower priority position.

10. (B) Some states allow owners to redeem the property after the foreclosure sale. However, in some states with a nonjudicial foreclosure, there is no redemption.

11. (D) If a borrower defaults on a trust deed or mortgage with an acceleration clause, the payment period is accelerated and the entire note is due and payable. This permits foreclosure.

12. (C) The total cash outlay by the buyer was $17,000.
$$\$115,000 - \$15,000 = \$100,000$$
$$\$100,000 \times 2\% = \$2,000$$
$$\$15,000 + 2,000 = \$17,000$$

13. (D) If the satisfaction of mortgage is not recorded, then the public record still reflects a lien on the property.

14. (A) A traditional mortgage has two parties while a deed of trust has three.

15. (C) A person who assumes an existing mortgage steps into the financial shoes of the seller, that is, he or she becomes personally obligated for the payment of the entire debt. However, if the lender has not released the original borrower, then that person may also be responsible for paying the debt.

16. (D) Equity is the difference between what is owned and what it is worth.

17. (D) The lender must seek a deficiency judgment to recover the difference.

18. (A) The alienation clause is also known as the due-on-sale clause. The note must be paid upon transfer to another person. This clause prevents a loan assumption without the lender's permission.

19. (B) A defeasance clause requires the lender to execute a release when the note has been satisfied.

20. (B) Under an installment sale (a.k.a. contract for deed), the vendor (seller) retains legal title to the property and the vendee (buyer) takes possession and receives equitable title. When the buyer has made all the payments, legal title passes. The contract should be recorded in order to prevent the seller from selling the property to another buyer before this buyer has the opportunity to perform under the contract.

21. (A) As an alternative to foreclosure, the lender may accept a deed in lieu of foreclosure from the borrower. However, in doing so, the lender forfeits rights to PMI, MIP, VA guarantees, and a suit for deficiency. Plus, the borrower still has a stain on the borrower's credit history.

22. (C) The lender may collect $\frac{1}{12}$ of the taxes monthly and deposit the money into the impound account, also known as an escrow account. Therefore, when the taxes are due, the money has already been collected.

23. (C) Hypothecation is pledging the property as security for an obligation or loan without giving up possession of it.

24. (C) An installment land contract is similar to a contract for deed. The owner transfers the title when the debt is paid.

25. (B) An option is a unilateral contract in which the optionee (purchaser) buys the optionor's (seller's) promise to sell IF the purchaser chooses to buy. Thus, the optionee may not recover the consideration paid for the option right.

26. (B) The leader will charge $2,000.
$$\$50,000 \times 4\% = \$2,000$$

27. (B) Priority of liens is established by the date and time of recordation.

28. (A) The mortgage is the pledge of property to secure the note.

29. (B) If a property sold at foreclosure does not see for enough money to satisfy the loan, the lender may sue to seek a deficiency judgment for the difference.

30. (A) The borrower pays simple interest based on the unpaid principal over the life of the loan.

31. (B) Loan Amount ÷ Value = Loan to Value (LTV). The sales price in the contract is used as value until the lender establishes a value via an appraisal.

32. (D) RESPA is a consumer protection law that requires lenders to give borrowers advance notice of closing costs.

33. (D) The loan principal is $120,000.
    $3,150 × 4 ÷ 10.5% = $120,000

34. (B) Fannie Mae purchases loans, they do not make the loans. Fannie Mae is part of the secondary market. (Note that FNMA has changed its name to Fannie Mae.)

35. (C) In a sale and leaseback arrangement, the property is sold and the old owner (grantor) becomes the tenant (lessee). The sale and leaseback is a method by which the owner can recover equity to use for other purposes.

36. (A) Interim financing provides financing during construction before permanent financing is obtained.

37. (B) The terms of the mortgage are open ended and additional items may be added if need be.

38. (D) Anyone can assume a VA mortgage. Some newer VA loans require the buyer to qualify financially for the assumption.

39. (B) The Truth-in-Lending Act exempts business loans. Disclosures under the law do apply to loans on residential property.

40. (C) Any approved lender may offer an FHA-insured loan. The FHA does not make loans, it insures loans.

41. (B) Fannie Mae, Ginnie Mae, and Freddie Mac are the major players in the secondary market. They purchase loans made by primary lenders.

42. (B) A mortgage broker does not have the money to lend. Mortgage brokers bring the lenders and borrowers together for a fee.

43. (D) The veteran would need to obtain the difference but could not borrow it under the VA program. The VA purchaser may withdraw from the transaction, come up with the down payment or negotiate with the seller to reduce the price.

44. (C) A partially amortized loan is also called a balloon loan. The remaining balance is due at the prescribed time.

45. (D) A VA buyer cannot finance the points into a VA loan.

46. (B) The primary lender makes the loans to the public while the secondary market buys these loans from the institutions that originated the loans.

47. (D) An amortized loan is one in which the principal as well as the interest is payable in monthly or other periodic installments over the term of the loan.

48. (B) A purchase-money mortgage (PMM) is a note secured by a mortgage or deed of trust given by the buyer as borrower, to the seller as lender, as part of the purchase price of the real estate.

49. (D) The impound amounts are based on the actual amounts needed to pay taxes, insurance, etc.

50. (B) The principal is $147,339.
$1,412 × 12 ÷ 11.5% = $147,339

51. (A) Effective July 1999, lenders must stop charging PMI when a borrower's LTV reaches 22%.

52. (D) Savings associations have a fiduciary obligation to protect and preserve their depositors' funds. Mortgage loans are perceived as secure investments for generating income and thus enable these institutions to pay interest to their depositors.

53. (D) The Truth-in-Lending Act, implemented by Regulation Z, applies to personal purchases under $25,000. It does not apply to business or commercial loans or real estate sales agreements.

54. (C) Fannie Mae can and does purchase FHA, VA and conventional mortgages at a discount.

55. (C) Federal Home Loan Mortgage Corporation (FHLMC or Freddie Mac) was set up to buy mortgage loans from savings and loan associations.

56. (C) Under a graduated payment loan, the payments graduate (increase) according to the terms of the loan. This type of loan is excellent for a person whose income is expected to rise and who expects to remain in the same location for a number of years, e.g., a doctor just starting a practice.

57. (B) The semiannual interest payment is $506.25.
$13,500 × 7.5% ÷ 2 = $506.25

58. (B) A package mortgage is secured by both real and personal property. As an example, it is often used when selling a fully furnished condominium unit in a resort area.

59. (A) Federal Reserve requirements and discount rates limit the supply by the cost of funds and the availability.

60. (B) Lenders who make home loans directly to the public are called primary lenders. These primary lenders then can sell their loans to the secondary market.

61. (B) The buyer will pay $2,160 in points.
$72,000 × 3% = $2,160

62. (C) In this balloon mortgage, the remaining balance balloons at the end of 20 years. The borrower can pay the amount or refinance.

63. (D) In a sale-and-leaseback arrangement, the buyer (grantee) becomes the new owner (lessor) and the seller (grantor) becomes the tenant (lessee).

64. (C) The annual rate of interest is 8.25%.
$412.50 × 12 ÷ 60,000 = .0825 or 8.25%

65. (B) A reverse-annuity mortgage provides the homeowner with a monthly income. When the person dies, the property will be sold to pay off the debt. This is useful for a person who is house-rich and cash-poor.

66. (D) Traditionally, conventional loans have had the lowest loan-to-value ratio; in other words, requiring a larger down payment. FHA and VA loans are designed to allow people to buy with the least amount down.

67. (A) Private mortgage insurance protects the lender against a loss in the event of a foreclosure and deficiency.

68. (A) Under the Equal Credit Opportunity Act (ECOA) a lender may **NOT** discriminate based on marital status.

69. (C) The servicing company's duties are to service the existing mortgage. The actual lender would need to negotiate any change in rates.

70. (A) A developer will often use a blanket loan. This is a mortgage secured by more than one parcel of real estate, providing for each parcel's partial release from the mortgage lien upon repayment of a definite portion of the debt.

Closing/Settlement and Transferring Title

8

■ CONTENT OUTLINE

VII. Closing/Settlement and Transferring Title

A. Settlement statement and other critical documents—each time a residential property is closed, the closing agent should use a standardized form or settlement statement.

B. Closing/settlement

1. Purpose of closing/settlement

   a. Seller's deed is delivered in exchange for purchase price.

   b. Buyer signs loan documents, and lender disburses mortgage funds.

   c. Proration of financial responsibility between buyer and seller for taxes, interest, and rent and expenses or items paid by seller or buyer.

   d. Both parties sign all required documents. For title to be transferred, the deed must be delivered. However, if the buyer does not accept the delivery of the deed the title has not been transferred.

   e. Escrow—a method of closing a real estate transaction in which a disinterested third party is authorized to act as escrow agent and has the responsibility of coordinating closing activities. Not all states close the property in escrow. Some states allow the transaction to be closed by any third party. In those states the escrow agent primarily holds trust funds for the parties such as earnest money.

2. Legal requirements (includes RESPA)

   a. The Real Estate Settlement and Procedures Act (RESPA)—is the federal law that protects consumers from abusive lending practices.

      (1) RESPA requires lenders to use a Uniform Settlement Statement. This is designed to protect consumers by standardizing the closing documents state to state. This must be available to the buyer one business day before closing.

      (2) Applies to all federally related loans of first-lien residential mortgage loans on one- to four-family dwellings, either for investment or occupancy.

      (3) Prohibits kickbacks and payment of unearned fees

      (4) Lenders must provide good-faith estimate within three business days of completed loan application.

           (5) Lenders must retain statements for two years.

    b. Truth in Lending (Regulation Z)—requires lending institutions to inform borrowers of the true cost of borrowing.

         (1) The most common method is providing an APR (annual percentage rate) calculated using the certain closing fees and the interest cost.

         (2) Commercial and agriculture loans are not subject to Regulation Z.

         (3) Personal property credit transactions over $25,000 are exempt.

C. Transferring title

1. Methods of transfer (includes deeds)

    a. Voluntary transfer

         (1) Sale or gift

         (2) Devise by will

    b. Involuntary alienation

         (1) Person dies intestate; property escheats to the state or county.

         (2) Eminent domain (through condemnation suit and payment of just compensation)

         (3) Foreclosure for nonpayment of a debt secured by real property

         (4) Adverse possession of another's property for a prescribed period of time that is open, notorious, and hostile.

    c. Laws of inheritance, descent and distribution

         (1) Intestate—the legal designation of a person who has died without leaving a will

         (2) Testate—the legal designation of a person who died with a will

         (3) Probate—a legal process by which a court determines the validity of a will or the order of descent if there is not will

         (4) Devise—the transfer of real property by a will

         (5) Devisee—the person who receives property by a will

         (6) Descent or intestate succession—real estate (other than community property) located in the state and owned as separate property by the deceased owner who died intestate is distributed according to the descent statutes.

    d. Title search

         (1) Chain of title—the history of ownership of a property from some starting point. As with a chain, each link would be transfer of ownership.

         (2) Search begins with present owner and traces back to the origin of title.

         (3) Length of search depends on local custom or laws.

    e. Title evidence—documentary proof of whether or not seller is conveying marketable title. Forms of evidence are abstract of title, abstract and attorney's opinion and title insurance policy.

         (1) Abstract of title—a condensed history of all the recorded instruments affecting title to a property. An abstract does not guarantee the quality of the tile but provides a summary of recorded documents affecting the property.

         (2) Abstract and attorney's opinion—attorney's opinion issued on basis of abstract

         (3) Title insurance policy—insures the policyholder against loss due to defects in the title other than those exceptions identified in the policy.

f. Types of deeds

    (1) General warranty deed—grantor fully warrants good and clear title to the property from the sovereignty of the soil. Offers the most protection to the owner. Basic warranties:

        (a) Covenant of seisin—the owner has full ownership and the legal right to convey the title.

        (b) Covenant against encumbrances—the title is free from all liens and encumbrances except those specifically stated.

        (c) Covenant of quiet enjoyment—the grantor assumes responsibility for protecting the title against the claims of third parties.

        (d) Covenant of further assurance—the grantor will furnish whatever is needed to make the title good.

        (e) Covenant of warranty forever—the grantor is liable for reimbursing the grantee for any title interest lost in the future.

    (2) Special warranty deed—grantor warrants against defects in title only during his or her ownership.

    (3) Bargain and sale deed—only implies that the grantor holds title and possession, contains no warranties against encumbrances unless stated.

    (4) Quitclaim deed—conveys whatever interest, if any, grantor has but makes no warranties or guarantees; used to convey less than fee simple title or remove clouds on the title.

        (a) Provides the least protection to the grantee

        (b) Used to cure a defect, called a cloud on the title, such as a misspelled name

    (5) Deed in trust—used by a trustor to convey property to a trustee for the benefit of a beneficiary

    (6) Trustee's deed—used to convey property out of a trust to anyone other than the trustor

    (7) Reconveyance deed—executed by the trustee to return (reconvey) title property held in trust to the trustor

    (8) A deed executed pursuant to a court order—usually a statutory deed form used to convey title, includes executor's deeds, administrator's deeds, sheriff's deeds and others

2. Recording title—recording the deed is not a requirement in all states. However, if a deed is **NOT** recorded, the property owner is at risk of someone else recording a deed. By recording the deed, the owner is telling the world that he or she is the owner.

    a. Documents must be recorded in the county where the real estate is located.

    b. Constructive notice—presumption that information is available and by diligent inquiry, an individual can obtain it.

    c. Actual notice—includes knowing what has been recorded and personal inspection of the property

D. Title insurance

1. Purpose and scope of title insurance—a title insurance policy is a contract by which a title insurance company agrees, subject to the terms of its policy, to compensate or reimburse the insured against any losses sustained as a result of defects in the title other than those exceptions listed in the policy.

    a. Mortgagor's (borrower's) policy—insures the owner for the amount of the sales price.

    b. Mortgagee's (lender's) policy—insures the lender for the amount of the loan (decreases as the loan is paid off).

    c. Premium paid one time, at closing.

2. Essentials of title insurance—title policies generally contain three sections:

    a. First, the agreement to insure the title and indemnify against loss

    b. Second, the description of the estate and the property insured

    c. Third, a listing of conditions and exclusions to the coverage being issued

    d. Standard coverage policy insures against

       (1) Defects found in public records
       (2) Forged documents
       (3) Incompetent grantors
       (4) Incorrect marital statements
       (5) Improperly delivered deeds

    e. Extended coverage policy insures against

       (1) All perils insured against by the standard coverage policy
       (2) Property inspection, including unrecorded rights of persons in possession
       (3) Examination of survey
       (4) Unrecorded liens not known of by the policyholder

■ QUIZ

1. The title to real estate passes when a valid deed is

    (A) signed and recorded.
    (B) delivered and accepted.
    (C) filed and microfilmed.
    (D) executed and mailed.

2. The primary purpose of a deed is to

    (A) prove ownership.
    (B) transfer title rights.
    (C) give constructive notice.
    (D) prevent adverse possession.

3. A special warranty deed differs from a general warranty deed in that the grantor's covenant in the special warranty deed

    (A) applies only to a definite limited time.
    (B) covers the time back to the original title.
    (C) is implied and is not written in full.
    (D) protects all subsequent owners of the property.

4. The law that requires transfers of real property ownership to be in writing is the

    (A) parol evidence rule.
    (B) statute of limitations.
    (C) rule of civil procedure.
    (D) statute of frauds.

5. A third party holds title to property on behalf of someone else through the use of a

    (A) devise.   (C) bequest.
    (B) quitclaim deed.   (D) trust deed.

6. In a real estate transaction, any transfer taxes that are due are usually the responsibility of the

    (A) buyer.   (C) escrow agent
    (B) seller.   (D) licensee.

7. Title to real estate that is inherited from a person who died intestate is referred to as a

    (A) legacy.   (C) descent.
    (B) bequest.   (D) demise.

8. Which of the following documents is signed by the owner of the real estate?

   (A) A gift deed
   (B) A trustee's deed
   (C) A reconveyance deed
   (D) A tax deed

9. Which of the following deeds contains no expressed or implied warranties?

   (A) A bargain and sale deed
   (B) A quitclaim deed
   (C) A warranty deed
   (D) A grant deed

10. Which of the following is **NOT** required for a deed to be valid?

   (A) Date
   (B) Legal description
   (C) Name of the grantee
   (D) Signature of the grantee

11. The reversion of real estate to the state because of its lack of heirs or other persons legally entitled to own the property is called

   (A) eminent domain.   (C) attachment.
   (B) escheat.   (D) estoppel.

12. What is the purpose of the acknowledgment by a notary public on a deed?

   (A) To make the deed eligible for recording
   (B) To assure that the title is valid
   (C) To show the genuineness of the grantor's signature
   (D) To prove that the property has not been encumbered

13. A person owns a one-quarter undivided interest in a parcel of land, and he wants his interest transferred to his sister. As a general rule, which of the following actions will transfer the undivided interest out of his name?

   (A) The redemption from a foreclosure sale
   (B) The making and the signing of a will
   (C) The delivery of the deed during the owner's lifetime
   (D) The acceptance by signature of an offer to purchase

14. A valid will devises the decedent's real estate after the payment of all debts, claims, inheritance taxes and expenses through the

   (A) administrator of the estate.
   (B) law of testate succession.
   (C) granting clause established in the will.
   (D) court action known as probate.

15. When the grantor does not wish to convey certain property rights, he or she

   (A) must note the exceptions in a separate document.
   (B) may not do so, as the deed conveys the entire premises.
   (C) may note the exceptions in the deed of conveyance.
   (D) must convey the entire premises and have the grantee reconvey the rights to be retained by the grantor.

16. A person bought acreage in a distant county, never went to see it, and did not use it, although he regularly paid the real estate taxes on it. Another person moved his mobile home onto the property, drilled a well for water, and lived there for many years. The person who moved on to the property and drilled a well may have become the owner of the acreage if he has complied with the state laws regarding

   (A) intestate succession.
   (B) adverse possession.
   (C) the statute of frauds.
   (D) the statute of limitations.

17. In which of the following situations would a quitclaim deed be the **MOST** appropriate type of deed to use?

   (A) To convey a marketable title
   (B) To release a nominal real estate interest
   (C) To remove a cloud on title
   (D) To warrant that a title is valid

18. The condemnation of private property for public use is exercised under the government right of

   (A) taxation.
   (B) escheat.
   (C) manifest destiny.
   (D) eminent domain.

19. A trespasser built a log cabin in a national park and occupied the structure for over 15 years. That person will never be able to claim the property under adverse possession statutes because

    (A) the possession was not "notorious."
    (B) the possession was not "hostile."
    (C) the property was not privately owned.
    (D) the property was not properly fenced.

20. Grantee is to a deed as devisee is to

    (A) a trust
    (B) a will
    (C) an estate
    (D) a leasehold.

21. Which of the following is **NOT** true about adverse possession?

    (A) The person taking possession of the property must do so without its owner's consent.
    (B) Occupancy of the property must be continuous over a specified period of time.
    (C) The person taking possession must compensate the owner at the end of the possessory period.
    (D) The person taking possession may become the owner of the property.

22. Which of the following would **NOT** be a method of transferring property upon the owner's death?

    (A) By devise
    (B) By dedication
    (C) By descent
    (D) By escheat

23. A deed must be signed by the

    (A) grantor.
    (B) grantee.
    (C) grantor and grantee.
    (D) grantee and two witnesses.

24. Normally a deed will be considered valid even if

    (A) it is signed by an attorney-in-fact rather than the seller.
    (B) the grantor is not a legal entity.
    (C) the grantor is a minor.
    (D) the grantor did not deliver the deed.

25. In order for a deed to be valid

    (A) the grantor must be legally competent.
    (B) the signature of the grantor must be witnessed.
    (C) the deed must be recorded.
    (D) the grantee must sign the deed.

26. The seller conveyed a quitclaim deed to the buyer. Upon receipt of the deed, the buyer may be certain that

    (A) the seller owned the property.
    (B) there are no encumbrances against the property.
    (C) the buyer now owns the property subject to certain claims of the seller.
    (D) all of the seller's interests in the property belong to the buyer.

27. The type of deed in which the grantor defends the title back to its beginning is a

    (A) trustee's deed.
    (B) quitclaim deed.
    (C) special warranty deed.
    (D) general warranty deed.

28. Which of the following is **TRUE** regarding a special warranty deed?

    (A) The grantor is making additional warranties beyond those given in a warranty deed.
    (B) The grantor retains an interest in the ownership.
    (C) The grantor is warranting that no encumbrances exist against the property.
    (D) The grantor's warranties are limited to the time the grantor owned the property.

29. Two people own a building as joint tenants with right of survivorship. One of the tenants dies intestate. The other tenant now owns the building

    (A) as a joint tenant with right of survivorship.
    (B) in severalty.
    (C) in absolute ownership under the law of descent.
    (D) subject to the terms of the deceased's will.

30. A single person owned a parcel of land. Subsequent to the owner's death, the probate court determined the distribution of the land in accordance with the state's statutes. This person

    (A) died testate.
    (B) died intestate.
    (C) was the devisee.
    (D) was the grantee.

31. Which of the following is an involuntary alienation of property?

    (A) Quitclaim
    (B) Inheritance
    (C) Eminent domain
    (D) Gift

32. The type of deed in which the granting clause states "grant, bargain and sell" is a

    (A) special warranty deed.
    (B) bargain and sale deed.
    (C) general warranty deed.
    (D) reconveyance deed.

33. The type of deed in which the granting clause states "remise, release, alienate and convey" is a

    (A) special warranty deed.
    (B) bargain and sale deed.
    (C) quitclaim deed.
    (D) sheriff's deed.

34. A grantor does not wish to be responsible for defects in the title that arise from previous owners, but will guarantee the title for the time the grantor has the ownership. What type of deed would the grantor convey?

    (A) Bargain and sale deed
    (B) Quitclaim deed
    (C) Reconveyance deed
    (D) Special warranty deed

35. Which of the following is an example of involuntary alienation?

    (A) Selling a property to pay off debts
    (B) Giving a piece of land to the zoo
    (C) Having a piece of land sold for delinquent taxes
    (D) Letting another person plant crops on an unused portion of a piece of land

36. The clause in the deed that conveys the rights and privileges of ownership is called the

    (A) habendum clause.
    (B) appurtenance clause.
    (C) granting clause.
    (D) acknowledgment.

37. Which of the following deeds can be executed without subjecting the grantor to legal warranties?

    (A) Quitclaim
    (B) Bargain and sale
    (C) Trust
    (D) Trustee's deed

38. The deed that "grants and releases" and implies that the grantor has title is a

    (A) special warranty deed.
    (B) bargain and sale deed.
    (C) quitclaim deed.
    (D) trust deed.

39. The deed states that the grantor is conveying all rights and interests of the grantor to have and to hold by the grantee. This is the

    (A) acknowledgment clause.
    (B) restriction clause.
    (C) covenant of seisin.
    (D) habendum clause.

40. What will happen to the real estate if the deceased owner did not write a will and has no heirs?

    (A) The ownership will pass by devise.
    (B) The ownership will escheat to the state.
    (C) The courts will seize the ownership.
    (D) The ownership will revert to the previous owner.

41. Under the terms of a trust established by a will, the trustee is required to sell the real estate the trust holds. The deed that will be delivered at settlement is a

    (A) deed of release.
    (B) warranty deed.
    (C) trustee's deed.
    (D) trustor's deed.

42. Which of the following is acceptable as the evidence of marketable title?

    (A) A trust deed
    (B) A warranty deed
    (C) A title insurance policy
    (D) An affidavit

43. When a claim is settled by a title insurance company, the company acquires all rights and claims of the insured against any other person who is responsible for the loss. This is known as

    (A) caveat emptor.   (C) subordination.
    (B) surety bonding.   (D) subrogation.

44. Which of the following would be used to clear a defect from the title records?

    (A) A lis pendens
    (B) An estoppel certificate
    (C) A suit to quiet title
    (D) A writ of attachment

45. The part of the title insurance policy that sets forth all of the encumbrances and defects that will **NOT** be insured against is called the

    (A) schedule of defects.
    (B) citation clause.
    (C) nonexclusionary clause.
    (D) schedule of exceptions.

46. An abstract of title does **NOT** provide evidence of title unless it is accompanied by a

    (A) copy of the title insurance policy.
    (B) letter of insurance coverage.
    (C) letter of warranty.
    (D) legal opinion of title.

47. A bill of sale is used to transfer the ownership of

    (A) real property.
    (B) fixtures.
    (C) personal property.
    (D) appurtenances.

48. A title insurance policy delivered at closing does **NOT** include

    (A) a list of outstanding mortgage loans against the property.
    (B) a record of all of the previous owners of the property.
    (C) a report of the existing tax liens against the property.
    (D) a list of the easements held by utility companies.

49. A written summary of the history of all conveyances and legal proceedings affecting a specific parcel of real estate is called

    (A) an affidavit of title.
    (B) a certificate of title.
    (C) an abstract of title.
    (D) a title insurance policy.

50. When the preliminary title report reveals the existence of an easement on the property, it indicates that the easement is

    (A) a lien.
    (B) an encumbrance.
    (C) an encroachment.
    (D) a tenement.

51. The recorded history of owners that affect the title to a specific parcel of real property is called

    (A) a chain of title.
    (B) a certificate of title.
    (C) a title insurance policy.
    (D) an abstract of title.

52. Generally, if some defect is found in the title to real property, the effect on a sales contract is that

    (A) the contract is immediately void.
    (B) a new contract must be written.
    (C) the buyer has a reasonable time to find another property.
    (D) the seller has a reasonable time to correct the defect.

53. Which of the following would **NOT** be considered evidence of marketable title?

    (A) An abstract of title with a legal opinion
    (B) A title commitment or title insurance policy
    (C) A certificate of title by a real estate broker
    (D) A certificate of title by a real estate attorney

54. The recordation of a warranty deed

    (A) guarantees ownership.
    (B) protects the interests of the grantee.
    (C) prevents claims of parties in possession.
    (D) provides defense against adverse possession.

55. Documents affecting real estate are recorded or filed with the county in which the property is located to

    (A) satisfy the legal requirements for recording.
    (B) give constructive notice of the real estate interest.
    (C) comply with the terms of the statute of frauds.
    (D) prove the execution of the document.

56. Which one of the following would **NOT** be acceptable as evidence of marketable title?

    (A) A Torrens certificate
    (B) A title insurance policy
    (C) An abstract and legal opinion
    (D) A property owner's warranty deed

57. Under the Torrens system,

    (A) title passes when the registrar approves the grantor's deed for registration.
    (B) the Torrens official performs exactly the same functions as the recorder of deeds.
    (C) the original deed is mailed to the buyer after it has been registered.
    (D) the registration of a title can be canceled by the owner at any time.

58. The **BEST** assurance of good title that a real estate purchaser can obtain is a

    (A) valid warranty deed signed by the seller.
    (B) valid quitclaim deed signed by the seller.
    (C) policy of title insurance.
    (D) certificate of title.

59. A document that protects against hidden risks such as forgeries and loss due to defects in the title, subject to specific exceptions, is called

    (A) a chain of title.
    (B) an abstract of title.
    (C) a certificate of title.
    (D) a title insurance policy.

60. The body of law that covers such topics as security agreements, financing statements and bulk transfers is the

    (A) American Land Title Association.
    (B) Uniform Commercial Code.
    (C) parol evidence rule.
    (D) statute of limitations.

61. The recording of a deed

    (A) is all that is required to transfer the title to real estate.
    (B) gives constructive notice of the ownership of real property.
    (C) insures the interest in a parcel of real estate.
    (D) warrants the title to real property.

62. A buyer took delivery of the deed to his new house but forgot to record the deed. Under these circumstances

    (A) the transfer of the property from the seller is ineffective.
    (B) the buyer's interest is not fully protected against third parties.
    (C) the deed is invalid after 90 days.
    (D) the deed in invalid after six months.

63. The mortgagee purchases a title insurance policy on the property a buyer is pledging as security for the mortgage loan. Which of the following is **TRUE?**

    (A) The policy is issued for the benefit of the buyer.
    (B) The policy guarantees that the buyer's equity will be protected.
    (C) The amount of coverage is commensurate with the loan amount.
    (D) The amount of coverage increases as the borrower's equity increases.

64. Which of the following is an example of proof of ownership?

    (A) An abstract of title   (C) Title insurance
    (B) A deed   (D) A title search

65. A defect or a cloud on the title may be cured by

    (A) obtaining quitclaim deeds from all interested parties.
    (B) bringing an action to register title.
    (C) paying cash for the property at closing.
    (D) obtaining title insurance.

66. Which of the following is **NOT TRUE** regarding public records?

    (A) They give notice of encumbrances.
    (B) They establish priority of liens.
    (C) They guarantee marketable title.
    (D) They provide constructive notice about interests in the property.

67. The primary reason a buyer obtains title insurance is

    (A) because the mortgage lender requires it.
    (B) to ensure that the buyer has marketable title.
    (C) to ensure that the abstractor has prepared a complete summary of title.
    (D) to pay future liens that may be filed.

68. A sales contract requires the seller to deliver marketable title. Which of the following is **TRUE?**

    (A) The delivery of a general warranty deed will provide this assurance.
    (B) A search of the public records will prove that the title is marketable.
    (C) The seller will pay all liens that are pending.
    (D) All encumbrances will be removed by the seller.

69. An outstanding claim or encumbrance that, if valid, would impair an owner's title is a

    (A) color of title.   (C) quiet title.
    (B) cloud on the title. (D) subrogation.

70. *Quieting a title* refers to

    (A) a title insurance company's search of the title.
    (B) a mortgagor relinquishing title after foreclosure.
    (C) the deposit of a title with an escrow agent.
    (D) the removal of a cloud on the title by court action.

71. A person agrees to purchase a property for $85,500. The buyer deposits the purchase price with an attorney, and the property owner deposits a warranty deed for the property with the attorney. The attorney is instructed to record the deed in the buyer's favor when the owner shows good title to the property. The attorney is also instructed to pay the purchase price, less some agreed prorations, to the owner when the buyer has received the deed. This transaction is called

    (A) provisional sale.
    (B) escrow.
    (C) installment sale.
    (D) option.

72. At the closing, the seller's attorney informed him that he would be giving credit to the buyer for certain accrued items. These items represent

    (A) bills related to the real estate that have already been paid by the seller.
    (B) bills related to the real estate that have not been paid as of the time of the closing.
    (C) all of the seller's outstanding bills.
    (D) all of the buyer's outstanding bills.

73. The Real Estate Settlement Procedures Act (RESPA) applies to the activities of

    (A) licensed real estate brokers when selling commercial and industrial buildings.
    (B) licensed securities salespeople when selling limited partnership interests.
    (C) lenders financing the purchase of a borrower's residence.
    (D) Fannie Mae and Freddie Mac when purchasing residential mortgages.

74. The details of a sales transaction are always governed by

   (A) the wishes of the seller as expressed orally.
   (B) the wishes of the buyer as expressed orally.
   (C) the escrow instructions that both the seller and the buyer sign.
   (D) the terms of the properly executed purchase contract.

75. At the closing, the real estate broker's commission generally appears as a

   (A) credit to the seller.
   (B) debit to the seller.
   (C) credit to the buyer.
   (D) debit to the buyer.

76. The condition of the seller's title is generally determined from

   (A) a title commitment or title insurance policy.
   (B) a physical inspection of the property by the buyer.
   (C) a closing statement prepared by an escrow agent.
   (D) an escrow report prepared by an attorney.

77. The Real Estate Settlement Procedures Act (RESPA) provides that

   (A) all real estate purchasers be able to view their closing statements the day before closing.
   (B) real estate advertisements must include the annual percentage rate, including all charges.
   (C) the borrower must be given an estimate of the closing costs before the time of the closing.
   (D) real estate syndicates must comply with the disclosure of "blue sky" laws.

78. The accrued interest on an assumed mortgage loan is entered on the closing statement as a

   (A) credit to the seller and a debit to the buyer.
   (B) debit to the seller and a credit to the buyer.
   (C) credit to both the seller and the buyer.
   (D) debit to both the seller and the buyer.

79. As provided in a valid purchase contract, the real estate transaction must be closed. This does **NOT** mean that

   (A) the seller must clear the title so that the condition of the title complies with the terms of the contract.
   (B) the purchaser must pay the balance of the purchase price to the seller.
   (C) the broker must attend the closing to receive any commission.
   (D) the seller must deliver the deed to the purchaser.

80. The process by which expenses are handled at the settlement of a real estate transaction so that both the buyer and the seller pay their respective portions of the debts is called

   (A) assessment.   (C) balancing.
   (B) proration.   (D) reconciliation.

81. Which of the following items is **NOT** usually prorated between the buyer and seller at closing?

   (A) Recording charges (C) Rents
   (B) Real estate taxes   (D) Utility bills

82. The Real Estate Settlement Procedures Act (RESPA) may apply to a loan assumption if the

   (A) terms of the assumed loan are modified by the lender.
   (B) lender charges less than $50 for the assumption.
   (C) buyer must be qualified by the lender for the assumption to occur.
   (D) seller does **NOT** want to be liable for the loan in the future.

83. The principal balance on an assumed mortgage loan is entered on the closing statement as a

   (A) credit to the seller and a debit to the buyer.
   (B) debit to the seller and a credit to the buyer.
   (C) credit to both the seller and the buyer.
   (D) debit to both the seller and the buyer.

84. The Real Estate Settlement Procedures Act (RESPA) is a regulation of the

    (A) state government.
    (B) federal government.
    (C) Department of Housing and Urban Development.
    (D) Department of Veteran Affairs.

85. The closing statement involves the debits and credits to the parties in the transaction. A debit is

    (A) a refund.
    (B) an expense.
    (C) an adjustment for an expense paid outside of closing.
    (D) a proration.

86. The Real Estate Settlement Procedures Act requires

    (A) that the closing of a transaction be held within 90 days of the date of the sales contract.
    (B) that disclosure be made of all closing costs within three days of the completed loan application.
    (C) the lender to disclose the annual percentage rate the borrower will be paying.
    (D) that lenders follow certain advertising procedures when advertising credit.

87. Which of the following statements is **NOT TRUE** regarding the Real Estate Settlement Procedures Act?

    (A) Lenders must provide borrowers with a good-faith estimate of closing costs.
    (B) A uniform settlement form must be used at loan closings.
    (C) The borrower may cancel the loan transaction within five days after settlement.
    (D) No kickbacks may be paid to any party in connection with a loan transaction.

88. An example of a *kickback* that is prohibited by RESPA is a

    (A) fee paid by Broker A to Broker B for referring a buyer to Broker A.
    (B) share of the commission paid by Broker A to her salesperson.
    (C) fee paid by a surveyor to a broker for a lead on a property to be surveyed.
    (D) flower arrangement that a salesperson sends to the buyer as a house warming gift.

89. Services offered by *computerized loan origination* (CLO) systems are permitted under RESPA as long as certain conditions are met. These conditions do **NOT** include

    (A) the broker may charge whatever fee the broker determines is fair for the service.
    (B) the borrower must pay whatever fees are charged for the service.
    (C) the mortgage broker may pay a referral fee for the mortgage loan.
    (D) the broker is required to disclose the existence of other loan products that are **NOT** part of the CLO.

90. In a closing statement, an accrued item is

    (A) an item paid in advance.
    (B) an item that is unpaid but is due.
    (C) a prepaid expense.
    (D) a proration.

91. Controlled business arrangements are permitted by RESPA as long as

    (A) consumers are unaware of these arrangements.
    (B) consumers are required to use the services of the affiliated companies.
    (C) the companies pay referral fees between them.
    (D) the companies make a written disclosure to the consumers of their relationship with one another.

■ ANSWER KEY WITH EXPLANATIONS

1. **(B)** Title to real estate passes when a valid deed is delivered and accepted during the grantor's lifetime.

2. **(B)** The primary purpose of a deed is to transfer title rights.

3. **(A)** A general warranty deed is one in which the grantor fully warrants good clear title to the premises. In a special warranty deed, the grantor only warrants the title against defects arising during the period of the grantor's ownership. A general warranty deed offers the greatest protection of any deed.

4. **(D)** The statute of frauds is the law that requires that the transfer of real property be in writing to be enforceable.

5. **(D)** A trust deed or deed of trust is an instrument by which title is conveyed to a third party who holds it on behalf of the lender.

6. **(B)** Transfer taxes, also known as tax stamps or conveyance taxes, are imposed by the state at the time of transfer and usually are paid by the seller.

7. **(C)** If a person dies without a will, the property is transferred by the statute of descent.

8. **(A)** In a voluntary transfer such as a gift deed, the owner is the person who signs the deed.

9. **(B)** In a quitclaim deed, the grantor transfers an interest, "if any," to the buyer. The quitclaim deed offers little or no protection to the grantee.

10. **(D)** Only the grantor must sign the deed. The grantee's signature is not required.

11. **(B)** When a person dies without a will and with no heirs, the property escheats to the state.

12. **(C)** The notary public acknowledges the grantor's signature to verify that the signature is voluntary and genuine. Generally, the grantor's signature must be acknowledged before the deed can be recorded.

13. **(C)** In this situation, the deed must be signed by the grantor and delivered to and accepted by the grantee during the grantor's lifetime.

14. **(D)** The probate process reviews and validates the terms and distribution of assets required by a will.

15. **(C)** A valid deed must specifically note any encumbrances, reservations or limitations that affect the title being conveyed.

16. **(B)** An owner has an obligation to inspect his or her property from time to time to protect his or her rights. After a certain period of time, which varies from state to state, title may be claimed by the adverse possessor.

17. **(C)** A quitclaim deed is frequently used to cure a defect, called a cloud on the title.

18. **(D)** Eminent domain is the police power used by governments to acquire property for the public good.

19. **(C)** Adverse possession cannot be claimed on government-held land.

20. **(B)** The grantee receives the property through a deed, and the devisee receives the proceeds of a will.

21. **(C)** An adverse possessor will not owe the original owner any compensation. The adverse possessor must prove that he or she occupied the property for a certain period of time, without the owner's consent, and that the use was open, notorious, and hostile.

22. (B) Dedication is the voluntary transfer of private property by a property owner to the government for some public use, such as streets or schools.

23. (A) The grantor must sign away his or her rights to the property. Since the grantee receives the deed/property, the grantee is not required to sign the deed.

24. (A) An attorney-in-fact holds a power of attorney who has been given authority to sign on behalf of the seller.

25. (A) The seller/grantor must be legally competent or the document is void.

26. (D) A seller may transfer any and all his or her interests via a quitclaim deed. However, the quitclaim deed offers no warranties or obligations.

27. (D) A general warranty deed offers the greatest protection of any deed.

28. (D) In a special warranty deed, the owner warrants the title for the term that the seller owned the property.

29. (B) Under joint tenancy, at the moment of death, the surviving tenant (owner) becomes an owner in severalty.

30. (B) A person who dies intestate did not leave a valid will. The decedent's property is distributed according to the state laws of descent.

31. (C) Eminent domain, the right by which government has the right to acquire private property for public use, is an involuntary alienation.

32. (B) A bargain and sale deed contains no express warranties against encumbrances, although it does imply that the grantor holds title and possession of the property.

33. (A) With a special warranty deed, the seller grants a warranty only for the period of time he or she owned the property.

34. (D) A special warranty deed only warrants the title during the time the seller owned the property.

35. (C) The property is sold by the government for back taxes. The owner did not volunteer to sell, and the property is alienated from the owner.

36. (C) The seller is the grantor and the buyer is the grantee. Therefore the language is referred to as the granting clause.

37. (A) In a quitclaim deed, the owner transfers all interest, "if any," with no warranties or guarantees.

38. (B) A bargain and sale deed contains no express warranties against encumbrances. It does, however, imply that the grantor holds title and possession of the property.

39. (D) The habendum clause means to have and to hold, which means the buyer can occupy and own the rights passed by the seller.

40. (B) In the event there is no will and no heirs, the property escheats to the state.

41. (C) In a trustee's deed, the trustee agrees to sell the property and he or she assumes no liability for condition of the property. The estate may be liable for problems in the deed but not the trustee.

42. (C) A title insurance policy is acceptable as evidence of marketable title. The insurance company writes a policy insuring good and clear title.

43. (D) Once the title company makes a payment to settle a claim covered by a policy, the company generally acquires the right to any remedy or damages available to the insured. This is called subrogation, a process by which a person releases his or her rights to damages to the insurance company.

44. (C) A suit to quiet title is used to clear a defect from the title records.

45. (D) The insurance company lists certain uninsurable losses that they will not cover in the event of a claim in the schedule of exceptions.

46. (D) The abstract of title is simply a list of recorded documents. The legal opinion addresses the quality of the title.

47. (C) A bill of sale transfers personal property and a deed transfers real property.

48. (B) The list of owners is found in the abstract. The title insurance policy will include a list of outstanding mortgage liens, existing tax liens, and a list of easements.

49. (C) The abstract of title is a list of recorded conveyances and legal proceedings affecting a specific real estate parcel.

50. (B) An easement is an encumbrance.

51. (A) A chain of title is the record of a property's ownership.

52. (D) If a title search finds a title defect, the seller is usually given a reasonable time to correct the defect, if possible. A seller may not have known of the problem.

53. (C) A broker does not have authority to guarantee good title. Ways of showing evidence of marketable title include an abstract with legal opinion, a title commitment or policy, or a certificate of title by a real estate attorney.

54. (B) Recording the deed serves constructive notice to the public as to the current owner.

55. (B) Since land is immovable, records pertaining to the property are recorded in the county where the property is located. Constructive notice is served by recording the deed.

56. (D) A property owner's warranty deed is not acceptable as evidence of marketable title. From the time the deed was issued, clouds or encumbrances may have been filed against the property.

57. (A) Under the Torrens system, title passes when the registrar of titles is directed to issue a certificate of title. Registration in the Torrens system provides evidence of title without the need to search the public record.

58. (C) The best assurance of good title is obtaining a title insurance policy. In the event there is a problem with the title, the owner can file a claim with the insurance company which assumes financial responsibility.

59. (D) In the event there is a problem with the title, the owner can file a claim with the insurance company.

60. (B) The Uniform Commercial Code is a commercial law statute that governs personal property when used as security for a loan. It does not apply to real estate transactions.

61. (B) Recording a deed serves constructive ownership of the ownership of real property.

62. (B) Failure to record a deed does not affect the transfer of the property. However, it is possible that the property could be sold to another. If the new buyer records his or her deed, the new party could be granted legal ownership.

63. (C) The mortgagee (lender) desires coverage to cover their loan amount.

64. (C) Title insurance is commonly used to prove ownership. Generally, a title insurance policy will not be issued without a detailed title search. The insurance company is willing to assume financial risk if it is wrong.

65. (A) A quitclaim deed from each of the parties would clear the defects by releasing the claims causing the problems.

66. (C) Public records do not guarantee validity of documents; they serve to notify the public of documents that affect the property.

67. (B) The primary reason that buyers obtain title insurance is to transfer the financial risk to the insurance company in the event that their title is challenged.

68. (C) The seller must pay off existing liens before conveying marketable title.

69. (B) A cloud on title is an outstanding claim or encumbrance that, if valid, would impair an owner's title.

70. (D) Removing a cloud on title by court action is also referred to as "quieting a title."

71. (B) Escrow is the closing of a transaction through a third party called an escrow agent, who receives certain funds and documents to be delivered upon the performance of certain conditions outlined in the escrow instructions.

72. (B) Accrued items on a closing statement are items of expense that have been incurred and not yet paid, such as interest on a mortgage loan or real estate taxes.

73. (C) RESPA is the federal law that requires certain disclosures to consumers about mortgage loan settlements. The law applies to one- to four-unit owner-occupied dwellings and prohibits the payment or receipt of kickbacks and certain kinds of referral fees.

74. (D) The contract is the blueprint of the transaction.

75. (B) A debit is a charge. Because the commission is owed by the seller, it is debited from the sale proceeds.

76. (A) The title company will research the owner's title before it issues a commitment or policy.

77. (A) RESPA provides that all real estate purchasers be able to view their closing statement (HUD-1) the day before closing. A good-faith estimate of closing costs must be given to the buyer within three business days of the completed loan application. The buyer should not be surprised by fees at the closing table.

78. (A) The accrued interest on an assumed mortgage loan is a credit to the seller and a debit to the buyer. The interest is the responsibility of the seller, but because it is paid in arrears the buyer would be required to pay the interest on the closing month's payment.

79. (C) A broker does not have to attend closing. Broker's fees are earned when they produce a ready and willing buyer under the terms of listing agreement.

80. (B) Proration is the process by which expenses, either prepaid or paid in arrears, are divided or distributed between the buyer and the seller at closing.

81. (A) Recording charges are not prorated; they are one-time fees and are paid as provided in the contract. Prorated items may include real estate taxes, rents and utility bills.

82. (A) RESPA requirements may apply to a loan assumption if a lender modifies the terms of an assumed loan. If the terms of the loan do not change, then RESPA requirements were met at the closing of the initial loan.

83. (B) The principal balance on an assumed loan is entered as a debit to the seller and a credit to the buyer. The outstanding loan amount must be paid from the seller's proceeds.

84. (B) RESPA is a federal law that applies in all states.

85. (B) A debit is a charge or an amount owed at closing.

86. (B) Under RESPA, the lender must provide a disclosure of all closing costs within three days of completed loan application.

87. (C) RESPA does not provide for a right of rescission for a purchase loan.

88. (C) RESPA prohibits kickback fees, or any unearned fees, in any real estate settlement service.

89. (C) Under CLO arrangements, fees earned by the real estate agent must be for service performed, not just a referral.

90. (B) On a closing statement, an accrued item is an expense that has been incurred but not yet paid, such as interest on a mortgage loan or real estate taxes.

91. (D) RESPA permits a controlled business arrangement as long as a consumer is clearly informed of the relationship among the service providers and that other providers are available. Fees may not be exchanged among the affiliated companies simply for referring business to one another.

Property Management

9

■ CONTENT OUTLINE

VIII. Property Management

A. Leases, estates, tenancies

1. Lease—a contract between an owner (lessor) and tenant (lessee) that transfers the right to exclusive possession and use of the property for a specified period of time in exchange for rent

   a. Types of leases

      (1) Gross lease—tenant pays fixed rent and landlord pays all taxes, insurance, mortgage payments, repairs, etc. (property charges). This is the most commonly used lease for residential properties.
      (2) Net lease—tenant pays rent and most or all property charges; generally, used for commercial or industrial properties.
      (3) Percentage lease—tenant pays fixed rent plus a percentage of gross or net income that exceeds a stated minimum—generally used for retail leases.

   b. Types of estates and tenancies

      (1) Estate for years—a lease for a definite period of time; it does not automatically renew itself at the end of the lease, has a specific termination date, is not terminated by the sale of the property or death of either party.
      (2) Estate from period to period—an interest that continues from period to period, such as a month-to-month tenancy, and continues for an indefinite period of time until proper notice of termination is given
      (3) Tenancy/estate at will—gives the lessee the right to possession until the lease is terminated by either party; term is indefinite. No definite initial period is specified as is the case of a periodic tenancy. An estate at will is automatically terminated by the death of either the landlord or tenant.
      (4) Tenancy/estate at sufferance—holdover tenant without consent of the landlord

   c. Requirements of a valid lease (Study tip: CLOAC)

      (1) Capacity to contract
      (2) Legal objectives

       (3) Offer and acceptance

       (4) Consideration

    d. Assignment—transfers all the lessee's interest for the entire term

    e. Subletting—transfers all or part of a lessee's interest for the remaining term; original lessee liable to lessor

B. Property manager and owner relationships—a fiduciary relationship is created between the property manager and the property owner in the management agreement.

  1. Property manager responsibilities

    a. Securing suitable tenants

    b. Collecting the rents

    c. Caring for the premises

      (1) Preventive maintenance—regularly scheduled activities to maintain the structure

      (2) Repair or corrective maintenance—fixing items that are broken

      (3) Routine maintenance—routine cleaning and repairs

    d. Budgeting and controlling expenses

      (1) Fixed expenses include employees' salaries, real estate taxes and insurance premiums.

      (2) Variable expenses include repairs, decorating and supplies.

    e. Hiring and supervising employees

    f. Keeping proper accounts

    g. Making periodic reports to the owner

C. Laws affecting property management

  1. Fair housing laws—apply to residential properties

    a. It is illegal to discriminate on basis of physical disabilities.

    b. Tenants may make reasonable modifications to property but must restore at end of lease term.

  2. Americans with Disabilities Act (ADA)—applies to commercial properties

    a. Adopting nondiscriminatory employment procedures (by July 26, 1994, if have 15 or more employees)

    b. Ensuring access to services and facilities for people with disabilities

      (1) Removing barriers and providing accommodations when they can be accomplished in a *readily achievable* manner

  3. State property code laws

  4. Tax laws

  5. Health and building codes

■ QUIZ

1. A couple's apartment lease has expired, but their landlord has indicated to them that they may remain on the premises until a sale of the building is closed. The couple will be charged their normal monthly rental during this period. The tenancy held by the couple is called

   (A) a year-to-year holdover.
   (B) an estate for term.
   (C) an estate at sufferance.
   (D) an estate at will.

2. Generally, an oral lease for five years is

   (A) illegal.
   (B) unenforceable.
   (C) a short-term lease.
   (D) renewable only in writing.

3. An office rents for $450 per month and measures 12 feet by 20 feet. The advertised annual rent per square foot would be

   (A) $1.875.   (C) $18.750.
   (B) $4.500.   (D) $22.500.

4. Rent is **BEST** defined as

   (A) the contractual consideration to a third party.
   (B) the consideration for the use of real property.
   (C) all monies paid by the lessor to the lessee.
   (D) the total amount owed under the terms of a lease.

5. Which of the following tenancies does **NOT** involve a lessor-lessee?

   (A) Tenancy at will
   (B) Tenancy in common
   (C) Tenancy from month to month
   (D) Tenancy from year to year

6. The tenant leases a heated apartment, but the landlord fails to provide heat because of a defective central heating plant. The tenant vacates the premises and refuses to pay any rent. This is an example of

   (A) abandonment.
   (B) actual eviction.
   (C) constructive eviction.
   (D) lessor negligence.

7. Which of the following will terminate a lease?

   (A) The sale of the leased premises
   (B) The death of the tenant
   (C) The abandonment of the leased premises by the tenant
   (D) The expiration of the term of the lease

8. For a written lease to be valid, it must contain

   (A) the signatures of both the lessor and the lessee.
   (B) a statement of the specific length of time.
   (C) a statement of the retention of the reversionary interest by the lessor.
   (D) a complete legal description of the premises.

9. The authority to carry out the eviction of a delinquent tenant from rented property is held by the

   (A) court.   (C) sheriff.
   (B) landlord.   (D) property owner.

10. Which of the following acquires a personal right in real property but **NOT** title to real property?

    (A) The grantee
    (B) The devisee
    (C) The beneficiary
    (D) The lessee

11. A tenant's lease has expired, but the tenant has not vacated the premises or negotiated a renewal lease. The landlord has declared that he does not want the tenant to remain in the building. This type of occupancy is referred to as an estate

    (A) for years.
    (B) from year to year.
    (C) at will.
    (D) at sufferance.

12. A barber leases a barbershop in a shopping center. The lease does not specifically indicate who is responsible for making repairs to the premises. The expense of making such repairs is generally

    (A) paid by the lessor.
    (B) paid by the lessee.
    (C) shared by the lessor and the lessee.
    (D) paid by the lessee who will be reimbursed by the lessor.

13. When a tenant sublets all or any part of the premises rented under a written lease,

    (A) the tenant assigns all rights, title and interest in the rented property to the new lessee.
    (B) the sublessee becomes primarily responsible to the landlord for the payment of rent and maintenance of the property.
    (C) the original lease is automatically canceled and the sublessee takes possession of the property on a month to month basis.
    (D) the original lease is unaffected unless it contains a provision that prohibits such subletting.

14. A lessee who pays some or all of the property expenses of the leased property has a

    (A) gross lease.
    (B) net lease.
    (C) percentage lease.
    (D) sublease.

15. The principal difference between an estate for years and an estate from year to year is that

    (A) an estate for years is a life estate.
    (B) an estate for years cannot be terminated.
    (C) an estate from year to year must be in writing.
    (D) an estate from year to year has no expiration date.

16. The covenant implied in a lease that ensures that the tenant will not be evicted by someone claiming ownership of the property prior to that of the lessor is the covenant

    (A) of seisin.
    (B) of quiet enjoyment.
    (C) of warranty forever.
    (D) against encumbrances.

17. A tenant has an estate for years. According to the written one-year lease, the tenancy will expire on May 1st. For the landlord to obtain possession as of that date, he or she must give the tenant

    (A) 30 days' notice.
    (B) 60 days' notice.
    (C) no notice.
    (D) notice as of April 15th.

18. The owner of real estate who leases it to another is called the

    (A) vendor.   (C) grantor.
    (B) lessor.   (D) trustor.

19. A lease that will terminate within one year of its inception

    (A) is invalid.
    (B) violates the provisions of the statute of frauds.
    (C) must be in writing.
    (D) can be an oral lease.

20. Which of the following is the **BEST** definition of actual eviction?

    (A) The right of a landlord to use the rental premises
    (B) The enforcement of a court order to remove a lessor
    (C) The landlord's reversionary right in the rental premises
    (D) The enforcement of a court order to remove a lessee

21. A tenant holds possession of a landlord's property without a definite lease term but with the consent of the landlord. This type of lease is called a

    (A) tenancy in common.
    (B) tenancy at sufferance.
    (C) tenancy at will.
    (D) trespass.

22. In the event that it is necessary for a landlord to remove a tenant from the premises, the landlord does so by

    (A) refunding any rents paid.
    (B) refunding any security or other deposits paid.
    (C) filing an eviction suit.
    (D) using the minimum amount of physical force necessary.

23. A leased building collapsed, and the tenant was forced to move out. This is an example of

    (A) constructive eviction.
    (B) effective eviction.
    (C) actual eviction.
    (D) detainer.

24. What type of notice must be given under a tenancy for years?

    (A) No notice is required to terminate the lease.
    (B) At least 30 days' notice must be given.
    (C) At least 180 days' notice is required to terminate the lease.
    (D) A year's notice must be given.

25. Under a percentage lease, the lessee may be requested to pay

    (A) a portion of maintenance.
    (B) some of the real estate taxes.
    (C) insurance on the building.
    (D) a percent of sales.

26. A lessee is in possession of property under a tenancy at will. Which of the following is **TRUE?**

    (A) The lessee has not received the consent of the landlord to possess the property.
    (B) The tenancy will terminate if the lessee dies.
    (C) The tenancy was created by the death of the lessor.
    (D) The tenancy has a definite termination date.

27. A tenant's lease does not terminate for five more years. The premises, however, have become too small to accommodate the tenant's growing business. Another business owner is interested in leasing the premises from the tenant for three years. Which of the following would the parties use for the tenant to lease the space to the business owner?

    (A) An assignment
    (B) A novation
    (C) A sublease
    (D) A tenancy at sufferance

28. A young couple with a toddler and an infant want to lease an apartment in a complex that is occupied primarily by adults. The rental agent shows the couple apartments only on the first floor. Which of the following is **TRUE?**

    (A) The rental agent is protecting the other adults from the disruption of the children.
    (B) The rental agent should charge a higher security deposit for this family.
    (C) The rental agent should have suggested that the couple look elsewhere.
    (D) The rental agent should have inquired about the couple's preference for apartments.

29. The landlord's lease prohibits tenants from altering the property in any way. A young woman who uses a wheelchair cannot maneuver over the doorstep into the apartment by herself. Nor can she use the bathroom facilities in her wheelchair. Which of the following is **TRUE?**

    (A) The landlord is responsible for making all apartments accessible to people with disabilities.
    (B) The tenant cannot remedy these conditions because of the terms of the lease.
    (C) The landlord should not have rented this apartment to the tenant.
    (D) The tenant is entitled to make the necessary alterations.

30. A tenant is leasing a house until he has saved enough money for the down payment to perform on the sales contract. What type of an arrangement is this?

    (A) Lease with an option
    (B) Lease purchase agreement
    (C) Periodic tenancy
    (D) Purchase-money mortgage

31. A lease agreement is signed by a lessee who is 17 years of age. This lease agreement is

    (A) void because a 17-year-old person cannot sign a lease.
    (B) voidable by the minor.
    (C) valid, but unenforceable.
    (D) voidable by the landlord.

32. An individual rents an apartment for one year. The landlord sells the building during the one-year lease term. What effect does the sale have on the lease?

    (A) The sale does not affect the lease.
    (B) The lease is automatically terminated.
    (C) The new landlord may decide whether to honor the existing lease.
    (D) The lease is terminated after 60 days' notice from the new owner.

33. The purpose of a security deposit is to

    (A) provide additional revenue for the landlord.
    (B) repair damage to the property caused by the tenant.
    (C) pay for the last month's rent.
    (D) ensure that the lease is valid.

34. The lessor and lessee have agreed to a lease term of five years. How can the lessor ensure that the rental income during the term is reflective of the market conditions?

    (A) Negotiate a new lease each year
    (B) Collect an additional security deposit each year
    (C) Negotiate an index lease
    (D) Negotiate a gross lease

35. A management agreement is to a property manager like

    (A) a listing agreement is to a broker.
    (B) a lease is to a tenant.
    (C) a deed is to a buyer.
    (D) an assignment.

36. A real estate broker acting as an owner's property manager

    (A) must not profit from private contracts at the expense of the owner.
    (B) may manage the client's property to the broker's own advantage.
    (C) need not maintain complete and accurate trust account records.
    (D) can personally collect the interest earned on trust account funds.

37. Adaptations of property specifications to suit tenant requirements are

    (A) tax-exempt improvements.
    (B) tenant improvements.
    (C) prohibited by most nonresidential leases.
    (D) generally not a good idea.

38. Which of the following is the **LEAST** likely cause for a high vacancy rate?

    (A) Inept management
    (B) Poor location
    (C) Excessive rent
    (D) Strong amenities

39. In determining rental amounts, a property manager considers the economic principle of

    (A) marginal contribution.
    (B) supply and demand.
    (C) conformity.
    (D) balance.

40. Which of the following is **NOT** an important function of a property manager?

    (A) Supervising the maintenance of the property
    (B) Protecting the physical integrity of the property
    (C) Meeting the functional requirements of the tenants
    (D) Preparing the owner's income tax returns

41. When dealing with risk, a property manager should **NOT** do which of the following?

    (A) Avoid risky situations
    (B) Retain it
    (C) Ignore it
    (D) Transfer it

42. The property manager's chief concern should be that the property

    (A) is seldom vacant because it is consistently rented at the lowest possible rents.
    (B) is managed to achieve the highest rate of return possible for the owner's investment.
    (C) manager's time is maximized in his or her management of the property.
    (D) exhibits the proper amount of the owner's pride of ownership.

43. The type of maintenance that is **MOST** often overlooked is

    (A) corrective maintenance.
    (B) repairs.
    (C) routine maintenance.
    (D) preventive maintenance.

44. A property manager's primary obligation is to

    (A) the tenants.
    (B) the owner.
    (C) the banker.
    (D) government authorities.

45. Which of the following should be **NOT** a consideration in selecting a tenant for the property?

    (A) Size of the available space relative to the tenant's requirements
    (B) Tenant's ability to make the rental payments
    (C) Compatibility of the tenant's business with those of other tenants
    (D) Ethnic background of the tenant and his or her employees

46. A property management firm **CANNOT** receive its income from a

    (A) fixed fee.
    (B) percentage of the net rentals collected.
    (C) fixed fee with a percentage on new rentals.
    (D) percentage of purchases made from suppliers.

47. The manager of a commercial building has many responsibilities in connection with the operation and maintenance of the structure. The manager would normally be considered the agent of the

    (A) lessor of the building.
    (B) lessee of the building.
    (C) lessor and the lessee.
    (D) resident manager.

48. The successful property manager does **NOT**

    (A) screen the tenants' ability to pay.
    (B) study rental rates in the area.
    (C) consider the type of business the tenant has.
    (D) appease the tenants by repairing their equipment.

49. Despite the complexity of the laws that affect today's properties, a property manager does **NOT** need to be familiar with

    (A) environmental hazards.
    (B) accessible construction.
    (C) nondiscriminatory practices.
    (D) investment securities laws.

50. The duties of a property manager generally do **NOT** include

    (A) renting space to tenants.
    (B) preparing a budget.
    (C) developing a management plan.
    (D) repairing a tenant's fixture.

■ ANSWER KEY WITH EXPLANATIONS

1. (D) The couple holds an estate at will. Either they or the landlord may terminate at either time.

2. (B) A valid lease over one year must be in writing in order to be enforceable.

3. (D) The annual rent per square foot would be $22.50.
$450 \times 12 = \$5,400$
$\$5,400 \div [12 \times 20] = \$22,500$

4. (B) In return for rent, the owner gives up the right of possession but not of ownership.

5. (B) Tenancy in common is an *ownership* right not a leasehold right.

6. (C) Constructive eviction results from the action or inaction of the landlord making the property uninhabitable. The tenant has the right to terminate the lease.

7. (D) Expiration of the lease term will terminate the lease. Even if the tenant abandons the property, the landlord may be owed rent through the original term of the lease.

8. (A) Both lessor and lessee must sign the lease. One person cannot bind another to a lease without his or her consent.

9. (C) The court gives the authority to the sheriff to evict the tenant. The sheriff cannot make the determination, just carry out the action.

10. (D) A lessee holds leasehold rights, not ownership rights.

11. (D) The landlord must suffer because of the tenant's refusal to leave.

12. (B) If not specifically indicated, who makes such repairs will usually fall to the tenant (lessee), particularly in a commercial or industrial lease.

13. (D) The person who executed the lease is still responsible unless they received a release from the lessor. The lessee can give up rights, but not responsibilities.

14. (B) A net lease is one in which the tenant pays a certain amount of rent to the landlord and also some or all of the expenses of the building. A net lease is often used for industrial properties.

15. (D) The estate for years has an ending date while an estate from year to year goes until terminated by either party.

16. (B) In a lease, the landlord implies ownership and the tenant can expect to enjoy occupancy without worrying about another person claiming ownership or occupancy.

17. (C) By definition, the tenant occupies the property at the "will" of the landlord and either party may terminate the lease on May 1st with no notice. However, some states mandate some notice.

18. (B) The landlord is the lessor; the tenant is the lessee.

19. (D) Generally, under the statute of frauds, a lease for less than one year can be enforceable even if it is an oral lease.

20. (D) The court gives authority to an officer of the court to actually remove the tenant from the property.

21. (C) The tenant has possession of the property for an indefinite time until the lease is terminated by either party or the death of either party.

22. (C) If the landlord "has" to remove the tenant, he or she must take legal action through the court system.

23. (A) Constructive eviction is the action or inaction of the landlord making the property uninhabitable, resulting in the tenant having to move out.

24. (A) No notice is required to terminate an estate for years, since there is a specific termination date in the lease.

25. (D) A common retail property lease is the percentage lease, under which the tenant pays a rental fee plus a percent of sales.

26. (B) A tenancy at will is an agreement between the lessor and lessee that is not binding on the lessor's or lessee's heirs.

27. (C) In a sublease, a person rents from the tenant, not the landlord. It is a lease "under" the primary lease.

28. (D) Families are a protected category under fair housing laws. If they want to live upstairs, then it is their choice not the landlord's.

29. (D) The handicapped tenant can make necessary changes. However, the tenant must comply with building and safety codes, and the landlord can require the property to be restored.

30. (B) Under a lease purchase, the tenant has contracted to buy the house while he is leasing. If he is applying the rent toward a down payment, the lender may allow only the portion of the rent that exceeds a reasonable amount for normal rent to be applied as the down payment.

31. (B) The lease is voidable at the option of the minor; it is binding and enforceable against the owner.

32. (A) Unless otherwise prohibited, a lease will survive a sale of the property.

33. (B) In the event the property is damaged, the landlord already has funds in the form of the security deposit to do repairs.

34. (C) An index lease allows rents to change based on a change in the consumer price index or other agreed-upon index. This is particularly useful in long-term leases.

35. (A) Both the listing agreement and the management agreement establish the employment status between principal and agent.

36. (A) The property manager has a fiduciary relationship to the owner and should not profit by receiving kickbacks without the owner's knowledge and consent.

37. (B) Tenant improvements are improvements mandated by the tenant, not other outside forces.

38. (D) Strong amenities should cause tenants to stay, not leave. Reasons for a high vacancy rate may include inept management, poor location or excessive rents.

39. (B) With a small supply and large demand, rents go up. With a large supply and small demand, rents go down.

40. (D) The manager may supply information, but the owner or the owner's accountant is responsible for preparing income tax returns.

41. (C) A manager should not ignore a risk. A manager may avoid risky situations, retain the risk or transfer the risk by buying insurance.

42. (B) The primary reason to have investment property is to receive a return on investment.

43. (D) Preventive maintenance is many times the last to be addressed because of the expense.

44. (B) The manager has a fiduciary relationship to the owner.

45. (D) Questions about race or ethnic backgrounds are prohibited by fair housing laws.

46. (D) A property management firm should **NOT** base its fees on a percentage of purchases from suppliers. Rather, the fees can be a fixed fee, a percentage of collected rents, or a combination of both.

47. (A) The lessor is the owner who hires the manager as agent. Generally, the manager has a fiduciary relationship to the owner.

48. (D) The upkeep of the tenants' personal (trade fixtures) property is not the responsibility of the owner's agent.

49. (D) Because the property manager is not an investment manager, he or she does **NOT** need to be familiar with investment security laws. The manager should be aware of environmental concerns, accessibility issues and nondiscriminatory practices.

50. (D) The upkeep of the tenants' personal (trade fixtures) property is not the responsibility of the owner's agent. A manager is often responsible for preparing a budget, developing a management plan, and renting space to tenants, among many other duties.

Mini-Review Exams

10

■ MINI-REVIEW EXAM #1

1. Which of the following is **NOT** a cost or capital expense of owning a home?

   (A) Interest paid on borrowed capital
   (B) Homeowner's insurance
   (C) Maintenance and repairs
   (D) Taxes on personal property

2. A borrower is told to make a payment for the same amount every month for 30 years, at which time the borrower will have paid off both principal and interest. What kind of loan is this?

   (A) Term   (C) Amortized
   (B) Straight   (D) Hypothecated

3. A building that is remodeled into residential units and is no longer used for the purpose for which it was originally built is an example of

   (A) a converted use property.
   (B) an urban homesteading.
   (C) a planned unit development.
   (D) a modular home.

4. A high-rise development that includes office space, stores, theaters and apartment units is an example of which of the following?

   (A) Planned unit development
   (B) Mixed-use development
   (C) Proprietary lease properties
   (D) Special cluster zoning

5. A house was preassembled at a factory, driven to the building site on a truck, then lowered onto its foundation by a crane. Later, workers finished the structure and connected plumbing and wiring. Which of the following terms **BEST** describes this type of home?

   (A) Mobile   (C) Manufactured
   (B) Modular   (D) Converted

6. Five years ago, a person bought a home for $250,000. Home values in the area have improved, and the current market value of the house has increased by 15%. If the owner has $95,875 left on the mortgage loan, what is the owner's current equity in the home?

   (A) $138,712   (C) $191,625
   (B) $154,125   (D) $250,000

7. For which of the following risks would a homeowner have to purchase a special policy in addition to a typical basic or broad-form homeowner's insurance policy?

   (A) The cost of medical expenses for a person injured in the policyholder's home
   (B) Theft
   (C) Vandalism
   (D) Flood damage

8. A person wants to buy his first home, but he doesn't know how much he can afford to pay. He has a gross monthly income of $1,800. According to the lender's 28% house-payment-to-income ratio, what is the total housing expense (principal, interest, taxes and insurance) the buyer can bear?

(A) $181.44
(B) $504.00
(C) $ 648.00
(D) $1,152.00

9. A married couple bought their house ten years ago for $150,000. Last week, they sold their home for $225,500. Based on these facts, how much capital gains tax will the couple have to pay this year?

(A)   0
(B) $ 7,550
(C) $11,325
(D) $75,500

10. Which of the following **BEST** expresses the concept of equity?

(A) Current market value minus capital gain
(B) Current market value minus property debt
(C) Current market value minus cost of land
(D) Replacement cost minus depreciation

11. A person purchases 100 acres and plans to subdivide them into 120 lots. In the deed to convey each lot, what method will the subdivider use in describing the lots?

(A) Rectangular-survey
(B) Metes-and-bounds
(C) Lot-and-block
(D) Fractional-sections

12. A developer received a loan that covers five parcels of real estate and provides for the release of the mortgage lien on each parcel when certain payments are made on the loan. This type of loan arrangement is called a

(A) purchase-money loan.
(B) blanket loan.
(C) package loan.
(D) wraparound loan.

13. Theft, smoke damage and damage from fire are covered under which type of homeowner's insurance policy?

(A) Basic form
(B) Broad form
(C) Coinsurance
(D) National Flood Insurance Program policies

14. By which of the following can a subdivider increase the amount of open or recreational space in a development?

(A) Density zoning
(B) Clustering
(C) Planned unit development
(D) Deed restrictions

15. The following groups of people wish to rent an apartment. Which group is considered a protected class under the current fair housing laws?

(A) Two sisters, ages 35 and 40
(B) Husband and wife
(C) Daughter (age 45) who is guardian of her mother (age 70)
(D) Man who is caring for two foster children, ages 8 and 10

16. Which of the following statements **BEST** explains the meaning of this sentence: To recover a commission for brokerage services, a broker must be employed as the agent of the seller?

    (A) The broker must work in a real estate office.
    (B) The seller must have made an express or implied agreement to pay a commission to the broker for selling the property.
    (C) The broker must have asked the seller the price of the property and then found a ready, willing and able buyer.
    (D) The broker must have a salesperson employed in the office.

17. A licensee who is paid in a lump sum and who is personally responsible for paying his or her own taxes is probably

    (A) a transactional broker.
    (B) a buyer's agent.
    (C) an independent contractor.
    (D) an employee.

18. Two licensees were found guilty of conspiring with each other to allocate real estate brokerage markets. A consumer suffered a $90,000 loss because of their activities. If the consumer brings a civil suit against the two licensees, what can she expect to recover?

    (A) Nothing; a civil suit cannot be brought for damages resulting from antitrust activities.
    (B) Only $90,000—the amount of actual damages the consumer suffered
    (C) Actual damages plus attorney's fees and costs
    (D) $270,000 plus attorney's fees and costs

19. A state has recently updated its rules and regulations for the real estate profession. Assuming this state is like all other states and provinces, which of the following statements is **TRUE** regarding this publication?

    (A) The rules and regulations are state laws enacted by the legislature.
    (B) The rules and regulations are a set of administrative rules adopted by the state real estate commission and do not have the same force and effect as the statutory license law.
    (C) The rules and regulations are a set of administrative rules adopted by the state real estate commission that define the statutory license law and have the same force and effect as the license law itself.
    (D) The rules and regulations create a suggested level of competence and behavior but are not enforceable against real estate licensees.

20. After a particularly challenging transaction finally closes, the client gives the listing agent a check for $500 "for all your extra work." Which of the following statements is accurate?

    (A) While such compensation is irregular, it is appropriate for the listing agent to accept the check.
    (B) The listing agent may receive compensation only from her broker.
    (C) The listing agent should accept the check and deposit it immediately in a special escrow account.
    (D) The listing agent's broker is entitled to 80% of the check.

21. A broker has established the following office policy: "All listings taken by any salesperson associated with this real estate brokerage must include compensation based on a 7% commission. No lower commission rate is acceptable." If the broker attempts to impose this uniform commission requirement, which of the following statements is **TRUE?**

    (A) A homeowner may sue the broker for violating the antitrust law's prohibition against price-fixing.
    (B) The salespersons associated with the brokerage will not be bound by the requirement and may negotiate any commission rate they choose.
    (C) The broker must present the uniform commission policy to the local professional association for approval.
    (D) The broker may, as a matter of office policy, legally set the minimum commission rate acceptable for the firm.

22. A local realty firm has adopted a 100% commission plan. The monthly desk rent required of sales associates is $900, payable on the last day of the month. In August, a sales associate closed an $89,500 sale with a 6% commission and a $125,000 sale with a 5.5% commission. The salesperson's additional expenses for the month were $1,265. How much of the salesperson's total monthly income did he or she keep?

    (A) $10,080   (C) $11,345
    (B) $10,980   (D) $12,245

23. A salesperson sold a house for $129,985 with a commission rate of 8 percent. The split between the listing and selling brokers was 60/40 with 60 percent going to the listing broker. The split in the listing office is 30/70 with the broker retaining 30 percent. How much does the listing agent earn on this sale?

    (A) $1,247.86   (C) $4,367.50
    (B) $2,911.66   (D) $6,239.28

24. On the sale of any property, a salesperson's compensation is based on the total commission paid to the broker. The salesperson receives 30 percent of the first $2,500, 15 percent of any amount between $2,500 and $7,500, and 5 percent of any amount exceeding $7,500. If a property sells for $234,500 and the broker's commission rate is 6.5 percent, what is the salesperson's total compensation?

    (A) $1,887.13   (C) $6,626.67
    (B) $4,609.13   (D) $7,621.25

25. Two competing real estate brokers meet for lunch and decide that a local property developer is gaining too much influence in the market. The two brokers decide to try to drive the developer out of business. One of the brokers happens to own a parcel of farmland that is key to the success of the developer's new subdivision. The other broker owns 17 acres of polluted swamp next to an oil refinery. When the developer offers to buy the farmland, the broker responds that the property is for sale only if the developer also buys the other broker's swamp at the same time. Without the farmland, the new subdivision will fail. Unfortunately, the developer doesn't have enough cash to pay the price demanded for the swamp. Rather than risk bankruptcy, the developer leaves town. This scenario is an example of which of the following violations of the antitrust laws?

    (A) Group boycotting and allocation of markets
    (B) Price-fixing and tie-in agreements
    (C) Tie-in agreements only
    (D) Allocation of customers and price-fixing

■ ANSWER KEY WITH EXPLANATIONS

1. (D) Taxes on personal property are not a cost or capital expense of owning a home.

2. (C) An amortized loan is a loan in which the principal as well as the interest is payable in monthly or other periodic installments over the term of the loan.

3. (A) A property whose use has been changed to something totally different is a converted use property.

4. (B) A high-rise building that includes offices, stores, theaters and apartments is considered a mixed-use building.

5. (B) The sections (modules) are constructed off site and then assembled at the building site.

6. (C) The owner's equity is $191,625.
[$250,000 × 115%] – $95,875 = $191,625

7. (D) Rising water (flood) damage is not covered in a standard homeowner's policy.

8. (B) The buyer is assumed to be able to afford $504 per month.
$1,800 × 28% = $504

9. (A) Under current laws, there is no tax on the first $500,000 of capital gains when selling a home for married taxpayers filing jointly.

10. (B) Equity is the difference between value and the loan amount.

11. (C) Although the subdivider may have purchased the 100 acres described by the rectangular survey method, the subdivider will do doubt describe the property by identifying each lot by reference to lot and block numbers within a subdivision as specified on a recorded subdivision plat. This description is also known as a recorded plat.

12. (B) A blanket loan is a mortgage covering more than one parcel of real estate, providing for each parcel's release from the mortgage lien upon repayment of a definite portion of the debt.

13. (A) These are standard losses covered by a basic policy.

14. (B) Clustering or grouping home sites within a subdivision on lots smaller than normal permits the developer to use the remaining land for recreation or common areas.

15. (D) Under HUD rules, familial status refers to the presence of one or more individuals who have not reached the age of 18 and who live with either a parent or guardian. Thus, the man caring for two foster children qualifies. While the others are "family," they do not qualify under HUD for protection because they do not involve children under 18.

16. (B) A broker cannot pursue a commission unless the consumer agreed that a commission would be paid.

17. (C) Real estate licensees who are treated as independent contractors for tax purposes receive the entire commission and are responsible for paying all Social Security and income taxes.

18. (D) Intentional antitrust violations may result in up to three times the amount in damages plus attorney's fees and costs.

19. (C) Generally, through "enabling acts," state legislatures authorize the real estate commission to adopt a set of administrative rules that define the statutory license law and that have the same force and effect as the license law itself.

20. (B) Commissions must be paid "through" the sponsoring/employing broker.

21. (D) Brokers are allowed to set the commissions they charge. What is illegal is when brokers "conspire" to fix prices between companies.

22. (A) The salesperson kept $10,080.
$$[\$89,500 \times 6\%] + [\$125,000 \times 5.5\%] - [\$900 + \$1,265] = \$10,080$$

23. (C) The listing agent earned $4,367.50.
$$[\$129,985 \times 8\%] \times .60 \times .70 = \$4,367.50$$

24. (A) The salesperson's total commission is $1,887.13.
$$\$234,500 \times 6.5\% = \$15,242.50 \text{ (broker's commission)}$$
$$\$15,242.50 - \$7,500 = \$7,742.50 \times 5\% = \$387.13$$
$$\$5,000 \times 15\% = \$750$$
$$\$2,500 \times 30\% = \$750$$
$$\$387.13 + \$750 + \$750 = \$1,887.13$$

25. (C) This story is a good illustration of "tying," a prohibited practice under antitrust laws.

■ MINI-REVIEW EXAM #2

1. A listing taken by a real estate salesperson is technically an employment agreement between the seller and the

   (A) broker.
   (B) local multiple-listing service.
   (C) salesperson.
   (D) salesperson and broker together.

2. Which of the following is a similarity between an exclusive-agency listing and an exclusive-right-to-sell listing?

   (A) Under both, the seller retains the right to sell the real estate without the broker's help and without paying the broker a commission.
   (B) Under both, the seller authorizes only one particular salesperson to show the property.
   (C) Both types of listings give the responsibility of representing the seller to one broker only.
   (D) Both types of listings are open listings.

3. The listing agreement on a residential property states that it expires on May 1. Which of the following will terminate this listing agreement?

   (A) The owner renews the agreement on April 25.
   (B) The broker brings an offer to the owner.
   (C) The owner tells the broker that the advertising is inadequate.
   (D) The house burns down on May 1.

4. A seller has listed a property under an exclusive-agency listing with a broker. If the seller sells the property personally during the term of the listing to someone who learns about the property through the seller, the seller will owe the broker

   (A) no commission.
   (B) the full commission.
   (C) a partial commission.
   (D) only reimbursement for the broker's costs.

5. A broker sold a residence for $85,000 and received $5,950 as commission in accordance with the terms of the listing. What was the broker's commission rate?

(A) 6.00%   (C) 7.25%
(B) 7.00%   (D) 7.50%

6. Which federal law prohibits racial discrimination in any type of housing under any circumstances?

(A) Fair Housing Amendments Act
(B) Civil Rights Act of 1866
(C) Civil Rights Act of 1964
(D) Civil Rights Act of 1968

7. Which of the following is a similarity between an open listing and an exclusive-agency listing?

(A) Under both, the seller avoids paying the broker a commission if the seller sells the property to someone the broker did not procure.
(B) Both grant a commission to any broker who procures a buyer for the seller's property.
(C) Under both, the broker earns a commission regardless of who sells the property, as long as it is sold within the listing period.
(D) Both grant the exclusive right to sell to whatever broker procures a buyer for the seller's property.

8. The final decision on a property's listed price should be made by the

(A) listing agent.
(B) appraised value.
(C) seller.
(D) seller's attorney.

9. Which of the following statements is **TRUE** of a listing contract?

(A) It is an employment contract for the professional services of the broker.
(B) It obligates the seller to convey the property if the broker procures a ready, willing and able buyer.
(C) It obligates the broker to work diligently for both the seller and the buyer.
(D) It automatically binds the owner, broker and MLS to the agreed provisions.

10. A broker sold a property and received a 6.5% commission. The broker gave the listing salesperson 30% of the commission, or $3,575. What was the selling price of the property?

(A) $55,000   (C) $152,580
(B) $95,775   (D) $183,333

11. A seller hired a broker under the terms of an open listing. While that listing was still in effect, the seller—without informing the first broker—hired a second broker under an exclusive-right-to-sell listing for the same property. If the first broker produces a buyer for the property whose offer the seller accepts, then the seller must pay a

(A) full commission only to the first broker under the open listing.
(B) full commission only to the second broker under the exclusive-right-to sell listing.
(C) full commission to both brokers.
(D) split the commission between both brokers.

12. A seller listed a home with a broker. The broker brought an offer from buyers who are ready, willing and able to pay cash for the property. However, the seller decided to reject the buyers' offer. In this situation, the seller

(A) must sell his or her property.
(B) owes a commission to the broker.
(C) is liable to the buyers for specific performance.
(D) is liable to the buyers for compensatory damages.

13. Which of the following is **TRUE** of an open buyer agency listing?

(A) The buyer may enter into agreements with multiple brokers and is obligated to pay only the broker who locates the property that the buyer ultimately purchases.
(B) While the buyer may enter into agreements with multiple brokers, he or she is under no obligation to pay the broker; the seller bears all brokerage expenses.
(C) Because multiple brokers may be involved, an open buyer agency agreement involves reduced fiduciary duties.
(D) The buyer may not look for or make offers on properties on his or her own.

14. A broker and a buyer enter into an exclusive-agency buyer agency agreement. What does this mean?

   (A) The buyer is obligated to compensate the broker, regardless of who locates the property ultimately purchased.
   (B) The broker is entitled to payment only if she or any broker acting under her authority locates the property the buyer ultimately purchases.
   (C) The buyer may enter into similar agreements with any number of other brokers.
   (D) If the buyer finds the property without any help from the broker, the buyer may pay the broker a reduced compensation.

15. Which of the following statements is **TRUE** of a competitive market analysis (CMA)?

   (A) A CMA is the same as an appraisal.
   (B) A CMA can help the seller price the property.
   (C) By law in most states a CMA must be completed for each listing taken.
   (D) A CMA should not be retained in the property's listing file.

16. A property was listed with a broker who belonged to a multiple-listing service and was sold by another member broker for $53,500. The total commission was 6% of the sales price. The selling broker received 60% of the commission, and the listing broker received the balance. What was the listing broker's commission?

   (A) $1,284   (C) $1,926
   (B) $1,464   (D) $2,142

17. The seller enters into a listing agreement. If the home sells for $120,000, what is the net amount to the seller after paying the broker a 7% commission?

   (A) $ 36,000   (C) $111,600
   (B) $102,877   (D) $120,000

18. A real estate broker and a seller enter into a listing agreement that contains the following language: "Seller will receive $100,000 from the sale of the subject property. Any amount greater than $100,000 will constitute Broker's sole and complete compensation." Which of the following statements is **TRUE** regarding this agreement?

   (A) This agreement is an example of an option listing.
   (B) If the seller's home sells for exactly $100,000, the broker will still be entitled to receive the standard commission in the area.
   (C) The broker may offer the property for any price over $100,000, but the listing agreement may be illegal.
   (D) This type of listing is known as an open listing, because the selling price is left open.

19. Which of the following listings opens the broker to charges of fraud unless the broker is scrupulous in fulfilling all obligations to the owner?

   (A) Open listing
   (B) Option listing
   (C) Exclusive-agency listing
   (D) Exclusive-right-to-sell listing

20. A written agreement between a broker and a client includes the following language: "In return for the compensation agreed upon, Broker will assist Client in locating and purchasing a suitable property. Broker will receive the agreed compensation regardless of whether Broker, Client or some other party locates the property ultimately purchased by Client." What kind of agreement is this?

   (A) Exclusive-agency listing
   (B) Exclusive-agency buyer agency agreement
   (C) Exclusive buyer agency agreement
   (D) Open buyer agency agreement

21. The right of a government body to take ownership of real estate for public use is called

   (A) escheat.
   (B) eminent domain.
   (C) condemnation.
   (D) police power.

22. A purchaser of real estate learned that his ownership rights could continue forever and that no other person claims to be the owner or has any ownership control over the property. This person owns a

    (A) fee simple interest.
    (B) life estate.
    (C) determinable fee estate.
    (D) fee simple on condition.

23. A property owner owned the fee simple title to a vacant lot adjacent to a hospital and was persuaded to make a gift of the lot. She wanted to have some control over its use, so her attorney prepared her deed to convey ownership of the lot to the hospital "so long as it is used for hospital purposes." After completion of the gift the hospital will own a

    (A) fee simple absolute estate.
    (B) license.
    (C) fee simple determinable.
    (D) leasehold estate.

24. An owner of property lets his neighbor regularly use the owner's driveway to reach a garage located on the neighbor's property. The ownership of the neighbor's real estate includes an easement for the use of the driveway. The owner's property is properly called

    (A) the dominant tenement.
    (B) a freehold.
    (C) a leasehold.
    (D) the servient tenement.

25. A license is an example of

    (A) an appurtenant easement.
    (B) an encroachment.
    (C) a temporary use right.
    (D) a restriction.

■ ANSWER KEY WITH EXPLANATIONS

1. (A) The parties to a listing agreement are the seller (principal) and broker (agent). The salesperson is acting as agent of the broker, i.e., as a subagent.

2. (C) The seller hires only one broker to represent the seller under both the exclusive-agency listing and an exclusive-right-to-sell listing.

3. (D) A listing is generally terminated if the property burns down. It is **NOT** terminated if the owner renews the listing prior to expiration or by seller complaints. Because an offer may be turned down, bringing an offer also does not terminate the listing.

4. (A) The seller only owes a commission if an agent finds a buyer.

5. (B) The broker's commission rate was 7%.
   $$\$5,950 \div \$85,000 = .07 \text{ or } 7\%$$

6. (B) The Civil Rights Act of 1866 prohibits all racial discrimination, private as well as public. This law was reaffirmed by the *Jones v. Mayer* Supreme Court decision in 1968.

7. (A) In either the open listing or exclusive-agency listing, the seller is obligated to pay a commission only if an agent found a buyer.

8. (C) The seller gets to decide what price he or she wants to place on the property.

9. (A) A listing contract is an employment contract for the professional services of the broker.

10. (D) The property sold for $183,333.
    $$\$3,575 \div .30 \div .065 = \$183.333$$

11. (C) Both listings obligate the seller to pay a commission if the first agent finds a buyer.

12. (B) The seller agreed to pay a commission if the broker produced a ready and willing buyer, which the broker did. The seller is not obligated to sell the property; however, the seller is obligated to pay the commission.

13. (A) The open buyer listing has the same obligations as an open seller listing.

14. (B) Under an exclusive-agency buyer agency agreement, if the buyer finds a property without the aid of the broker, then no commission is owed.

15. (B) The CMA gives the seller valuable market information that assists the seller in setting a fair marketing price.

16. (A) The listing broker's commission was $1,284.
    $53,500 \times .06 \times .40 = \$1,284$

17. (C) After paying the broker's 7% commission, the seller nets $111,600.
    $120,000 \times .93 = \$111,600$

18. (C) This is a good example of the potential conflict of interest inherent in a net listing. The broker may offer the property for any amount over $100,000 and keep the difference as a commission. The broker may possibly not be looking out for the best interests of the seller.

19. (B) An option listing gives the broker the right to purchase the listed property. Generally, the broker should inform the property owner of the broker's potential profit in the transaction. It is best that the broker secure in writing the owner's agreement.

20. (C) An exclusive buyer agency agreement follows the same guidelines as a exclusive right-to-sell listing. In both situations, the consumer is obligated to pay a commission, even if the consumer finds his or her own property/buyer.

21. (B) The right for a public entity to acquire private property for public use is called eminent domain. The action is condemnation. The government's police powers include the right to enforce zoning, building and occupancy codes in order to protect the public.

22. (A) Fee simple ownership is the highest form of ownership. Fee simple is inheritable.

23. (C) The hospital holds the property as fee simple determinable. The grantor has determined the future use of the property.

24. (D) To provide access, the owner's property must serve the neighbor's property.

25. (C) A license is a temporary use right that may be revoked at any time. An example of a license is movie ticket. You have permission to stay and watch the movie but when it is over you have to leave.

■ MINI-REVIEW EXAM #3

1. An owner conveys to her brother a life estate that will expire when their uncle dies. However, shortly after taking over, the brother dies, although the uncle is still living. The brother's will states that everything he owns is to go to his wife. At this point, what are the interests that the owner, her uncle, and the wife possess?

   (A) The brother possessed a life estate pur autre vie measured by the life of the uncle. Because the uncle is still living, the brother's wife now holds this estate. The original owner holds a reversionary interest.
   (B) The brother possessed a life estate pur autre vie measured by the life of the uncle. The brother's wife is the remainderman and holds a nonpossessory estate until the uncle dies. After the uncle's death, the property escheats to the state.
   (C) The brother possessed a determinable life estate, and the uncle is the measuring life. When the brother dies, his interest passes directly to his wife. When the uncle dies, the original owner may regain the property only by suing the brother's wife.
   (D) The original owner has a remainder interest in the conventional life estate granted to her brother. Because the grant was to the brother only, the estate may not pass to his wife. When the brother died before the uncle, the estate automatically ended and the original owner now owns the property in fee simple.

2. In a state that recognizes a limited homestead exemption, what happens if a property owner is sued by his or her creditors?

   (A) The creditors can have the court sell the owner's home and apply the full proceeds of sale to the debts.
   (B) The creditors have no right to have the owner's home sold.
   (C) The creditors can force the owner to sell the home to pay them.
   (D) The creditors can request a court sale and apply the sale proceeds, in excess of the statutory exemption and secured debts, to the owner's unsecured debts.

3. If the owner of real estate does not take action against a trespasser before the statutory period has passed, the trespasser may acquire the legal authority to continue using the property through

   (A) an easement by necessity.
   (B) a license.
   (C) title by eminent domain.
   (D) an easement by prescription.

4. A property owner wants to use water from a river that runs through the property to irrigate a potato field. To do so, the owner is required by state law to submit an application to the department of water resources describing in detail the beneficial use he plans for the water. If the department approves the owner's application, it will issue a permit allowing a limited amount of river water to be diverted onto the property. Based on these facts, it can be assumed that this property owner's state relies on which of the following rules of law?

   (A) Common-law riparian rights
   (B) Common-law littoral rights
   (C) Doctrine of prior appropriation
   (D) Doctrine of highest and best use

5. Which of the following is a private restriction and **NOT** an example of the government powers?

   (A) Dedication
   (B) Police power
   (C) Eminent domain
   (D) Taxation

6. Property deeded to a town "for recreational purposes only" conveys a

   (A) fee simple absolute.
   (B) fee simple on condition precedent.
   (C) leasehold interest.
   (D) fee simple determinable.

7. If a property owner has the legal right to cross over land owned by his or her neighbor, he or she holds

   (A) an estate in land.
   (B) an easement.
   (C) a police power.
   (D) an encroachment.

8. Which of the following is **NOT** a legal life estate?

   (A) A leasehold
   (B) The husband's curtesy
   (C) A homestead
   (D) The wife's dower

9. A father conveys ownership of his residence to his daughter but reserves for himself a life estate in the residence. The interest the daughter owns during her father's lifetime is

   (A) pur autre vie.   (C) a reversion.
   (B) a remainder.   (D) a leasehold.

10. When the back fence was installed, it was placed, inadvertently, one foot over the property line into the neighbor's yard. The fence is an example of

    (A) a license.
    (B) an encroachment.
    (C) adverse possession.
    (D) an easement by prescription.

11. A homeowner may be allowed certain protection from judgments of creditors as a result of his or her state's

    (A) littoral rights.
    (B) curtesy rights.
    (C) homestead rights.
    (D) dower rights.

12. A farmer gives permission to a person to hunt on his farm during the hunting season. The person holds

    (A) an easement by necessity.
    (B) an easement by condemnation.
    (C) riparian rights.
    (D) a license.

13. Which of the following statements about encumbrances on real estate is **TRUE?**

    (A) Encumbrances include easements and encroachments.
    (B) The presence of an encumbrance makes it impossible to sell the encumbered property.
    (C) All encumbrances must be removed before the title can be transferred.
    (D) An encumbrance is of no monetary value to its owner.

14. A tenant who rents an apartment from the owner of the property holds

    (A) an easement.
    (B) a license.
    (C) a freehold interest.
    (D) a leasehold interest.

15. Because a homeowner failed to pay her real estate taxes on time, the taxing authority imposed a claim against her property. This claim is known as

    (A) a deed restriction.
    (B) a lien.
    (C) an easement.
    (D) a reversionary interest.

16. The four unities of possession, interest, time and title are associated with which of the following?

    (A) Community property
    (B) Severalty ownership
    (C) Tenants in common
    (D) Joint tenancy

17. Two friends purchased a property. On the deed, their names were listed without any further explanation. The two friends took title as

    (A) joint tenants.
    (B) tenants in common.
    (C) tenants by the entirety.
    (D) community property owners.

18. Three owners hold title as joint tenants with rights of survivorship. One of the owners transfers his interest to a fourth person. What is the relationship between the new owner and the remaining owners?

    (A) The remaining original owners are still joint tenants with the new owner who is a tenant in common.
    (B) The original owners and the new owners are joint tenants.
    (C) All three owners are now tenants in common.
    (D) The new owner now has severalty ownership of the property.

19. A person owns a townhouse in fee simple along with a 5% ownership share of the parking facilities, recreation center and grounds. What kind of property ownership does this person own?

    (A) Cooperative   (C) Time-share
    (B) Condominium   (D) Land trust

20. A brother transfers a vineyard in trust to his attorney with instructions that any income derived from the vineyard be used for his sister's medical care. What is the relationship of the brother, the attorney and the sister?

    (A) The brother is the trustee, the attorney is the trustor, and the sister is the beneficiary.
    (B) The brother is the trustor, the attorney is the trustee, and the sister is the beneficiary.
    (C) The brother is the beneficiary, the attorney is the trustor, and the sister is the trustee.
    (D) The brother is the trustor, the attorney is the beneficiary, and the sister is the trustee.

21. Under the laws of one state, any real property that either member of a married couple owns at the time of their marriage remains separate property. Further, any real property acquired by either party during the marriage (except by gift or inheritance) belongs to both of them equally. What is this form of ownership called?

    (A) Partnership
    (B) Joint tenancy
    (C) Tenancy by the entirety
    (D) Community property

22. Three people were concurrent owners of a parcel of real estate. When one of the owners died, his interest became part of his estate and ultimately passed to his nephew. The deceased owner held title as a

    (A) joint tenant.
    (B) tenant in common.
    (C) tenant by the entirety.
    (D) severalty owner.

23. A legal arrangement under which the title to real property is held to protect the interests of a beneficiary is a

    (A) trust.
    (B) corporation.
    (C) limited partnership.
    (D) general partnership.

24. A condominium form of ownership is officially established when

    (A) the construction of the improvements is completed.
    (B) the owner files a declaration in the public record.
    (C) the condominium owners' association is established.
    (D) all the unit owners file their documents in the public record.

25. An owner purchased an interest in a house in Beachfront. The owner is only entitled to the right of possession between July 10 and August 4 of each year. Which of the following is **MOST** likely the type of ownership that has been purchased?

    (A) Cooperative   (C) Time-share
    (B) Condominium   (D) Trust

■ ANSWER KEY WITH EXPLANATIONS

1. (A) The brother possessed a life estate pur autre vie measured by the life of the uncle. Since the uncle is still living, the brother's wife inherits his interest and will hold it until the uncle dies. The original owner holds a reversionary interest and she will get the property when the uncle dies.

2. (D) In states that recognize a homestead estate, some portion of the family home is protected from the claims of unsecured creditors.

3. (D) If a trespasser is permitted access over a long enough period of time, the trespasser may acquire permanent legal rights with an easement by prescription.

4. (C) Doctrine of prior appropriation is a concept of water ownership in which the landowner's right to use available water is based on a government-administered permit system.

5. (A) Dedication is an action in which a property owner voluntarily transfers ownership of property to the public for some public use, such as for streets or schools.

6. (D) The grantor has determined the future use of the property.

7. (B) An easement is a right to use but not to own.

8. (A) A leasehold estate is the right a tenant obtains under a lease. Legal life estates are created by statute and include curtesy, dower and homestead.

9. (C) Because the property has been conveyed to the daughter, she retains a reversionary right during her father's lifetime. It reverts to her upon his death.

10. (B) The misplaced fence is an example of an encroachment. It "encroaches" on someone else's property.

11. (C) The homestead is protected from unsecured creditors as per state law.

12. (D) A license is the revocable, personal permission to enter another's property.

13. (A) An encumbrance is anything that may diminish the value or use and enjoyment of a property.

14. (D) A tenant holds a leasehold estate.

15. (B) The taxing authority will file a lien to enforce payment of the debt.

16. (D) Possession, interest, time and title are all requirements to create a joint tenancy ownership.

17. (B) Tenants in common is the default form of ownership between two or more owners. Each owns "as if in severalty."

18. (A) The remaining owners are still joint tenants with right of survivorship, and the new owner is a tenant in common.

19. (B) Condominium ownership is characterized by ownership of the airspace that the unit actually occupies plus an undivided interest in the ownership of the common elements.

20. (B) The brother is the trustor (owner), the attorney is the trustee, and the sister is the beneficiary.

21. (D) Community property is the Spanish common-law concept treating ownership of property acquired during the marriage as equal ownership. There are some exceptions as per state law.

22. (B) Under tenancy in common, each owner owns "as if in severalty." This means that his or her interest can be willed and does not revert to the surviving owners.

23. (A) A trust is a fiduciary arrangement whereby property is conveyed to a person or institution, called a trustee, to be held and administered on behalf of another person, called a beneficiary. The one who conveys the trust is called the trustor.

24. (B) Condominium ownership is established when the owner files a declaration in the public record. However, this may vary from state to state.

25. (C) A time-share is a form of ownership that allows the use of the property for a fixed or variable stated period of time.

■ MINI-REVIEW EXAM #4

1. Because a corporation is a legal entity, title to real estate owned by it is taken in

   (A) trust.
   (B) partnership.
   (C) severalty.
   (D) survivorship tenancy.

2. Which of the following refers to ownership by one person?

   (A) Tenancy by the entirety
   (B) Community property
   (C) Tenancy in common
   (D) Severalty

3. A husband and wife co-own a farm with a right of survivorship. Theirs is **MOST** likely

   (A) severalty ownership.
   (B) community property.
   (C) a tenancy in common.
   (D) an estate by the entirety.

4. Which of the following is a nonfreehold estate?

   (A) Ownership in severalty
   (B) Cooperative ownership
   (C) Condominium ownership
   (D) Tenancy in common

5. Three partners are in total disagreement as to how to dispose of the property. Since they cannot agree, the solution is to

   (A) file a quiet title suit.
   (B) issue quitclaim deeds.
   (C) file a partition suit.
   (D) order a survey and divide up the property according to each person's interest.

6. Which of the following **BEST** proves the ownership in a cooperative?

   (A) Tax bill for the individual unit
   (B) Existence of a reverter clause
   (C) Shareholder's stock certificate
   (D) Right of first refusal

7. Which of the following ownership interests includes a proprietary lease?

   (A) Condominium unit
   (B) Cooperative unit
   (C) Time-share
   (D) Leasehold

8. Which of the following is used as evidence that a loan was made?

   (A) Promissory note
   (B) Mortgage
   (C) Deed of trust
   (D) Hypothecation

9. Which of the following increase the interest yield to the lender?

   (A) Loan origination fees
   (B) Usury
   (C) Discount points
   (D) Impound accounts

10. A lender does not want another person to assume the loan. What clause can the lender include in the mortgage to prevent the loan from being assumed?

(A) Subordination clause
(B) Defeasance clause
(C) Acceleration clause
(D) Alienation clause

11. The owner of the property knows that he cannot meet his mortgage payment obligations. He seeks an alternative to foreclosure. If the lender agrees, such an alternative could be

(A) deed in lieu of foreclosure.
(B) equitable right of redemption.
(C) release or satisfaction.
(D) a deficiency judgment.

12. When a property manager is establishing a budget for the building, which of the following is **NOT** an operating expense?

(A) Heating oil
(B) Cleaning supplies
(C) Window replacement
(D) Management fees

13. A property manager is offered a choice of three insurance policies: One has a $500 deductible, one has a $1,000 deductible, and one has a $5,000 deductible. If the property manager selects the policy with the highest deductible, which risk management technique is he or she using?

(A) Avoiding risk
(B) Retaining risk
(C) Controlling risk
(D) Transferring risk

14. Contaminated groundwater, toxic fumes from paint and carpeting and lack of proper ventilation are all examples of

(A) issues beyond the scope of a property manager's job description.
(B) problems faced only by newly constructed properties.
(C) issues that arise under the ADA.
(D) environmental concerns that a property manager may have to address.

15. In the case of commercial or industrial properties, tenant improvements are

(A) tenant-owned fixtures.
(B) adaptations of space to suit tenants' needs.
(C) illegal unless authorized.
(D) landlord obligations.

16. In preparing a budget, a property manager should set up which of the following for variable unexpected expenses?

(A) Control account
(B) Floating allocation
(C) Cash reserve fund
(D) Asset account

17. In most market areas, rents are determined by

(A) supply and demand factors.
(B) the local apartment owners' association.
(C) HUD.
(D) a tenants' union.

18. What federal law protects the rights of consumers by prohibiting kickbacks?

(A) Real Estate Settlement Procedures Act
(B) Truth-in-Lending Act
(C) Fair Housing Act
(D) Americans with Disabilities Act

19. A property manager hires a full-time maintenance person. While repairing a faucet in one of the apartments, the maintenance person steals a television set, and the tenant sues the owner. The property manager could protect the owner against this type of loss by purchasing

(A) liability insurance.
(B) workers' compensation insurance.
(C) a surety bond.
(D) casualty insurance.

20. Commercial leases are usually expressed as

(A) a monthly rate per unit.
(B) a percentage of total space available.
(C) an annual or monthly rate per square foot.
(D) an annual rate per room.

21. An appraiser is hired to determine the value of a large apartment complex. The appraiser will likely analyze the property using several approaches and will give the greatest weight to the

    (A) cost approach.
    (B) income approach.
    (C) sales comparison approach.
    (D) market data approach.

22. Every deed must be signed by the

    (A) grantor.
    (B) grantee.
    (C) grantor and grantee.
    (D) devisee.

23. A minor has inherited several properties. If the minor enters a deed conveying his interest in one of the properties to a purchaser, the conveyance is considered

    (A) valid.   (C) invalid.
    (B) void.   (D) voidable.

24. An instrument authorizing one person to act for another is called

    (A) a power of attorney.
    (B) a release deed.
    (C) a quitclaim deed.
    (D) an acknowledgment.

25. The grantee receives greatest protection with what type of deed?

    (A) Quitclaim
    (B) General warranty
    (C) Bargain and sale with covenant
    (D) Executor's

■ ANSWER KEY WITH EXPLANATIONS

1. (C) Because a corporation is a single entity, it owns property in severalty. The stockholders own shares of stock, which is personal property.

2. (D) Ownership of real property by one person or a single entity, such as a corporation, is ownership in severalty.

3. (D) Tenancy by the entireties is a special form of joint tenancy limited to married couples. This form of ownership is not recognized in all states.

4. (B) Cooperative ownership is a nonfreehold estate. The corporation is the owner of the real property, and the residents lease their unit as shareholders.

5. (C) If co-owners disagree, they may file a suit to partition to terminate their ownership.

6. (C) A shareholder's stock certificate may be used to show ownership in a cooperative.

7. (B) In a cooperative, a tenant owns a share of stock that contains a proprietary lease to a specific unit.

8. (A) A promissory note shows evidence that a loan was made. Security for the loan is provided by a mortgage or deed of trust. Using property as security without giving up possession is called hypothecation.

9. (C) Discount points increase the interest yield to the lender.

10. (D) A lender often includes an alienation clause in the mortgage or deed of trust to prevent the assumption of the loan. This clause is also known as the due-on-sale clause because it requires that the balance of the secured debt becomes immediately due and payable at the lender's option if the property is sold by the borrower.

11. (A) One way for a debtor to avoid foreclosure is to offer the deed in lieu of foreclosure. If the lender accepts, there is no foreclosure.

12. (C) Replacing windows would not be a normal maintenance of the property.

13. (B) By opting for a higher deductible, the manager is "retaining" the risk in return for lower premiums. The manager must have the financial ability to pay the higher deductible.

14. (D) The property manager and owner may be faced with legal actions if they do not address environmental issues.

15. (B) In commercial or industrial properties, tenant improvements are adaptations of space to suit the tenant's needs.

16. (C) The cash reserve fund is a cushion in the event of unexpected expenses.

17. (A) Rents are based on market indicators, such as variables caused by changing supply and demand.

18. (A) The Real Estate Settlement Procedures Act (RESPA) prohibits kickbacks.

19. (C) A surety bond protects the owner from claims due to contractors doing work on the property.

20. (C) Commercial rent is generally expressed by an annual or monthly rate per square foot.

21. (B) When appraising a large apartment complex, or any income-generating property, the appraiser will generally assign the greatest weight to the income approach.

22. (A) The grantor must sign away his or her rights forever. In many states, the deed may not be recorded unless the grantor's signature is acknowledged, i.e., that the signature is both voluntary and genuine.

23. (D) Any contract signed by the minor is voidable, at the minor's option.

24. (A) The legal document conveying the right to sign for another is called a power of attorney.

25. (B) A general warranty deed is the strongest deed available and offers the most protection.

Salesperson Exams

■ SALESPERSON EXAM #1

1. After the foreclosure sale, a borrower who has defaulted on a loan may seek to pay off the debt plus any accrued interest and costs under the right of

   (A) equitable redemption.
   (B) defeasance.
   (C) usury.
   (D) statutory redemption.

2. A tenant signs a lease that requires a percentage of gross monthly sale plus a base rent. If the base rent is $1,000 per month, the percentage is 5% of gross sales over $10,000, and the gross sales for the month was $15,000, what is the rent due for that month?

   (A) $ 250   (C) $1,750
   (B) $1,250   (D) $2,250

3. A licensee lists a residence. For various reasons, the owner must sell the house quickly and confides to the licensee that although the asking price is reasonable, a lower price would probably be acceptable. To expedite the sale, the licensee tells a prospective purchaser that the seller will accept up to $5,000 less than the asking price for the property. Based on these facts,

   (A) the licensee has not violated any agency responsibilities to the seller.
   (B) the licensee should have disclosed this information, regardless of its accuracy.
   (C) the disclosure was improper and possibly illegal, regardless of the licensee's motive.
   (D) the relationship between the licensee and the seller ends automatically if the purchaser submits an offer.

4. A buyer who is a client of the broker wants to purchase a house that the broker has listed for sale. What is the proper course of action?

   (A) The broker may proceed to write an offer on the property and submit it.
   (B) The broker should refer the buyer to another broker to negotiate the sale.
   (C) Both the seller and buyer must be informed of the situation and agree to the broker's representing both of them.
   (D) The buyer should not be shown a house listed by the broker.

5. What does the phrase "the law of agency is a common-law doctrine" mean?

   (A) It is a legal doctrine that is not unusual.
   (B) It is one of the rules of society enacted by legislatures and other governing bodies.
   (C) It is a body of law established by tradition and court decisions.
   (D) It may not be superseded by statutory law.

6. A seller lists a home with a licensee for $98,000. Later that week, an acquaintance comes into the broker's office and asks for general information about homes for sale in the $90,000 to $100,000 price range. Based on these facts, which of the following statements is **TRUE?**

   (A) Both the seller and the buyer are the broker's customers.
   (B) The seller is the broker's customer; the buyer is a client.
   (C) The buyer is the broker's customer; the seller is the broker's client.
   (D) If the buyer asks the broker to present an offer to the seller, the broker must ask both parties to sign a disclosed dual agency agreement.

7. A real estate licensee was representing a buyer. At their first meeting, the buyer explained that he planned to operate a dog-grooming business out of any house he bought. The licensee did not check the local zoning ordinances to determine in which parts of town such a business could be conducted. Which common-law duty did the licensee violate?

   (A) Care   (C) Loyalty
   (B) Obedience   (D) Disclosure

8. A seller listed her residence with a broker. The broker brought an offer at full price and met all the terms of the listing from buyers who are ready, willing and able to pay cash for the property. However, the seller changed her mind and rejected the buyers' offer. In this situation, the seller

   (A) must sell her property.
   (B) owes a commission to the broker.
   (C) is liable to the buyers for specific performance.
   (D) is liable to the buyers for compensatory damages.

9. A buyer wants to enter into an open buyer agency agreement. What are the consequences?

   (A) The buyer may enter into agreements with multiple brokers and is obligated to pay only the broker who locates the property that the buyer ultimately purchases.
   (B) While the buyer may enter into agreements with multiple brokers, he or she is under no obligation to pay the broker; the seller bears all brokerage expenses.
   (C) Because multiple brokers may be involved, an open buyer agency agreement involves reduced fiduciary duties.
   (D) The buyer may not look for or make offers on properties on his or her own.

10. A broker and a buyer enter into an exclusive-agency buyer agency agreement. What does this mean?

   (A) The buyer is obligated to compensate the broker, regardless of who locates the property ultimately purchased.
   (B) The broker is entitled to payment only if she or any broker acting under her authority locates the property the buyer ultimately purchases.
   (C) The buyer may enter into similar agreements with any number of other brokers.
   (D) If the buyer finds the property without any help from the broker, the buyer must pay the broker a reduced compensation.

11. "I hear *they're* moving in. There goes the neighborhood! Better put your house on the market before values drop!" This is an example of an illegal practice called

   (A) steering.
   (B) blockbusting.
   (C) redlining.
   (D) fraudulent advertising.

12. The act of directing home seekers toward or away from particular areas either to maintain or to change the character of the neighborhood is

   (A) blockbusting.
   (B) redlining.
   (C) steering.
   (D) permitted under the Fair Housing Act of 1968.

13. A seller signs a listing agreement with a broker to sell her home. The agreement states that the broker will receive a 7% commission. The home sells for $120,000. What is the net amount that seller will receive from the sale?

    (A) $ 36,000   (C) $111,600
    (B) $102,877   (D) $120,000

14. A real estate broker and a seller enter into a listing agreement that contains the following language: "Seller will receive $100,000 from the sale of the subject property. Any amount greater than $100,000 will constitute Broker's sole and complete compensation." Which of the following statements is **TRUE** regarding this agreement?

    (A) This agreement is an example of an option listing.
    (B) If the seller's home sells for exactly $100,000, the broker will still be entitled to receive the standard commission in the area.
    (C) The broker may offer the property for any price over $100,000, but the listing agreement may be illegal.
    (D) This type of listing is known as an *open listing*, because the selling price is left open.

15. Which of the following would **NOT** permit a listing agreement for residential property to be terminated?

    (A) Destruction of the listed property
    (B) Seller dissatisfaction with the wording of a newspaper advertisement
    (C) Seller's unreasonable refusal to permit showings of the property during any time other than 6:00 A.M. to 7:30 A.M.
    (D) Abandonment by the broker

16. A written agreement between a broker and a client includes the following language: "In return for the compensation agreed upon, Broker will assist Client in locating and purchasing a suitable property. Broker will receive the agreed compensation regardless of whether Broker, Client or some other party locates the property ultimately purchased by Client." What kind of agreement is this?

    (A) Exclusive-agency listing
    (B) Exclusive-agency buyer agency agreement
    (C) Exclusive buyer agency agreement
    (D) Open buyer agency agreement

17. The physical characteristic of land that makes it easy to tax at a local level is

    (A) uniqueness.
    (B) indestructibility.
    (C) scarcity.
    (D) immobility.

18. Two unmarried brothers take title as joint tenants. Upon the death of one brother, his interest in the property

    (A) is divided equally among his heirs.
    (B) escheats to the state if he leaves no will.
    (C) goes to whomever is named in his will.
    (D) goes to the surviving brother.

19. In describing real estate, the system that uses a property's physical features to determine boundaries and measurements is

    (A) rectangular survey.
    (B) metes-and-bounds.
    (C) government survey.
    (D) lot-and-block.

20. If a farm described as "the NW¼ of the SE¼ of Section 10, Township 2 North, Range 3 West of the 6th P.M." sold for $1,500 an acre, what would the total sales price be?

    (A) $15,000   (C) $45,000
    (B) $30,000   (D) $60,000

21. Which of the following is **NOT** a power of the government?

    (A) Dedication
    (B) Police power
    (C) Eminent domain
    (D) Taxation

22. A homeowner may be allowed certain protection from judgments of creditors as a result of his or her state's

    (A) littoral rights.
    (B) curtesy rights.
    (C) homestead rights.
    (D) dower rights.

23. Two salespeople agree to divide their town into a northern region and a southern region. One will handle listings in the northern region, and the other will handle listings in the southern region. Which of the following statements is **TRUE** regarding this agreement?

    (A) The agreement between the two agents does not violate antitrust laws.
    (B) The agreement between the two agents constitutes illegal price-fixing.
    (C) The two agents have violated the Sherman Antitrust Act and are liable for triple damages.
    (D) The two agents are guilty of group boycotting with regard to other salespersons in their office.

24. After a particularly challenging transaction finally closes, the client gives the listing agent a check for $500 "for all your extra work." Which of the following statements is accurate?

    (A) While such compensation is irregular, it is appropriate for the listing agent to accept the check.
    (B) The listing agent may receive compensation only from his or her broker.
    (C) The listing agent should accept the check and deposit it immediately in a special escrow account.
    (D) The listing agent's broker is entitled to 80% of the check.

25. Which of the following liens affects all real and personal property of a debtor?

    (A) Specific
    (B) Voluntary
    (C) Involuntary
    (D) General

26. Priority of liens refers to the

    (A) order in which a debtor assumes responsibility for payment of obligations.
    (B) order in which liens will be paid if property is sold to satisfy a debt.
    (C) dates liens are filed for record.
    (D) fact that specific liens have greater priority than general liens.

27. Which of the following liens on real estate is made to secure payment for a specific municipal improvement project?

    (A) Mechanic's lien
    (B) Special assessment
    (C) Ad valorem tax
    (D) Utility lien

28. A property owner has the right to drive on his neighbor's driveway to get to his garage. This right is

    (A) a lien.
    (B) an encroachment.
    (C) an easement.
    (D) a license.

29. Which of the following liens usually would be given highest priority in disbursing funds from a foreclosure sale?

    (A) Mortgage dated last year
    (B) Real estate taxes due
    (C) Mechanic's lien for work started before the mortgage was made
    (D) Judgment rendered the day before foreclosure

30. A specific parcel of real estate has a market value of $80,000 and is assessed for tax purposes at 35% of market value. The tax rate for the county in which the property is located is 30 mills. The tax bill will be

    (A) $50.   (C) $720.
    (B) $60.   (D) $840.

31. The highest interest recognized by law is

   (A) a life estate.
   (B) pur autre vie.
   (C) fee simple absolute.
   (D) fee simple defeasible.

32. A carpet dealer has installed two rooms of carpet in a home that was just sold. The contractor is avoiding the carpet dealer who has not been paid. In this situation, the carpet dealer may

   (A) tear out the carpets.
   (B) record a notice of the lien.
   (C) record a notice of the lien and file a court suit within the time required by state law.
   (D) have personal property of the owner sold to satisfy the lien.

33. What is the annual real estate tax on a property valued at $135,000 and assessed for tax purposes at $47,250, with an equalization factor of 125%, when the tax rate is 25 mills?

   (A) $ 945   (C) $1,418
   (B) $1,181   (D) $1,477

34. Which of the following actions is legally permitted?

   (A) Advertising property for sale only to a special group
   (B) Altering the terms of a loan for a member of a minority group
   (C) Refusing to make a mortgage loan to a minority individual because of a poor credit history
   (D) Telling an individual that an apartment has been rented when in fact it has not

35. Which of the following statements is **TRUE** of complaints relating to the Civil Rights Act of 1866?

   (A) They must be taken directly to federal courts.
   (B) They are no longer reviewed in the courts.
   (C) They are handled by HUD.
   (D) They are handled by state enforcement agencies.

36. Why is the Civil Rights Act of 1866 unique?

   (A) It has been broadened to protect the aged.
   (B) It adds welfare recipients as a protected class.
   (C) It contains "choose your neighbor" provisions.
   (D) It provides no exceptions that would permit racial discrimination.

37. Which of the following statements is **TRUE** of a competitive market analysis (CMA)?

   (A) A CMA is the same as an appraisal.
   (B) A CMA can help the seller price the property.
   (C) By law in most states, a CMA must be completed for each listing taken.
   (D) A CMA should not be retained in the property's listing file.

38. A property was listed with a broker who belonged to a multiple-listing service and was sold by another member broker for $53,500. The total commission was 6% of the sales price. The selling broker received 60% of the commission, and the listing broker received the balance. What was the listing broker's commission?

   (A) $1,284   (C) $1,926
   (B) $1,464   (D) $2,142

39. A lender's refusal to lend money to potential homeowners attempting to purchase properties located in predominantly African-American neighborhoods is an illegal practice known as

   (A) redlining.   (C) steering.
   (B) blockbusting.   (D) prequalifying.

40. Which of the following is **NOT** permitted under the federal Fair Housing Act?

   (A) An expensive club in New York rents rooms only to members who are graduates of a particular university.
   (B) The owner of a 20-unit residential apartment building rents to men only.
   (C) A Catholic convent refuses to furnish housing for a Jewish man.
   (D) An owner refuses to rent the other side of her duplex to a family with children.

41. A real estate broker wants to end racial segregation. As an office policy, the broker requires that salespersons show prospective buyers from racial or ethnic minority groups only properties that are in certain areas of town where few members of their groups currently live. The broker has prepared a map illustrating the appropriate neighborhoods for each racial or ethnic group. Through this policy, the broker hopes to achieve racial balance in residential housing. Which of the following statements is **TRUE** regarding this broker's policy?

   (A) While the broker's policy may appear to constitute blockbusting, application of the effects test proves its legality.
   (B) Because the effect of the broker's policy is discriminatory, it constitutes illegal steering regardless of the broker's intentions.
   (C) The broker's policy clearly shows the intent to discriminate.
   (D) While the broker's policy may appear to constitute steering, application of the intent test proves its legality.

42. Which of the following appraisal methods uses a rate of investment return?

   (A) Sales comparison approach
   (B) Cost approach
   (C) Income approach
   (D) Gross income multiplier method

43. The elements of value include which of the following?

   (A) Competition   (C) Anticipation
   (B) Scarcity   (D) Balance

44. 457 and 459 Tarpepper Street are adjacent vacant lots, each worth approximately $50,000. If their owner sells them as a single lot, however, the combined parcel will be worth $120,000. What principle does this illustrate?

   (A) Substitution   (C) Regression
   (B) Plottage   (D) Progression

45. The amount of money a property commands in the marketplace is its

   (A) intrinsic value.
   (B) market value.
   (C) subjective value.
   (D) book value.

46 A homeowner constructs an eight-bedroom brick house with a tennis court, a greenhouse and an indoor pool in a neighborhood of modest two-bedroom and three-bedroom frame houses on narrow lots. The value of this house is likely to be affected by what principle?

   (A) Progression   (C) Change
   (B) Assemblage   (D) Regression

47. Owners of lesser-valued houses in a neighborhood may find that the values of their homes are affected by what principle?

   (A) Progression   (C) Competition
   (B) Increasing returns (D) Regression

48. For appraisal purposes, accrued depreciation is **NOT** caused by which of the following?

   (A) Functional obsolescence
   (B) Physical deterioration
   (C) External obsolescence
   (D) Accelerated depreciation

49. *Reconciliation* refers to which of the following?

   (A) Loss of value due to any cause
   (B) Separating the value of the land from the total value of the property to compute depreciation
   (C) Analyzing the results obtained by the different approaches to value to determine a final estimate of value
   (D) Process by which an appraiser determines the highest and best use for a parcel of land

50. Gaslight fixtures in every unit of an apartment building would result in depreciation due to which of the following?

   (A) Curable physical deterioration
   (B) Curable functional obsolescence
   (C) Incurable external obsolescence
   (D) Incurable functional obsolescence

51. A charge of three discount points on a $120,000 loan equals

   (A) $ 450.   (C) $ 4,500.
   (B) $3,600.   (D) $116,400.

52. A prospective buyer needs to borrow money to buy a house. The buyer applies for and obtains a real estate loan from a lender. Then the buyer signs a note and a mortgage. In this example, the buyer is referred to as the

   (A) mortgagor.   (C) mortgagee.
   (B) beneficiary   (D) vendor.

53. The institution that makes a loan for a property is the

   (A) mortgagor.   (C) mortgagee.
   (B) beneficiary.   (D) vendor.

54. Under a deed of trust, the borrower is known as the

   (A) trustor.   (C) beneficiary.
   (B) trustee.   (D) vendee.

55. Which of the following is **NOT TRUE** of the vendee in a land contract? The vendee

   (A) is responsible for the real estate taxes on the property.
   (B) must pay interest and principal.
   (C) obtains possession at closing.
   (D) obtains legal title at closing.

56. A state law provides that lenders cannot charge more than 24% interest on any loan. This kind of law is called

   (A) a Truth-in-Lending law.
   (B) a usury law.
   (C) the statute of frauds.
   (D) RESPA.

57. What document is available to the mortgagor when the mortgage debt is completely repaid?

   (A) Satisfaction of mortgage
   (B) Defeasance certificate
   (C) Deed of trust
   (D) Mortgage estoppel

58. Under a typical land contract, the vendor gives the deed to the vendee

   (A) when the contract is fulfilled.
   (B) at the closing.
   (C) when the parties approve the contract for deed.
   (D) after the first year's real estate taxes are paid.

59. If a borrower must pay a discount fee of $4,500 for points on a $90,000 loan, how many points is the lender charging for this loan?

   (A) 2   (C) 5
   (B) 3   (D) 6

60. Which of the following clauses in a mortgage may prevent a buyer from assuming a loan?

   (A) Seisin   (C) Acceleration
   (B) Defeasance   (D) Alienation

61. Which of the following allows a mortgagee to proceed to a foreclosure sale without having to go to court first?

   (A) Waiver of redemption right
   (B) Power-of-sale clause
   (C) Alienation clause
   (D) Hypothecation

62. Pledging property for a loan without giving up possession is referred to as

   (A) hypothecation.   (C) alienation.
   (B) defeasance.   (D) novation.

63. Discount points on a mortgage are computed as a percentage of the

   (A) selling price.
   (B) amount borrowed.
   (C) closing costs.
   (D) down payment.

64. *Chain of title* is **MOST** accurately defined as

   (A) a summary or history of all documents and legal proceedings affecting a specific parcel of land.
   (B) a report of the contents of the public record regarding a particular property.
   (C) an instrument or document that protects the insured parties (subject to specific exceptions) against defects in the examination of the record and hidden risks such as forgeries, undisclosed heirs, errors in the public records and so forth.
   (D) a record of a property's ownership.

65. Which of the following types of insurance coverage insures an employer against most claims for job-related injuries?

    (A) Consequential loss
    (B) Workers' compensation
    (C) Casualty
    (D) Surety bond

66. A contract is said to be *bilateral* if

    (A) one of the parties is a minor.
    (B) the contract has yet to be fully performed.
    (C) only one party to the agreement is bound to act.
    (D) both parties to the contract are bound to act.

67. During the period of time after a real estate sales contract is signed, but before title actually passes, the status of the contract is

    (A) voidable.   (C) unilateral.
    (B) executory.   (D) implied.

68. A contract for the sale of real estate that does not state the consideration to be paid for the property and is not signed by the parties is considered to be

    (A) voidable.   (C) void.
    (B) executory.   (D) enforceable.

69. A buyer and seller sign a contract under which the owner will sell a property to the buyer. The owner changes his mind, and the buyer sues for specific performance. What is the buyer seeking in this lawsuit?

    (A) Money damages
    (B) New contract
    (C) Deficiency judgment
    (D) Conveyance of the property

70. In a standard sales contract, several words were crossed out or inserted by the parties. To eliminate future controversy as to whether the changes were made before or after the contract was signed, the usual procedure is to

    (A) write a letter to each party listing the changes.
    (B) have each party write a letter to the other approving the changes.
    (C) redraw the entire contract.
    (D) have both parties initial or sign each change.

71. A buyer makes an offer on a house, and the owner accepts. Both parties sign the sales contract. At this point, the buyer has what type of title to the property?

    (A) Equitable   (C) Escrow
    (B) Voidable   (D) Contract

72. The sales contract says the buyer will purchase only if an attorney approves the sale by the following Saturday. The attorney's approval is a

    (A) contingency.   (C) warranty.
    (B) reservation.   (D) consideration.

73. A prospective buyer places an advertisement in the local paper. The ad reads: "I will pay $50,000 for any house, anywhere in town!" What kind of contract is this?

    (A) Unilateral
    (B) Option
    (C) Implied
    (D) It is not a contract.

74. A title search in the public records may be conducted by

    (A) anyone.
    (B) attorneys and abstractors only.
    (C) attorneys, abstractors and real estate licensees only.
    (D) anyone who obtains a court order under the Freedom of Information Act.

75. Which of the following statements **BEST** explains why instruments affecting real estate are recorded?

    (A) Recording gives constructive notice to the world of the rights and interests of a party in a particular parcel of real estate.
    (B) Failing to record will void the transfer.
    (C) The instruments must be recorded to comply with the terms of the statute of frauds.
    (D) Recording proves the execution of the instrument.

76. A purchaser went to the county building to check the recorder's records, which showed that the seller was the grantee in the last recorded deed and that no mortgage was on record against the property. The purchaser may assume which of the following?

    (A) All taxes are paid, and no judgments are outstanding.
    (B) The seller has good title.
    (C) The seller did not mortgage the property.
    (D) No one else is occupying the property.

77. The date and time a document was recorded help establish which of the following?

    (A) Priority
    (B) Abstract of title
    (C) Subrogation
    (D) Marketable title

78. An individual bought a house, received a deed and moved into the residence, but neglected to record the document. One week later, the seller died, and his heirs in another city, unaware that the property had been sold, conveyed title to another person, who recorded the deed. Who has the **BEST** claim on the property?

    (A) The first buyer
    (B) The second buyer
    (C) The owner's heirs
    (D) Both buyers

79. A property with encumbrances that will outlast the closing

    (A) cannot be sold.
    (B) can be sold only if title insurance is provided.
    (C) cannot have a deed recorded without a survey.
    (D) can be sold only if a buyer agrees to take it subject to the encumbrances.

80. Which of the following is **NOT** acceptable proof of ownership?

    (A) Attorney's opinion
    (B) Title insurance policy
    (C) Abstract
    (D) Deed signed by the last seller

81. A legally enforceable agreement under which two parties agree to do something for each other is known as

    (A) an escrow agreement.
    (B) a legal promise.
    (C) a valid contract.
    (D) an option agreement.

82. A buyer approaches a homeowner and says, "I'd like to buy your house." The homeowner says "sure," and they agree on a price. What kind of contract is this?

    (A) Implied
    (B) Unenforceable
    (C) Void
    (D) There is no contract.

83. Avoid, control, transfer or retain are the four alternative techniques of

    (A) tenant relations.
    (B) acquiring insurance.
    (C) risk management.
    (D) property management.

84. From a management point of view, apartment building occupancy that reaches as high as 98% would tend to indicate that

    (A) the building is poorly managed.
    (B) the building has reached its maximum potential.
    (C) building similar sites would not be profitable.
    (D) rents could be raised.

85. How much can a lender legally charge a borrower for the preparation of the federal Uniform Settlement Statement?

    (A) Nothing
    (B) ½ of 1%
    (C) 1%
    (D) No more than $25

86. Two brokers meet and agree not to show a competitor's listings because the competitor is charging less than a 6% commission. What does the law say about this practice?

    (A) This is acceptable so long as the two brokers do not agree on a commission rate they charge.
    (B) This is a violation of the antitrust laws.
    (C) This is acceptable so long as the brokers disclose that they will not show the competitor's listings.
    (D) This is acceptable because brokers can have any type of commission agreements they want.

87. Once a contract has been terminated by both parties, it is

    (A) voidable.   (C) void.
    (B) unenforceable.   (D) valid.

88. Who may give legal advice to either buyer or seller?

    (A) Their agent so long as the agent states that they are not an attorney
    (B) The title company
    (C) Attorneys
    (D) Brokers in an agent-client relationship

89. A real estate broker hired by an owner to sell a parcel of real estate must comply with

    (A) the common law of agency, even if a state agency statute exists.
    (B) dual agency requirements.
    (C) the concept of caveat emptor.
    (D) all lawful instructions of the owner.

90. A licensee is hired by a first-time buyer to help the buyer purchase a home. The buyer confides that being approved for a mortgage loan may be complicated by the fact that the buyer filed for bankruptcy two years ago. A **TRUE** statement about the licensee's responsibility regarding this information during the presentation of an offer to purchase a property is that the licensee is

    (A) required to disclose it under the Fair Credit Registry Act.
    (B) required to disclose it because bankruptcies are a matter of public record.
    (C) not required to disclose it owing to the client's request for confidentiality.
    (D) not required to disclose it because the licensee has no agency relationship with the seller.

■ ANSWER KEY WITH EXPLANATIONS

1. **(D)** Some states allow a statutory right of redemption, i.e., the delinquent borrower has the right to redeem the property within a certain time frame.

2. **(B)** The month's rent is $1,250.
   [$15,000 − $10,000] × 5% = $250
   $1,000 + $250 = $1,250

3. **(C)** An agent may not disclose the principal's financial condition. When the principal is the seller, the agent may not reveal such things as the principal's willingness to accept less than the listing price or anxiousness to sell the property, unless authorized by the principal.

4. **(C)** In states that permit dual agency, the broker may represent both buyer and seller only with the informed consent of both.

5. **(C)** Under the common law of agency or the statutory law governing real estate transactions, the agent owes the principal five duties of care, obedience, accounting, loyalty (including confidentiality), and disclosure. Not all states recognize common law of agency.

6. **(C)** When a seller contracts with a broker to market the seller's property, the broker becomes an agent of the seller; the seller is the principal, the broker's client. In single agency, a buyer who contacts the broker to see properties listed by that broker or his firm, the buyer would be a customer. At this point, the acquaintance is still a customer, not having hired the broker.

7. **(A)** The principal expects the agent's skill and expertise in real estate matters to be superior to that of the average person. The agent has a duty of care to know that zoning laws may determine how the property is used and to bring this to the attention of his client.

8. **(B)** By the employed broker producing a ready, willing and able buyer, the seller is obligated to pay the employed broker a commission.

9. **(A)** This agreement is a nonexclusive agency contract between a broker and a buyer. Only the broker who locates a property for the buyer is entitled to compensation.

10. **(B)** The broker is entitled to payment only if he or she locates the property the buyer ultimately purchases. Therefore, the buyer may find a suitable property without obligation to pay the agent.

11. **(B)** Blockbusting is the illegal practice of using racial or religious fears to induce homeowners to sell their properties.

12. **(C)** Steering is the illegal practice of channeling home seekers to particular areas, either to maintain the homogeneity of an area or to change the character of an area. It is also the practice of limiting choices and may be passive as when the property manager shows only ground-floor apartments to families with children.

13. **(C)** The seller's net is $111,600.
    $120,000 × 93% = $111,600

14. **(C)** This is an example of a net listing, which is illegal in many states and is discouraged in others.

15. **(B)** The seller hired the broker to market the property and to solicit offers to purchase. The seller may not terminate a listing simply by objecting to the wording of the ad. A listing may be terminated by the destruction of the listed property, the seller being unreasonable as to showing opportunities or abandonment by the broker.

16. (C) Because the buyer is legally bound to compensate the agent whenever the buyer purchases a property of the type described in the contract, the agent is entitled to payment even if the buyer finds the property independently.

17. (D) Immobility makes land easy to tax at a local level.

18. (D) As a joint tenant with right of survivorship, the surviving brother now owns the entire property upon the death of his brother. If they had held title as tenants in common, the deceased's interest could go to anyone named in his will. Property escheats to the state only when it becomes ownerless, which is not the case here.

19. (B) Metes and bounds is a legal description that begins at a well marked point and follows the boundaries, using distances and directions around the parcel, back to the point of beginning.

20. (D) The sales price of the described parcel of land is $60,000.
$[640 \div 4 \div 4] \times \$1,500 = \$60,000$

21. (A) Dedication is not a government power, rather it is defined as the voluntary transfer of private property to the public for a public use.

22. (C) In states that have homestead exemption laws, a portion of the area or value of the property occupied as the family home is exempt from certain judgments for debts such as charge accounts and personal loans.

23. (C) Allocation of customers or markets between brokers is illegal since it reduces competition.

24. (B) All compensation to a salesperson must be set by a mutual agreement between the salesperson and his or her broker. In addition, the salesperson must be paid by the broker unless otherwise permitted by license laws and agreed to by the employing broker.

25. (D) A general lien affects all real and personal property of a debtor. This includes estate and inheritance taxes, judgments, corporate franchise taxes and IRS taxes.

26. (B) Priority of liens refers to the order in which liens will be paid if the property is sold to satisfy a debt. Property tax liens are paid first even if they were filed after a mortgage lien.

27. (B) A special assessment is levied against the property owners who will benefit from the improvement. Such improvements could be street paving, installation of curbs or more lighting.

28. (C) The property owner who has the right to drive on his neighbor's driveway has an easement.

29. (B) The property taxes are first in line to be paid.

30. (D) The tax bill is $840.
$\$80,000 \times 35\% \times .030 = \$840$
(Mills must be converted to decimals, which is done by multiplying by 1,000 or moving the decimal three places to the left.)

31. (C) The highest interest recognized by law is fee simple absolute.

32. (C) The mechanic's lien must be filed to protect the carpet dealer's right to sue.

33. (D) The annual real estate tax is $1,477.
$\$47,250 \times 125\% \times .025 = \$1,476.56$ or $\$1,477$
(Remember to multiply the millage rate by 1,000 or move the decimal point three places to the left).

34. (C) A person must be financially qualified for a loan. It is not legal for lenders to alter the terms of a loan for a minority applicant.

35. (A) An aggrieved person who is alleging discrimination based on the 1866 law must take the case directly to federal court. HUD has no jurisdiction under the Civil Rights Act of 1866.

36. (D) The Civil Rights Act of 1866 provides no exemptions for racial discrimination. Under no circumstances is anyone allowed to discriminate in housing based on race.

37. (B) A comparative market analysis uses comparable properties that have sold, properties still on the market, and properties that have not sold, in the same area as the subject property that gives the seller information on homes to compare in order to set his or her listing price.

38. (A) The listing broker earned $1,284 as a commission.
$53,500 sales price × 6% = $3,210 gross commission
$3,210 gross commission × 40% = $1,284 listing broker's commission

39. (A) Lenders at one time would actually draw a red line around areas in which they would not make loans based on a protected category.

40. (B) The owner of a 20-unit apartment building may not rent to males only. The owner is not exempt since the building is more than four units.

41. (B) The effects of the broker's policy is discriminatory. It is not up to the broker to end segregation. The broker's policy does not allow free selection.

42. (C) The income approach uses a rate of investment return.

43. (B) The four elements of value include demand, utility, scarcity and transferability.

44. (B) Plottage is the principle that smaller properties will be valued less than being combined into a larger tract.

45. (B) Market value is the probable price a property will sell for.

46. (D) Regression is the principle that the better properties are affected by the lesser properties.

47. (A) Properties that are not as good as the surrounding properties often will still command a higher value than they would in another neighborhood. Progression is the opposite of the principle of regression.

48. (D) Accelerated depreciation is an accounting procedure and is not relevant for appraisal purposes.

49. (C) The appraiser *reconciles* the data from all three approaches to determine the value.

50. (B) Gaslight fixtures are curable functional obsolescence. The owner could upgrade the gas fixtures to current lighting standards.

51. (B) The cost of the discount points on a $120,000 loan is $3,600.
$120,000 × 3% = $3,600

52. (A) The buyer is the borrower, called a mortgagor in the mortgage.

53. (C) The lender is the mortgagee in a mortgage. The lender receives a mortgage from the buyer.

54. (A) The buyer/borrower is the trustor who gives the trustee the deed under a deed of trust.

55. (D) Under a land contract the seller retains ownership and does not transfer legal title until all the terms of the contract have been met.

56. (B) Usury laws limit the amount of interest that can be charged.

57. (A) A satisfaction or release is given to the borrower showing that the mortgage debt has been completely repaid.

58. (A) Under a typical land contract, the owner retains ownership until the terms of the contract have been fulfilled.

59. (C) The lender has charged 5 points for this loan.
$4,500 \div $90,000 = .05$ or 5 points

60. (D) The alienation clause is sometimes called the due-on-sale clause. It stipulates that the loan must be paid in full if title transfers, thus effectively prohibiting a loan assumption unless the lender approves.

61. (B) Some states allow nonjudicial foreclosure when the security instrument contains a power-of-sale clause.

62. (A) Hypothecation is the pledge of property to secure a debt without giving up possession.

63. (B) Discount points are charged on loan amounts.

64. (D) The chain is the recorded transfer from each seller to buyer.

65. (B) Workers' compensation is a specialty type of insurance for injuries on the job.

66. (D) A bilateral contract contains a promise for a promise.

67. (B) The contract is executory between the time that it has been executed but not closed.

68. (C) A valid contract is one that has been signed by both parties and contains legal consideration.

69. (D) In a specific performance suit, the buyer is seeking to have the owner perform as per the contract.

70. (D) Both parties should initial and/or sign any changes to the contract. This is a notice that all the parties knew of and accepted the change.

71. (A) Once the seller has promised to sell and the buyer promises to buy, the buyer has equitable interest in the property. The seller cannot sell it to someone else.

72. (A) A contingency is a provision in a contract that requires a certain act to be done or a certain event to occur before the contract becomes binding. Another example is "subject to financing"; i.e., the buyer will not have to buy IF the buyer cannot obtain a mortgage loan.

73. (D) There is no contract. This is an advertisement, not an agreement between the parties.

74. (A) A search of the public records may be done by anyone.

75. (A) Recording gives constructive notice to the world of the rights and interest of a party in a particular parcel of real estate.

76. (C) Apparently, there is no mortgage on the property. The lender should have filed a lien in relation to any note on the property.

77. (A) Priority of liens is determined by date and time recorded. The first filed is first in line.

78. (A) When the first buyer moved in, he gave constructive notice of his ownership. Still, it would be better if the first buyer had also recorded his or her deed.

79. (D) The buyer agrees to accept the encumbrances on the property.

80. (D) The deed alone is not sufficient proof of ownership. Acceptable proof of ownership includes an abstract with the attorney's opinion, or a title insurance policy.

81. (C) A valid contract is one that can be enforced by both parties.

82. (B) To be enforceable, contracts for the sale of real property must be reduced to writing.

83. (C) The manager creates procedures to limit the risk on the property.

84. (D) Apparently, with a 98% occupancy, there is sufficient demand to justify higher rents.

85. (A) Under the Real Estate Settlement Procedures Act, the lender is not permitted to charge for the preparation of the Uniform Settlement Statement.

86. (B) The Sherman Antitrust Act prohibits companies from grouping together to boycott a competitor.

87. (C) Once all the parties have agreed to terminate, the contract has no legal affect and is void.

88. (C) Only attorneys may give legal advice. In most cases, the title company has an attorney who provides them with legal advice. Real estate licensees should be careful to avoid the unauthorized practice of law.

89. (D) A licensee must follow the lawful instructions by the owner. The licensee should not follow unlawful instructions.

90. (C) Confidentiality about the principal's personal affairs is a key element of loyalty.

SALESPERSON EXAM #2

1. An owner is frantic because she cannot find her deed and now wants to sell the property. She

   (A) may need a suit to quiet title.
   (B) must buy title insurance.
   (C) does not need the deed to sell if it was recorded.
   (D) should execute a replacement deed to herself.

2. Mortgagee title policies protect which parties against loss?

   (A) Buyers
   (B) Sellers
   (C) Lenders
   (D) Buyers and lenders

3. Which of the following statements is **TRUE** of a real estate broker acting as the agent of the seller?

   (A) The broker is obligated to render faithful service to the seller.
   (B) The broker can disclose confidential information about the seller to a buyer if it increases the likelihood of a sale.
   (C) The broker can agree to a change in price without the seller's approval.
   (D) The broker can accept a commission from the buyer without the seller's approval.

4. A real estate broker lists a home for $189,500. Later that same day, a buyer comes into the broker's office and asks for general information about homes for sale in the $130,000 to $140,000 price range. Based on these facts, which of the following statements is **TRUE?**

   (A) Both the seller and the buyer are the broker's customers.
   (B) The seller is the broker's client; the buyer is a customer.
   (C) The broker owes fiduciary duties to both seller and buyer.
   (D) If the buyer asks the broker to be their buyer representative, the broker must decline because of the preexisting agreement with the seller.

5. In a dual agency situation, a broker may collect a commission from both the seller and the buyer if

   (A) the broker has informed either the buyer or the seller that he or she will receive a commission from both parties.
   (B) the buyer and the seller are related by blood or marriage.
   (C) both parties give their informed consent to the dual compensation.
   (D) both parties are represented by attorneys.

6. Which of the following events will terminate an agency in a broker-seller relationship?

   (A) The broker discovers that the market value of the property is such that he or she will not make an adequate commission.
   (B) The owner declares personal bankruptcy.
   (C) The owner abandons the property.
   (D) The broker appoints other brokers to help sell the property.

7. Confidentiality is included under which of the following fiduciary duties?

   (A) Care   (C) Disclosure
   (B) Obedience   (D) Loyalty

8. A listing taken by a real estate salesperson is technically an employment agreement between the seller and the

   (A) broker.
   (B) local multiple-listing service.
   (C) salesperson.
   (D) salesperson and broker together.

9. Which of the following is a similarity between an exclusive-agency listing and an exclusive-right-to-sell listing?

   (A) Under both, the seller retains the right to sell the real estate without the broker's help and without paying the broker a commission.
   (B) Under both, the seller authorizes only one particular salesperson to show the property.
   (C) Both types of listings give the responsibility of representing the seller to one broker only.
   (D) Both types of listings are open listings.

10. The listing agreement on a residential property states that it expires on May 2. Which of the following events would **NOT** terminate the listing?

    (A) The agreement is not renewed prior to May 2.
    (B) The owner dies on April 29.
    (C) On April 15 the owner tells the listing broker that the owner is dissatisfied with the broker's marketing efforts.
    (D) The house is destroyed by fire on April 25.

11. A seller has listed a property under an exclusive-agency listing with a broker. If the seller sells the property personally during the term of the listing to someone who learns about the property through the seller, the seller will owe the broker

    (A) no commission.
    (B) the full commission.
    (C) a partial commission.
    (D) only reimbursement for the broker's costs.

12. In two weeks, a general contractor will file a suit against a homeowner for nonpayment. The contractor just learned that the homeowner has listed the property for sale with a real estate broker. In this situation, which of the following will the contractor's attorney use to protect the contractor's interest?

    (A) Seller's lien
    (B) Buyer's lien
    (C) Assessment
    (D) Lis pendens

13. Which of the following statements **MOST** accurately describes special assessment liens?

    (A) They are general liens.
    (B) They are paid on a monthly basis.
    (C) They take priority over mechanics' liens.
    (D) They cannot be prepaid in full without penalty.

14. Which of the following is a similarity between an open listing and an exclusive-agency listing?

    (A) Under both, the seller avoids paying the broker a commission if the seller sells the property to someone the broker did not procure.
    (B) Both grant a commission to any broker who procures a buyer for the seller's property.
    (C) Under both, the broker earns a commission regardless of who sells the property, as long as it is sold within the listing period.
    (D) Both grant the exclusive right to sell to whatever broker procures a buyer for the seller's property.

15. The final decision on a property's listed price should be made by the

    (A) listing agent.   (C) seller.
    (B) appraised value.   (D) seller's attorney.

16. Which of the following statements is **TRUE** of a listing contract?

    (A) It is an employment contract for the professional services of the broker.
    (B) It obligates the seller to convey the property if the broker procures a ready, willing and able buyer.
    (C) It obligates the broker to work diligently for both the seller and the buyer.
    (D) It automatically binds the owner, broker and MLS to the agreed provisions.

17. A broker sold a property and received a 6.5% commission. The broker gave the listing salesperson 30% of the commission, or $3,575. What was the selling price of the property?

    (A) $55,000   (C) $152,580
    (B) $95,775   (D) $183,333

18. A buyer purchased a one-acre parcel for $2.15 per square foot. What was the selling price of the parcel?

    (A) $344   (C)$ 1,376
    (B) $774   (D)$93,654

19. How many acres are contained in the tract described as "beginning at the NW corner of the SW¼, then south along the west line to the SW corner of the section, then east along the south line of the section 2,640 feet, more or less, to the SE corner of the said SW¼, then in a straight line to the POB?"

    (A) 80   (C) 100
    (B) 90   (D) 160

20. A property contains ten acres. How many complete 50-foot by 100-foot lots could be subdivided from the property if 26,000 square feet were dedicated for roads?

    (A) 80   (C) 82
    (B) 81   (D) 83

21. A parcel of land is located in an area that is zoned multifamily. The parcel has a deed restriction stating that it can only be used for a single-family dwelling. In this situation

    (A) the parcel may be developed with an apartment building since it is zoned multifamily.
    (B) the parcel may only be used to build a single-family house because of the deed restriction.
    (C) the owner may choose to build either an apartment building or a single-family home.
    (D) the matter of which to build is decided by the community planning board.

22. The practice of locating families with children away from other buildings to one where other families with children reside is

    (A) most practical.   (C) redlining.
    (B) blockbusting.   (D) steering.

23. A property owner wants to use water from a river that runs through the property to irrigate a potato field. To do so, the owner is required by state law to submit an application to the department of water resources describing in detail the beneficial use he plans for the water. If the department approves the owner's application, it will issue a permit allowing a limited amount of river water to be diverted onto the property. Based on these facts, it can be assumed that this property owner's state relies on which of the following rules of law?

    (A) Common-law riparian rights
    (B) Common-law littoral rights
    (C) Doctrine of prior appropriation
    (D) Doctrine of highest and best use

24. Which of the following are **NOT** powers of the government?

    (A) Restrictive covenants
    (B) Police power
    (C) Eminent domain
    (D) Taxation

25. All of the following are violations of the federal antitrust laws **EXCEPT**

    (A) group boycotting.
    (B) allocation of customers.
    (C) commission splitting.
    (D) tie-in agreements.

26. A state has recently updated its rules and regulations for the real estate profession. Assuming this state is like all other states and provinces, which of the following statements is **TRUE** regarding this publication?

    (A) The rules and regulations are state laws enacted by the legislature.
    (B) The rules and regulations are a set of administrative rules adopted by the state real estate commission and do not have the same force and effect as the statutory license law.
    (C) The rules and regulations are a set of administrative rules adopted by the state real estate commission that define the statutory license law and have the same force and effect as the license law itself.
    (D) The rules and regulations create a suggested level of competence and behavior but are not enforceable against real estate licensees.

27. A seller sold a buyer a parcel of real estate. Title has passed, but to date the buyer has not paid the purchase price in full, as originally agreed on. If the seller wants to force payment, which of the following remedies would the seller be entitled to seek?

    (A) Attachment   (C) Lis pendens
    (B) Mechanic's lien   (D) Judgment

28. A broker sold a residence for $85,000 and received $5,950 as her commission in accordance with the terms of the listing. What was the broker's commission rate?

    (A) 6.00%   (C) 7.25%
    (B) 7.00%   (D) 7.50%

29. Under a listing agreement, the broker is entitled to sell the property for any price, as long as the seller receives $85,000. The broker may keep any amount over $85,000 as a commission. This type of listing is called

    (A) an exclusive-right-to-sell listing.
    (B) an exclusive-agency listing.
    (C) an open listing.
    (D) a net listing.

30. Which of the following is a lien on real estate?

    (A) Easement running with the land
    (B) Unpaid mortgage loan
    (C) License
    (D) Encroachment

31. Lumber, sand and bricks have been delivered to a property to be used when the owner builds an enclosed patio. At this point, the lumber, sand and bricks are considered

    (A) real property.
    (B) personal property.
    (C) trade fixtures.
    (D) fixtures.

32. A mechanic's lien would **NOT** be available to which of the following?

    (A) Subcontractor   (C) Surveyor
    (B) Contractor   (D) Broker

33. The right of a defaulted taxpayer to recover property before its sale for unpaid taxes is the

    (A) statutory right of reinstatement.
    (B) equitable right of appeal.
    (C) statutory right of assessment.
    (D) equitable right of redemption.

34. Which of the following is permitted under the antitrust laws?

    (A) Property management companies standardizing management fees
    (B) Brokers allocating markets based on the value of homes
    (C) Real estate companies agreeing not to cooperate with a broker because of the fees that broker charges
    (D) A broker deciding not to join a MLS

35. General real estate taxes levied for the operation of the government are called

    (A) assessment taxes.
    (B) ad valorem taxes.
    (C) special taxes.
    (D) improvement taxes.

36. Which of the following probably would **NOT** be exempt from real estate taxes?

    (A) Public hospital
    (B) Golf course operated by the park district
    (C) Community church
    (D) Apartment building

37. If a mortgage lender discriminates against a loan applicant on the basis of marital status, it violates what law?

    (A) ADA
    (B) Civil Rights Act of 1866
    (C) ECOA
    (D) Fair Housing Act

38. A Lithuanian-American real estate broker offers a special discount to Lithuanian-American clients. This practice is

    (A) legal in certain circumstances.
    (B) illegal.
    (C) legal, but ill-advised.
    (D) an example of steering.

39. Which of the following statements describes the Supreme Court's decision in the case of *Jones v. Alfred H. Mayer Company?*

    (A) Racial discrimination is prohibited by any party in the sale or rental of real estate.
    (B) Sales by individual residential homeowners are exempted, provided the owners do not use brokers.
    (C) Laws against discrimination apply only to federally related transactions.
    (D) Persons with disabilities are a protected class.

40. After a broker takes a sale listing of a residence, the owner specifies that he will not sell his home to any Asian family. The broker should do which of the following?

    (A) Advertise the property exclusively in Asian-language newspapers
    (B) Explain to the owner that the instruction violates federal law and that the broker cannot comply with it
    (C) Abide by the principal's directions despite the fact that they conflict with the fair housing laws
    (D) Require that the owner sign a separate legal document stating the additional instruction as an amendment to the listing agreement

41. The fine for a first violation of the federal Fair Housing Act could be as much as

    (A) $ 500.   (C) $ 5,000.
    (B) $1,000.   (D) $10,000.

42. A single man with two small children has been told by a real estate salesperson that homes for sale in a condominium complex are available only to married couples with no children. Which of the following statements is **TRUE**?

    (A) Because a single-parent family can be disruptive if the parent provides little supervision of the children, the condominium is permitted to discriminate against the family under the principal of rational basis.
    (B) Condominium complexes are exempt from the fair housing laws and can therefore restrict children.
    (C) The man may file a complaint alleging discrimination on the basis of familial status.
    (D) Restrictive covenants in a condominium take precedence over the fair housing laws.

43. The following ad appeared in the newspaper: "For sale: 4 BR brick home; Redwood School District; excellent Elm Street location; short walk to St. John's Church and right on the bus line. Move-in condition; priced to sell." Which of the following statements is **TRUE?**

    (A) The ad describes the property for sale and is very appropriate.
    (B) The fair housing laws do not apply to newspaper advertising.
    (C) The ad should state that the property is available to families with children.
    (D) The ad should not mention St. John's Church.

44. One method an appraiser can use to determine a building's cost as new construction involves the estimated cost of the materials needed to build the structure, plus labor and indirect costs. This is called the

    (A) square-foot method.
    (B) quantity-survey method.
    (C) cubic-foot method.
    (D) unit-in-place method.

45. If a property's annual net income is $24,000 and it is valued at $300,000, what is its capitalization rate?

   (A) 8.0%   (C) 12.5%
   (B) 10.5%   (D) 15.0%

46. An offeror has the right to

   (A) reject an offer.
   (B) control an offeree.
   (C) revoke an offer.
   (D) release an offer.

47. An appraiser who is asked to determine the value of an existing strip shopping center would probably give the **MOST** weight to which of the following approaches to value?

   (A) Cost approach
   (B) Sales comparison approach
   (C) Income approach
   (D) Index method

48. The market value of a parcel of real estate is

   (A) an estimate of its future benefits.
   (B) the amount of money paid for the property.
   (C) an estimate of the most probable price it should bring.
   (D) its value without improvements.

49. The primary purpose of Freddie Mac is to

   (A) guarantee mortgages by the full faith and credit of the federal government.
   (B) buy and pool blocks of conventional mortgages, selling bonds with such mortgages as security.
   (C) act in tandem with GNMA to provide special assistance in times of tight money.
   (D) buy and sell VA and FHA mortgages.

50. The federal Equal Credit Opportunity Act does **NOT** prohibit lenders from discriminating against potential borrowers on the basis on which of the following?

   (A) Race
   (B) Sex
   (C) Dependence on public assistance
   (D) Amount of income

51. The effective gross annual income from a property is $112,000. Total expenses for this year are $53,700. What capitalization rate was used to obtain a valuation of $542,325?

   (A) 9.75%   (C) 10.50%
   (B) 10.25%   (D) 10.75%

52. Of the following events which would **NOT** terminate an offer?

   (A) Revocation of the offer before acceptance
   (B) A counteroffer by the offeree
   (C) Death of the buyer before acceptance
   (D) An offer from a third party

53. The appraised value of a residence with four bedrooms and one bathroom would probably be reduced because of

   (A) external obsolescence.
   (B) functional obsolescence.
   (C) curable physical deterioration.
   (D) incurable physical deterioration.

54. Under the provisions of the Truth-in-Lending Act (Regulation Z), which of the following is **NOT** required to be disclosed to a residential buyer?

   (A) Discount points
   (B) The broker's commission
   (C) A loan origination fee
   (D) The loan interest rate

55. A home is purchased using a fixed-rate, fully amortized mortgage loan. Which of the following statements is **TRUE** regarding this mortgage?

   (A) A balloon payment will be made at the end of the loan.
   (B) Each payment amount is the same.
   (C) Each payment reduces the principal by the same amount.
   (D) The principal amount in each payment is greater than the interest amount.

56. Which of the following **BEST** defines the secondary market?

    (A) Lenders who deal exclusively in second mortgages
    (B) Institutional investors who buy and sell loans
    (C) The major lender of residential mortgages and deeds of trust
    (D) Institutional investors who supply money for FHA and VA loans

57. Which of the following is a **TRUE** statement about interest on a fully amortized mortgage or deed of trust loan?

    (A) Interest may be charged in arrears—that is, at the end of each period for which interest is due.
    (B) The interest portion of each payment increases throughout the term of the loan.
    (C) Only interest is paid each period.
    (D) The final interest payment will be determined after the last payment is made.

58. Independent contractors receive compensation for their services from the broker by

    (A) negotiated commissions or fees on transactions.
    (B) company-provided health insurance.
    (C) company-provided automobile.
    (D) a monthly salary or hourly wage.

59. From the reproduction or replacement cost of a building, the appraiser deducts depreciation, which represents

    (A) the remaining economic life of the building.
    (B) remodeling costs to increase rentals.
    (C) loss of value due to any cause.
    (D) costs to modernize the building.

60. A borrower obtains a $100,000 mortgage loan for 30 years at 7½% interest. If the monthly payments of $902.77 are credited first to interest and then to principal, what will be the balance of the principal after the borrower makes the first payment?

    (A) $99,097.32   (C) $ 99,723.00
    (B) $99,722.23   (D) $100,000.00

61. Using a factor of 7.81 per $1,000 what is the P&I payment on a 100,000 loan at 8⅛% over a term of 25 years?

    (A) $772   (C) $789
    (B) $781   (D) $806

62. Which of the following would automatically terminate a residential lease?

    (A) Total destruction of the property
    (B) Sale of the property
    (C) Failure of the tenant to pay rent
    (D) Death of the tenant

63. Which basic principle of value is noted in every appraisal because it notes the use that is the **MOST** profitable single use to which a property may be put in the near future?

    (A) Highest and best use
    (B) Competition
    (C) Substitution
    (D) Supply and demand

64. If a lender agrees to make a loan based on an 80% LTV, what is the amount of the loan if the property appraises for $114,500 and the sales price is $116,900?

    (A) $83,200   (C) $91,600
    (B) $91,300   (D) $92,900

65. The appraiser noted that the subject property is located very near a toxic site registered with the EPA. The value of the subject property will be influenced by

    (A) external obsolescence.
    (B) physical deterioration.
    (C) functional obsolescence.
    (D) physical proximity.

66. In which of the following types of loans is the loan amount divided into two parts, to be paid off separately by periodic interest payments followed by payment of the principal in full at the end of the term?

    (A) Amortized   (C) ARM
    (B) Straight   (D) GEM

67. An option to purchase binds which of the following parties?

    (A) Buyer only
    (B) Seller only
    (C) Neither buyer nor seller
    (D) Both buyer and seller

68. A buyer and seller enter into a real estate sales contract. Under the contract's terms, the buyer will pay the seller $500 a month for ten years. The seller will continue to hold legal title. The buyer will live on the property and pay all real estate taxes, insurance premiums and regular upkeep costs. What kind of contract do the buyer and seller have?

    (A) Option contract
    (B) Contract for mortgage
    (C) Unilateral contract
    (D) Land or installment contract

69. The purchaser of real estate under an installment contract

    (A) generally pays no interest charge.
    (B) receives title immediately.
    (C) is not required to pay property taxes for the duration of the contract.
    (D) has only an equitable interest in the property's title.

70. Under the statute of frauds, all contracts for the sale of real estate must be

    (A) originated by a real estate broker.
    (B) on preprinted forms.
    (C) in writing to be enforceable.
    (D) accompanied by earnest money deposits.

71. A couple offer in writing to purchase a house for $120,000, including its draperies, with the offer to expire on Saturday at noon. The seller replies in writing on Thursday, accepting the $120,000 offer, but excluding the draperies. On Friday, while the buyers consider this counteroffer, the seller decides to accept the original offer, draperies included, and states that in writing. At this point, the buyers

    (A) are legally bound to buy the house although they have the right to insist that the draperies be included.
    (B) are not bound to buy.
    (C) must buy the house and are not entitled to the draperies.
    (D) must buy the house, but may deduct the value of the draperies from the $120,000.

72. A buyer makes an offer to purchase a certain property listed with a broker and leaves a deposit with the broker to show good faith. The broker should

    (A) immediately apply the deposit to the listing expenses.
    (B) put the deposit in an account, as provided by state law.
    (C) give the deposit to the seller when the offer is presented.
    (D) put the deposit in the broker's personal checking account.

73. From June 5 through October 15, an individual suffered from a mental illness that caused delusions, hallucinations and loss of memory. On July 1, she signed a contract to purchase a farm, with the closing set for October 31. On September 24, she began psychiatric treatment. She was declared completely cured by October 15. Which of the following statements is **TRUE** regarding the contract to purchase the farm?

    (A) The contract is voidable.
    (B) The contract is void.
    (C) The contract lacks reality of consent.
    (D) The contract is fully valid and enforceable.

74. A broker has found a buyer for a seller's home. The buyer has indicated in writing a willingness to buy the property for $1,000 less than the asking price and has deposited $5,000 in earnest money with the broker. The seller is out of town for the weekend, and the broker has been unable to inform the seller of the signed document. At this point, the buyer has signed

   (A) a voidable contract.
   (B) an offer.
   (C) an executory agreement.
   (D) an implied contract.

75. A buyer and seller agree to the purchase of a house for $200,000. The contract contains a clause stating that time is of the essence. Which of the following statements is **TRUE**?

   (A) The closing must take place within a reasonable period before the stated date.
   (B) A "time is of the essence" clause is not binding on either party.
   (C) The closing date must be stated as a particular calendar date, and not simply as a formula, such as "two weeks after loan approval."
   (D) If the closing date passes and no closing takes place, the contract may be invalid.

76. A buyer signed a contract under which he may purchase an acreage for $30,000 any time in the next three months. He pays the current owner $500 at the time the contract is signed. Which of the following **BEST** describes this contract?

   (A) Contingency   (C) Installment
   (B) Option   (D) Sales

77. In a real estate transaction, the term fiduciary typically refers to the

   (A) sale of real property.
   (B) person who gives someone else the legal power to act on his or her behalf.
   (C) person who has legal power to act on behalf of another.
   (D) agent's relationship to principal.

78. The relationship between broker and seller is generally what type of agency?

   (A) Special   (C) Implied
   (B) General   (D) Universal

79. Which of the following are traditionally covered by a standard title insurance coverage policy?

   (A) Unrecorded rights of persons in possession
   (B) Improperly delivered deeds
   (C) Changes in land use due to zoning ordinances
   (D) Unrecorded liens not known of by the policyholder

80. General Title Company settled a claim against its insured. General Title made a substantial payment to the person who sued its client. Now, General Title may seek damages from the person who originally gave its insured a general warranty deed. Through what right can General Title recover the amount it paid out in the settlement?

   (A) Escrow   (C) Subordination
   (B) Encumbrance   (D) Subrogation

81. A title insurance policy with standard coverage generally does **NOT** cover which of the following?

   (A) Forged documents
   (B) Incorrect marital statements
   (C) Unrecorded rights of parties in possession
   (D) Incompetent grantors

82. The documents referred to as title evidence include

   (A) title insurance.
   (B) warranty deeds.
   (C) security agreements.
   (D) a deed.

83. To give notice of a security interest in personal property items, a lienholder must file which of the following?

   (A) Bill of sale
   (B) Financing statement
   (C) Chattel agreement
   (D) Quitclaim deed

84. An owner sells a portion of her property. The buyer promptly records the deed in the appropriate county office. If the owner tries to sell the same portion of her property to another person, which of the following statements is **TRUE?**

   (A) A second buyer has been given constructive notice of the prior sale because the first buyer promptly recorded it.
   (B) A second buyer has been given actual notice of the prior sale because first buyer promptly recorded it.
   (C) Because a second buyer's purchase of the portion of the owner's property is the more recent, it will have priority over the first buyer's interest, regardless of when the first buyer recorded the deed.
   (D) Because a second buyer purchased the property from its rightful owner, he is presumed by law to be aware of first buyer's prior interest.

85. An individual lives in Lake County, Wisconsin. While vacationing in Arlington County, Virginia, he finds a piece of property he likes very much. Its current owner lives in Orange County, California, and when he decides to buy the property, the closing is held in Omaha County, Nebraska. Assuming that he will maintain his permanent residence in Wisconsin, where should title for the property be recorded?

   (A) Lake County
   (B) Arlington County
   (C) Orange County
   (D) Omaha County

86. Which of the following statements regarding the Uniform Commercial Code is TRUE?

   (A) The UCC has been adopted in about half the states in the United States.
   (B) The UCC governs all transactions involving personal or real property.
   (C) The UCC is a legal registration system used to verify ownership and encumbrances.
   (D) The UCC applies to personal property transactions not real estate.

87. A tenant has a one-year leasehold interest in Harbor House. The interest automatically renews itself at the end of each year. The tenant interest is referred to as a tenancy

   (A) for years.
   (B) from period to period.
   (C) at will.
   (D) at sufferance.

88. A tenant has assigned her apartment lease to her friend, and the landlord has agreed to the assignment. If the friend fails to pay the rent, who is liable?

   (A) The new tenant is primarily liable; the original tenant is secondarily liable.
   (B) The original tenant is primarily liable; the friend is secondarily liable.
   (C) Only the original tenant is liable.
   (D) Only the friend is liable.

89. A seller delivered a title to the buyer at the closing. A title search disclosed no serious defects, and the title did not appear to be based on doubtful questions of law or fact or to expose the buyer to possible litigation. The seller's title did not appear to present a threat to the buyer's quiet enjoyment, and the title policy was sufficient to convince a reasonably well-informed person that the property could be resold. The title conveyed would commonly be referred to as

   (A) a certificate of title.
   (B) an abstract of title.
   (C) a marketable title.
   (D) an attorney's opinion of title.

90. The person who prepares an abstract of title for a parcel of real estate

   (A) searches the public records and then summarizes the events and proceedings that affect title.
   (B) insures the condition of the title.
   (C) inspects the property.
   (D) issues a certificate of title.

■ ANSWER KEY WITH EXPLANATIONS

1. (C) The official deed is recorded at the courthouse, and she can get a copy.

2. (C) The lender is the mortgagee. The mortgagee's policy protects the lender.

3. (A) Generally, the broker is obligated to render faithful service to the seller. The five common-law fiduciary duties that a real estate broker owes a client are care, obedience, accounting, loyalty and disclosure (COALD).

4. (B) When a seller contracts with a broker to market the seller's property, the broker becomes an agent of the seller; the seller is the principal, the broker's client. The buyer who contacts the broker to see properties listed by that broker or his firm is a customer.

5. (C) Real estate licensing laws may permit dual agency only if the buyer and seller are informed and consent to the broker's representation of both in the same transaction. Many states have passed laws that permit a broker to designate certain licensees within the firm who act as the legal representatives of the principal. Some states do not permit dual agency at all.

6. (B) Once an owner declares bankruptcy, he or she no longer has control over financial decisions regarding the property; thus, the listing is terminated. An agency may be terminated for any of the following: death or incapacity of either party, destruction or condemnation of the property, expiration of the terms of the agreement, mutual agreement, breach by one of the parties, operation of law, and completion or fulfillment of the agreement.

7. (D) The duty of loyalty requires that the agent place the principal's interests above those of all others, including the agent's own self interest. Confidentiality about the principal's personal affairs is a key element of loyalty.

8. (A) A listing agreement is between the seller and the broker. A salesperson may list property for sale for a seller only in the name of and under the supervision of his or her broker.

9. (C) The seller authorizes only one particular salesperson to represent the seller in both the exclusive-agency and exclusive-right-to-sell listings. From the broker's perspective, an exclusive-right-to-sell listing offers the greatest opportunity to receive a commission. Under an exclusive-agency listing, the broker may only earn a commission if he or she has been the procuring cause of a sale because the seller reserves the right to find the buyer without the aid of the broker.

10. (C) The owner could not simply terminate the listing because of dissatisfaction over the marketing efforts. Other reasons that may terminate a listing agreement include fulfillment, expiration, destruction of the property, bankruptcy, death, incapacitation or breach of contract by the other party.

11. (A) In an exclusive-agency listing the seller authorizes one broker to act as the exclusive agent of the principal, however, the seller retains the right to sell the property without being obligated to the broker.

12. (D) A lis pendens is the notice of the contractor's intent to file the suit, in other words, that the property will soon be the subject of a lawsuit.

13. (C) A special assessment lien is filed by the municipality and has priority over a contractor's mechanic's lien.

14. (A) In both an open listing and exclusive-agency listing, the seller reserves the right to find his or her own buyer and thus avoids paying the broker a commission.

15. (C) It is the seller who must determine the listing price of a property. It is the responsibility of the broker or salesperson to advise and assist the seller with his or her knowledge, information and expertise.

16. (A) A listing agreement is an employment contract rather than a real estate contract. This contract is for professional personal service by the broker, not for the transfer of real estate.

17. (D) The house sold for $183,333.
$3,575 ÷ .30 = $11,916.67
$11,916.67 ÷ 6.5% = $183,333

18. (D) The parcel sold for $93,654.
43,560 × $2.15 = $93,654

19. (A) The described parcel contains 80 acres.
[2,640 × 2,640] ÷ 2 = 3,484,800 sq. ft.
3,484,800 ÷ 43,560 = 80

20. (B) The developer can expect 81 complete lots.
[43,560 × 10] − 26,000 = 409,600 sq. ft.
409,600 ÷ [50 × 100] = 81.92 or 81 complete lots.

21. (B) The parcel may only be used to build a single-family home. If there is a conflict between a deed restriction and zoning, the more restrictive prevails.

22. (D) Locating families with children in one building only is an example of the illegal practice of steering.

23. (C) The doctrine of prior appropriation is used in states where water is scarce.

24. (A) Previous owner(s) may include restrictive covenants that limit the way that real estate may be used. These are privately enforced. Governmental powers include police power, eminent domain, taxation and escheat. A helpful way to remember these items is the acronym PETE.

25. (C) It is legal for agents to share and split commissions. However, price-fixing, allocation of customers, and group boycotting are illegal under the antitrust laws.

26. (C) Each state has a licensing authority or commission, a department, a division, a board or an agency for real estate brokers and salespersons. The legislature passes laws. Generally, the rules and regulations adopted by the licensing authority have the force of law.

27. (D) The seller would ask the court to file a judgment to force the buyer to pay.

28. (B) The broker's commission rate was 7%.
$5,950 ÷ $85,000 = .07 or 7%

29. (D) This type of listing can create a conflict of interest between the broker's fiduciary responsibility to the seller (to get the highest price) and the broker's profit motive (to make the most money). Net listings are illegal in many states and are discouraged in others.

30. (B) Liens are always monetary. All liens are encumbrances but not all encumbrances are liens. Encumbrances include easements, licenses and encroachments.

31. (B) Because the lumber, sand, and bricks are still [re]movable, they are considered personal property. Once they are used to build the enclosed patio, they become real property by annexation.

32. (D) Generally, brokers do not have the ability to file a mechanic's lien.

33. (D) Under the equitable right of redemption, the debtor has the right to bring the tax bill current to stop the foreclosure.

34. (D) The antitrust laws do not preclude a broker from deciding **NOT** to cooperate through a local multiple-listing service. However, a violation would occur if the MLS brokers decided to avoid cooperating with a discount broker (group boycotts) or if the MLS brokers agreed to set or standardize fees (price-fixing).

35. (B) An ad valorem tax is levied according to value, generally used for real estate taxes.

36. (D) The apartment building is taxed. Generally, nonprofit organizations, religious institutions and government properties are exempt from property taxes.

37. (C) When issuing credit, the Equal Credit Opportunity Act (ECOA) prohibits discrimination based on race, color, religion, national origin, sex, receipt of public assistance, age and marital status.

38. (B) The fair housing laws prohibit offering different terms and conditions based on national origin.

39. (A) In *Jones v. Mayer*, the Supreme Court reaffirmed the Civil Rights Act of 1866 prohibiting all racial discrimination, private as well as public.

40. (B) The fair housing laws do not provide for any exemptions for a real estate licensee. The broker cannot participate in the owner's discrimination nor may the broker obey an unlawful instruction.

41. (D) The fine for a first offense of the federal Fair Housing Act is up to $10,000. The fine for a second offense in five years is up to $25,000. The fine for a third offense in seven years is up to $50,000.

42. (C) The father of two children who is refused an apartment because he has children may file a complaint alleging discrimination on the basis of familial status. Families with children are a protected category.

43. (D) The ad should not mention the church. Describe the property, not the type of people or religions; doing so could lead to charges of steering.

44. (B) The quantity-survey method is an appraisal method of estimating building costs by calculating the cost of all of the physical components in the improvements, adding the cost to assemble them and then including the indirect costs associated with such construction.

45. (A) The cap rate used is 8%.
$24,000 ÷ $300,000 = .08 or 8%

46. (C) The offeror has the right to revoke an offer. One revokes offers, rescinds contracts. (It helps to look at the center letters of the two actions: rev*o*ke and res*c*ind. *O* for offers, *C* for contracts)

47. (C) The most common method to value income-producing property is the income method.

48. (C) Market value is the estimate of the most probable price that a property will bring.

49. (B) The primary purpose of Freddie Mac is to buy and pool blocks of conventional mortgages, selling bonds with such mortgages as security.

50. (D) ECOA does not prohibit using income as a means to qualify borrowers. Borrowers must be financially qualified to obtain a loan.

51. (D) The capitalization rate used is 10.75%.
[$112,000 − $53,700] ÷ $542,325 = .1075 or 10.75%

52. (D) All offers from a third party will **NOT** terminate an offer. The revocation before acceptance, a counteroffer, and the death of one of the parties will all terminate offers.

53. (B) A property with four bedrooms and only one bathroom will lose value because of functional obsolescence.

54. (B) Required disclosures under the Truth-in-Lending Act do **NOT** include the broker's commission. Required disclosures include the amount of discount points, loan origination fees and the loan interest rate. Disclosing the annual percentage rate (APR) supercedes all other disclosures because it presents the true cost of borrowing money.

55. (B) An amortized loan is characterized by requiring equal payment amounts. However, the payment is allocated to paying $\frac{1}{12}$ of the interest on the remaining principal and whatever is left reduces the principal balance.

56. (B) Institutional investors buy and sell loans secured by mortgages or deeds of trust on the secondary market. The primary market makes the loans directly to the public.

57. (A) In a fully amortized loan, interest may be charged in arrears—that is, at the end of each period for which interest is due. The interest portion decreases throughout the life of the loan since the principal is slowing paid off.

58. (A) Independent contractors receive compensation in the form of negotiated commissions or fees on transactions.

59. (C) Depreciation is defined as a loss of value by any cause.

60. (B) After the first payment, the remaining principal balance is $99,722.23.
$100,000 × 7.5% = $7,500 ÷ 12 = $625
$902.77 − $625 = $277.77
$100,000 − $277.77 = $99,722.23

61. (B) The monthly P&I payment is $781.
[$100,000 ÷ $1,000] × 7.81 = $781

62. (A) If the property has been totally destroyed, the landlord cannot provide possession, so the lease is thereby automatically terminated by constructive eviction.

63. (A) Used in every appraisal, highest and best use indicates the use of the property that will produce the greatest net income and thereby develop the highest value.

64. (C) The loan is $91,600.
$114,500 × 80% = $91,600
Generally, the loan-to-value ratio is determined as a percentage of the sale price or the appraised price, whichever is lower.

65. (A) The subject property will be adversely affected by a nearby toxic waste site; in other words, external obsolescence.

66. (B) A straight (or term) loan is repaid "interest only" during the term of the loan with the entire principal amount due with the final interest payment.

67. (B) An option binds the seller but not the buyer. The buyer gave compensation for the seller's promise to perform. An option is an example of a unilateral contract.

68. (D) Under a land or installment contract, possession is granted to the buyer, but legal title stays with the seller.

69. (D) Under a land or installment contract, the buyer (vendee) has an equitable interest in the property. The seller retains legal title to the property.

70. (C) The statute of frauds enacted in every state requires that any contract to convey a real estate interest must be in writing to be enforceable.

71. (B) Making a counteroffer implies a rejection of the first offer. Thus, if the seller makes a counteroffer, the seller cannot go back and undo his rejection. To bind the parties, a new agreement must be accepted by all parties.

72. (B) The broker must be able to account for all monies or property received. Most states regulate deposit timeliness.

73. (A) The contract is voidable at the option of the individual (buyer) who suffered from a mental illness. It is binding on the sellers who were fully competent when they signed.

74. (B) The document is still an offer. An offer is not binding until it is accepted in writing by both parties.

75. (D) "Time is of the essence" means that time limits should be strictly followed. If the closing date passes and no closing takes place, the contract may be invalid.

76. (B) An option is an example of a unilateral contract. The buyer may purchase but is not required to purchase. The seller is bound to sell at the agreed-upon price.

77. (D) Fiduciary is defined as the relationship in which the agent is held in a position or special trust and confidence by the client, who may be either the seller/landlord or the buyer/tenant.

78. (A) A special agency is defined as short term with limited authority. The listing agreement is a good example. A general agent is hired for a long time and given broader or wider authority. A property manager is an example of a general agent.

79. (B) The owner's title insurance policy with standard coverage protects against the following defects: defects found in public records, forged documents, incompetent grantors, incorrect marital statements and improperly delivered deeds.

80. (D) After paying a claim, the title insurance company generally acquires the right to any remedies or damages available to the insured through a process called subrogation.

81. (C) Title insurance standard coverage generally does **NOT** include unrecorded rights of parties in possession. That coverage is available under an "extended coverage" policy.

82. (A) A title insurance policy is generally accepted as proof of title.

83. (B) The UCC requires the borrower to sign a security agreement, including a complete description of the personal property. A short notice of this agreement is called a financing statement or a UCC-1, and it must be filed.

84. (A) The public record serves constructive notice to the world. It is the second buyer's responsibility to check.

85. (B) The deed is recorded in the county where the property is located.

86. (D) The UCC applies to personal property not real estate.

87. (B) The tenant has a period-to-period tenancy because it automatically renews unless either party gives notice to change any portion. A period-to-period lease may be month to month, year to year, etc.

88. (A) Since the landlord agreed to the assignment, the new tenant is primarily liable, but the original tenant is also liable. If the landlord had "released" the original tenant in accepting the assignment, then the original tenant is released from further liability.

89. (C) Because there is no evidence of a problem with the seller's ownership, the buyer receives a marketable title.

90. (A) The person who prepares the abstract does the research and then reports on what he or she has found.

Broker Exams

12

■ BROKER EXAM #1

1. Which of the following is a lien on real estate?

   (A) Recorded easement
   (B) Recorded mortgage
   (C) Encroachment
   (D) Deed restriction

2. After the first Hispanic family purchased in the neighborhood, the broker sent letters to the neighbors suggesting that they might want to sell, **NOW,** before the neighborhood changed any more. This is an example of

   (A) a good business practice to obtain listings.
   (B) an illegal practice called blockbusting.
   (C) a legal practice called channeling.
   (D) illegal net listings.

3. A broker receives a check for earnest money from a buyer and deposits the money in the broker's personal interest-bearing checking account over the weekend. This action exposes the broker to a charge of

   (A) commingling.   (C) subrogation.
   (B) novation.   (D) accretion.

4. A man and woman are preparing to buy a house. Each is putting up the same amount of down payment. Both incomes are included in the loan application. They ask the salesperson, "How should we take title?" In this situation, the salesperson should

   (A) ask how they would want the property divided if one should die.
   (B) refer the couple to a lawyer for advice.
   (C) advise them to go "joint tenancy with right of survivorship."
   (D) advise them to take title as "tenants in common" since they are equally involved.

5. If a borrower computed the interest charged for the previous month on a $60,000 loan balance as $412.50, what is the borrower's interest rate?

   (A) 7.50%   (C) 8.25%
   (B) 7.75%   (D) 8.50%

6. A broker signs a contract with a buyer. Under the contract, the broker agrees to help the buyer find a suitable property and to represent the buyer in negotiations with the seller. Although the buyer may not sign an agreement with any other broker, the buyer may look for and purchase a property without the broker's assistance. The broker is entitled to payment only if the broker locates the property that is purchased. What kind of agreement has this broker signed?

(A) Exclusive buyer agency agreement
(B) Exclusive-agency buyer agency agreement
(C) Open buyer agency agreement
(D) Option contract

7. A grantor conveys property by delivering a deed. The deed contains five covenants. This is **MOST** likely a

(A) general warranty deed.
(B) quitclaim deed.
(C) special warranty deed.
(D) deed in trust.

8. A real estate broker does not show non-Asian clients any properties in several traditionally Asian neighborhoods. The broker bases this practice on the need to preserve the valuable cultural integrity of Asian immigrant communities. Which of the following statements is **TRUE** regarding the broker's policy?

(A) The broker's policy is steering and violates the fair housing laws regardless of the motivation.
(B) Because the broker is not attempting to restrict the rights of any single minority group, the practice does not constitute steering.
(C) The broker's policy is steering, but it does not violate the fair housing laws because the broker is motivated by cultural preservation, not by exclusion or discrimination.
(D) The broker's policy has the effect, but not the intent, of steering.

9. When is a certificate of occupancy issued?

(A) When the owner of multifamily residential property wishes to limit the number of individuals who may live in a single unit
(B) At the time a property owner applies for a building permit
(C) After a newly constructed building has been inspected and found satisfactory by the municipal inspector
(D) When an application for a variance or conditional-use permit has been granted by the zoning board

10. A study that looks at properties that have sold and those that are currently on the market to assist a seller in determining the appropriate asking price is

(A) a conditional commitment.
(B) a certificate of reasonable value (CRV).
(C) an appraisal.
(D) a competitive market analysis (CMA).

11. A real estate salesperson who has a written contract with his broker that specifies that he will not be treated as an employee. The salesperson's entire income is from sales commissions rather than an hourly wage. Based on these facts, the salesperson is probably treated as

(A) a real estate assistant.
(B) an employee.
(C) a subagent.
(D) an independent contractor.

12. The appraiser is evaluating a 30-year home in a 50-year-old neighborhood. Which approach to value will the appraiser give the **MOST** weight?

(A) Sales comparison approach
(B) Cost approach
(C) Income approach
(D) Straight-line method

13. The form of tenancy that may expire on a specific date is a

(A) joint tenancy.
(B) tenancy for years.
(C) tenancy in common.
(D) tenancy by the entirety.

14. A suburban home that lacks sufficient indoor plumbing suffers from which of the following?

    (A) Functional obsolescence
    (B) Curable physical deterioration
    (C) Incurable physical deterioration
    (D) External obsolescence

15. A developer built a structure that has six stories. Several years later, an ordinance was passed in that area banning any building six stories or higher. This building is a

    (A) nonconforming use.
    (B) situation in which the structure would have to be demolished.
    (C) conditional use.
    (D) violation of the zoning laws.

16. Assuming that the listing broker and the selling broker in a transaction split their commission equally, what was the sales price of the property if the commission rate was 6.5% and the listing broker received $2,593.50?

    (A) $39,900   (C) $79,800
    (B) $56,200   (D) $88,400

17. A real estate broker specializes in helping both buyers and sellers with the necessary paperwork involved in transferring property. While the broker is not an agent of either party, the broker may not disclose either party's confidential information to the other. The broker is **BEST** described as

    (A) a buyer's agent.
    (B) an independent contractor.
    (C) a dual agent.
    (D) a transactional broker.

18. After the appraiser applies three approaches to value on the same property, the appraiser must then analyze and effectively weigh the findings. This last process is called

    (A) depreciation.
    (B) highest and best use.
    (C) reconciliation.
    (D) capitalization ratios.

19. The listing and selling brokers agree to split a 7% commission 50-50 on a $95,900 sale. The listing broker gives the listing salesperson 30% of the listing broker's share, and the selling broker gives the selling salesperson 35%. After deducting expenses of $35, how much does the selling salesperson earn from the sale?

    (A) $1,139.78   (C) $1,183.95
    (B) $1,174.78   (D) $1,971.90

20. Which of the following is a consequence of violating the antitrust laws by conspiring to fix prices?

    (A) $10,000 for the first offense
    (B) Up to $100,000 fine and three years in prison
    (C) Up to $50,000 fine for the third offense in seven years
    (D) Unlimited punitive damages

21. A seller wants to net $65,000 from the sale of a house after paying the broker's fee of 6%. The seller's gross sales price will be

    (A) $61,100.   (C) $68,900.
    (B) $64,752.   (D) $69,149.

22. A sales contract was signed under duress. Which of the following describes this contract?

    (A) Voidable   (C) Discharged
    (B) Breached   (D) Void

23. A buyer is purchasing a condominium unit in a subdivision and obtains financing from a local savings bank. In this situation, which of the following **BEST** describes this buyer?

    (A) Vendor   (C) Grantor
    (B) Mortgagor   (D) Lessor

24. The current value of a property is $40,000. The property is assessed at 40% of its current value for real estate tax purposes, with an equalization factor of 1.5 applied to the assessed value. If the tax rate is $4 per $100 of assessed valuation, what is the amount of tax due on the property?

    (A) $640   (C) $1,600
    (B) $960   (D) $2,400

25. A building was sold for $60,000, with the purchaser putting 10% down and obtaining a loan for the balance. The lending institution charged a 1% loan origination fee. What was the total cash used for the purchase?

   (A) $ 540   (C) $6,540
   (B) $6,000   (D) $6,600

26. A parcel of vacant land has an assessed valuation of $274,550. If the assessment is 85% of market value, what is the market value?

   (A) $315,732.50   (C) $323,000.00
   (B) $320,000.00   (D) $830,333.33

27. Which of the following **BEST** describes a capitalization rate?

   (A) Amount determined by the gross rent multiplier
   (B) Rate of return an income property will produce
   (C) Mathematical value determined by a sales price
   (D) Rate at which the amount of depreciation in a property is measured

28. A parcel of land described as "the NW¼ and the SW¼ of Section 6, T4N, R8W of the Third Principal Meridian" was sold for $875 per acre. The listing broker will receive a 5% commission on the total sales price. How much will the broker receive?

   (A) $1,750   (C) $14,000
   (B) $5,040   (D) $15,040

29. If a house was sold for $40,000 and the buyer obtained an FHA-insured mortgage loan for $38,500, how much money would the buyer pay in discount points if the lender charged four points?

   (A) $ 385   (C) $1,540
   (B) $1,500   (D) $1,600

30. The commission rate is 7¾% on a sale of $50,000. What is the dollar amount of the commission?

   (A) $3,500   (C) $4,085
   (B) $3,875   (D) $4,585

31. A prospective buyer signs an offer to purchase a residential property. Which of the following circumstances would **NOT** automatically terminate the offer?

   (A) The buyer signed a written offer to buy a house and then died.
   (B) The buyer revoked the offer between the presentation and a possible acceptance.
   (C) The seller made a counteroffer.
   (D) The seller received a better offer from another buyer.

32. A buyer purchased a home under a land contract. Until the contract is paid in full, the buyer

   (A) holds legal title to the premises.
   (B) has no legal interest in the property.
   (C) possesses a legal life estate in the premises.
   (D) has equitable title in the property.

33. A buyer and a seller sign a contract for the sale of real property. A few days later, they decide to change many of the terms of the contract, while retaining the basic intent to buy and sell. The process by which the new contract replaces the old one is called

   (A) assignment.
   (B) novation.
   (C) assemblage.
   (D) rescission.

34. Using the services of a mortgage broker, a person borrowed $4,000 from a private lender. After deducting the loan costs, the borrower received $3,747. What is the face amount of the note?

   (A) $3,747   (C) $4,253
   (B) $4,000   (D) $7,747

35. Whose signature is necessary for an offer to purchase real estate to become a contract?

   (A) Buyer's only
   (B) Buyer's and seller's
   (C) Seller's only
   (D) Seller's and seller's broker's

36. A borrower has just made the final payment on a mortgage loan. Regardless of this fact, the records will still show a lien on the mortgaged property until which of the following events occurs?

    (A) A satisfaction of the mortgage document is recorded.
    (B) A reconveyance of the mortgage document is delivered to the mortgage holder.
    (C) A novation of the mortgage document takes place.
    (D) An estoppel of the mortgage document is filed with the clerk of the county in which the mortgagee is located.

37. If the annual net income from a commercial property is $22,000 and the capitalization rate is 8%, what is the property worth if the income approach is used?

    (A) $176,000   (C) $200,000
    (B) $183,000   (D) $275,000

38. A broker enters into a listing agreement with a seller in which the seller will receive $120,000 from the sale of a vacant lot and the broker will receive any sale proceeds exceeding that amount. This is what type of listing?

    (A) Exclusive agency
    (B) Net
    (C) Exclusive right to sell
    (D) Multiple

39. Under a cooperative form of ownership, an owner

    (A) is a shareholder in the corporation.
    (B) owns his or her unit outright and a share of the common areas.
    (C) will have to take out a new mortgage loan on a newly acquired unit.
    (D) receives a fixed-term lease for the unit.

40. A known defect or a cloud on title to property may be cured by

    (A) obtaining quitclaim deeds from all appropriate parties.
    (B) recording the title after closing.
    (C) paying cash for the property at the settlement.
    (D) purchasing a title insurance policy at closing.

41. A buyer signed an exclusive-agency buyer agency agreement with a licensee. If the buyer finds a suitable property with no assistance, the licensee is entitled to

    (A) full compensation from the buyer.
    (B) full compensation from the seller.
    (C) partial compensation.
    (D) no compensation.

42. Under the terms of a net lease, a commercial tenant would usually **NOT** be directly responsible for paying which of the following property expenses?

    (A) Maintenance expenses
    (B) Mortgage debt service
    (C) Fire and extended-coverage insurance
    (D) Real estate taxes

43. The Civil Rights Act of 1866 prohibits discrimination based on

    (A) sex.   (C) race.
    (B) religion.   (D) familial status.

44. A borrower takes out a mortgage loan that requires monthly payments of $875.70 for 20 years and a final payment of $24,095. This is what type of loan?

    (A) Wraparound   (C) Balloon
    (B) Accelerated   (D) Variable

45. What is the difference between a general lien and a specific lien?

    (A) A general lien cannot be enforced in court, while a specific lien can.
    (B) A specific lien is held by only one person, while a general lien must be held by two or more.
    (C) A general lien is a lien against personal property, while a specific lien is a lien against real estate.
    (D) A specific lien is a lien against a certain parcel of real estate, while a general lien covers all of a debtor's property.

46. In an option to purchase real estate, which of the following statements is **TRUE** of the optionee?

    (A) The optionee must purchase the property but may do so at any time within the option period.
    (B) The optionee is limited to a refund of the option consideration if the option is exercised.
    (C) The optionee cannot obtain third-party financing on the property until after the option has expired.
    (D) The optionee has no obligation to purchase the property during the option period.

47. The local village board has decided that a parking lot would enhance the beauty, safety and vitality of the community by keeping cars from parking on the streets. Unfortunately, a house is located on the land needed for the new parking lot. Based on these facts, which of the following statements is **TRUE?**

    (A) The owner's constitutional rights to own property cannot be infringed by the village under any circumstances.
    (B) The village may tear down the house and build the lot without paying the owner any compensation, through the village's constitutional authority under the takings clause.
    (C) The village may tear down the house but must first pay the owner a fair amount for her home.
    (D) The village may not seize the house because it has insufficient reason to do so.

48. In the sales comparison approach to value, the appraiser must analyze for differences between the subject property and the comparables. This approach is a good example of what basic principle of value?

    (A) Competition
    (B) Highest and best use
    (C) Supply and demand
    (D) Substitution

49. A home is the smallest in a neighborhood of large, expensive houses. The effect of the other houses on the value of this home is known as

    (A) regression.   (C) substitution.
    (B) progression.   (D) contribution.

50. A lien that arises as a result of a judgment, estate or inheritance taxes, the decedent's debts or federal taxes is what sort of lien?

    (A) Specific   (C) Voluntary
    (B) General   (D) Equitable

51. The seller has accepted an offer from the buyer. No changes were made. Which of the following could terminate the accepted contract?

    (A) The buyer changes his or her mind.
    (B) A tornado destroys the property.
    (C) The seller decides not to sell.
    (D) The seller dies.

52. Two people are joint tenants. One person sells her interest to a third person. What is the relationship between the surviving owner and the new owner regarding the property?

    (A) Joint tenants
    (B) Tenants in common
    (C) Tenants by the entirety
    (D) No relationship exists because a person cannot sell his or her joint tenancy interest.

53. A tenant and landlord enter into a six-month oral lease. If the tenant defaults, the landlord

    (A) may not bring a court action because leases must be in writing for a court to review them.
    (B) may not bring a court action because the statute of frauds governs six-month leases.
    (C) may bring a court action because six-month leases need not be in writing to be enforceable.
    (D) may bring a court action because the statute of limitations does not apply to oral leases, regardless of their term.

54. On Monday, the buyer offers to purchase a vacant lot for $10,500. On Tuesday, the owner counteroffers to sell the lot for $12,000. On Friday, the owner withdraws the counteroffer and accepts the buyer's original offer of $10,500. Under these circumstances

(A) a valid agreement exists because the seller accepted the buyer's offer exactly as it was made, regardless of the fact that it was not accepted immediately.
(B) a valid agreement exists because the seller accepted before the buyer provided notice that the offer was withdrawn.
(C) no valid agreement exists because the buyer's offer was not accepted within 72 hours of its having been made.
(D) no valid agreement exists because the seller's counteroffer was a rejection of the buyer's offer and, once rejected, cannot be accepted later.

55. The neighbors use your driveway to reach their garage, which is on their property. Your attorney explains that the neighbors have the right to use the driveway. Your property is the

(A) dominant tenement.
(B) servient tenement.
(C) fee simple defeasible estate.
(D) fee simple determinable estate.

56. If the quarterly interest at 7.5% is $562.50, what is the principal amount of the loan?

(A) $ 7,500   (C) $30,000
(B) $15,000   (D) $75,000

57. A deed conveys ownership to the grantee "as long as the existing building is not torn down." What type of estate does this deed create?

(A) Fee simple determinable estate
(B) Homestead estate
(C) Fee simple absolute estate
(D) Life estate pur autre vie, with the measuring life being the building's expected structural lifetime

58. If the mortgage loan is 80% of the appraised value of a house and the interest rate of 8% amounts to $460 for the first month, what is the appraised value of the house?

(A) $69,000   (C) $86,250
(B) $71,875   (D) $92,875

59. Local zoning ordinances may **NOT** regulate which of the following?

(A) Height of buildings in an area
(B) Density of population
(C) Appropriate use of buildings in an area
(D) Market value of a property

60. A broker took a listing and later discovered that a court had declared the client incompetent. What is the current status of the listing?

(A) The listing is unaffected because the broker acted in good faith as the owner's agent.
(B) The listing is void.
(C) The listing entitles the broker to collect a commission from the client's guardian or trustee if the broker produces a buyer.
(D) The listing must be renegotiated between the broker and the client, based on the new information.

61. After a borrower's default on home mortgage loan payments, the lender obtained a court order to foreclose on the property. At the foreclosure sale, the property sold for $64,000; the unpaid balance on the loan at the time of foreclosure was $78,000. What must the lender do to recover the $14,000 that the borrower still owes?

(A) Sue for specific performance
(B) Sue for damages
(C) Seek a deficiency judgment
(D) Seek a judgment by default

62. Which of the following is **NOT** an exemption to the federal Fair Housing Act of 1968?

    (A) The sale of a single-family home where the property is not advertised by the listing broker
    (B) The restriction of noncommercial lodgings by a private club to members of the club
    (C) The rental of a unit in an owner-occupied three-family dwelling where an advertisement is placed in the paper
    (D) The restriction of noncommercial housing in a convent where a certified statement has not been filed with the government

63. A buyer purchases a $37,000 property, depositing $3,000 as earnest money. If the buyer obtains a 75% loan-to-value loan on the property, no additional items are prorated and there are no closing costs to the buyer, how much more cash will the buyer need at the settlement?

    (A) $3,250   (C) $5,250
    (B) $3,500   (D) $6,250

64. A broker arrives to present a purchase offer to the seller who is seriously ill and finds the owner's son and daughter-in-law also present. The son and daughter-in-law angrily urge the owner to accept the offer, even though it is much less than the asking price for the property. If the owner accepts the offer, she may not be bound by it because

    (A) the broker improperly presented an offer that was less than the asking price.
    (B) the broker's failure to protect the seller from the son and daughter-in-law constituted a violation of the broker's fiduciary duties.
    (C) the seller's rights under the ADA have been violated by the son and daughter-in-law.
    (D) the seller was under undue influence from the son and daughter-in-law, so the contract is voidable.

65. An owner sold a property to a buyer. The deed of conveyance contained only the following guarantee: "This property was not encumbered during the time seller owned it except as noted in this deed." What type of deed did the seller give to the buyer?

    (A) General warranty
    (B) Special warranty
    (C) Bargain and sale
    (D) Quitclaim

66. The practice of refusing to make mortgage loans or issue insurance policies in specific areas because of the racial or religious make up of the area is

    (A) a legal practice called hypothecation.
    (B) an illegal practice called blockbusting.
    (C) a reasonable business practice to protect the lender/insurance company.
    (D) an illegal practice called redlining.

67. A buyer agrees to purchase a house for $84,500. He pays $2,000 as earnest money and obtains a new mortgage loan for $67,600. The purchase contract provides for a March 15 settlement. The buyer and the sellers prorate the year's real estate taxes of $1,880.96, which have not been paid. The buyer has additional closing costs of $1,250, and the sellers have other closing costs of $850. How much cash must the buyer bring to the settlement? Use a banker's year. Round *up* to nearest dollar.

    (A) $15,759   (C) $17,639
    (B) $16,389   (D) $17,839

68. A broker listed a house for $47,900. A member of a racial minority group saw the house and was interested in it. When the prospective buyer asked the broker the price of the house, the broker said it was listed for $53,000 and that the seller was very firm on the price. Under the federal Fair Housing Act of 1968, such a statement is

    (A) legal because the law requires only that the buyer be given the opportunity to buy the house.
    (B) legal because the representation was made by the broker and not directly by the owner.
    (C) illegal because the difference in the offering price and the quoted price was greater than 10%.
    (D) illegal because the terms of the potential sale were changed for the prospective buyer.

69. A property owner placed a property in a trust. When she died, her will directed the trustee to sell the property and distribute the proceeds of the sale to her heirs. The trustee sold property in accordance with the will. What type of deed was delivered at settlement?

    (A) Trustee's deed
    (B) Trustor's deed
    (C) Deed in trust
    (D) Reconveyance deed

70. An appraiser has been hired to prepare an appraisal report of a property for loan purposes. The property is an elegant old mansion that is now used as a restaurant. To which approach to value should the appraiser probably give the greatest weight when making this appraisal?

    (A) Income
    (B) Sales comparison
    (C) Replacement cost
    (D) Reproduction cost

71. A borrower applies for a mortgage, and the loan officer suggests that the borrower might consider a term mortgage loan. Which of the following statements **BEST** explains what the loan officer means?

    (A) All of the interest is paid at the end of the term.
    (B) The debt is partially amortized over the life of the loan.
    (C) The length of the term is limited by state law.
    (D) The entire principal amount is due at the end of the term.

72. Valley Place is a condominium community with a swimming pool, tennis courts and biking trail. These facilities are **MOST** likely owned by the

    (A) Valley Place condominium board.
    (B) corporation in which the unit owners hold stock.
    (C) unit owners in the form of proportional divided interests.
    (D) unit owners in the form of undivided percentage interests.

In questions 73 and 74, identify how each item would be entered on a closing statement in a typical real estate transaction.

73. Buyer's earnest money deposit

    (A) Credit to buyer only
    (B) Credit to seller, debit to buyer
    (C) Credit to buyer and seller
    (D) Debit to buyer only

74. Prepaid insurance and tax reserves, where the buyer assumes the mortgage

    (A) Credit to buyer, debit to seller
    (B) Credit to seller only
    (C) Debit to seller only
    (D) Debit to buyer, credit to seller

75. The seller tells the listing broker that the roof leaks in hard rains and that the previous tenant in the house died of AIDS. When the broker takes the listing, what if anything must the broker tell prospective buyers?

    (A) Disclose the AIDS death only
    (B) Disclose the leaking roof only
    (C) Disclose both the AIDS death and the leaking roof
    (D) The broker is not obligated to disclose either item.

76. Which of the following is required by HUD in any place of business where real estate is offered for sale or rent?

    (A) Sign with broker's name larger than name of company
    (B) Poster stating that broker is equal opportunity employer
    (C) Fair housing poster
    (D) Sign with REALTOR® in larger letters

77. What is the cost of constructing a fence 6 feet, 6 inches high around a lot measuring 90 feet by 175 feet if the cost of erecting the fence is $1.25 per linear foot and the cost of materials is $.825 per square foot of fence?

    (A) $1,752   (C) $2,084
    (B) $2,054   (D) $3,505

78. An owner signs a listing agreement with a broker. Another broker obtains a buyer for the house, and the listing broker does not receive a commission. The listing broker does not sue the owner, even though the other broker was compensated. The listing agreement between the seller and the first broker was probably which of the following?

    (A) Exclusive right to sell
    (B) Open
    (C) Exclusive agency
    (D) Dual agency

79. Antitrust laws do **NOT** prohibit which of the following?

    (A) Real estate companies agreeing on fees charged to sellers
    (B) Real estate brokers allocating markets based on the value of homes
    (C) Real estate companies allocating markets based on the location of commercial buildings
    (D) Real estate salespersons within the same office agreeing on a standard commission rate

80. A tenant leased an apartment from a landlord. Because the landlord failed to perform routine maintenance, the apartment building's central heating plant broke down in the fall. The landlord neglected to have the heating system repaired, and the tenant had no heat for the first six weeks of winter. Although eight months remained on the tenant's lease, he moved out of the apartment and refused to pay any rent. If the landlord sues to recover the outstanding rent, which of the following would be the tenant's **BEST** defense?

    (A) Because the tenant lived in the apartment for more than 25% of the lease term, he was entitled to move out at any time without penalty.
    (B) The tenant was entitled to vacate the premises because the landlord's failure to repair the heating system constituted abandonment.
    (C) Because the apartment was made uninhabitable, the landlord's actions constituted actual eviction.
    (D) The landlord's actions constituted constructive eviction.

81. Title to real estate can be transferred at death by which of the following documents?

    (A) Warranty deed
    (B) Special warranty deed
    (C) Trustee's deed
    (D) Will

82. A bachelor died owning real estate that he devised by his will to his niece. In essence, at what point do title and possession pass to his niece?

(A) Immediately upon the bachelor's death
(B) After his will has been probated
(C) After the niece has paid all inheritance taxes
(D) When the niece executes a new deed to the property

83. An owner of real estate was declared legally incompetent and was committed to a state mental institution. While institutionalized, the owner wrote and executed a will. The owner later died and was survived by a spouse and three children. The real estate will pass

(A) to the owner's spouse.
(B) to the heirs mentioned in the owner's will.
(C) according to the state laws of descent.
(D) to the state.

84. When title to trust property is transferred back to the trustor by the trustee, which of the following deeds is used?

(A) Trustee's deed
(B) Trustor's deed
(C) Deed of transfer
(D) Reconveyance deed

85. Where does a probate proceeding involving real property properly take place?

(A) In the county where the trustee resides
(B) In the county in which the decedent resided and/or in which the property is located
(C) In the county in which the heir resides
(D) In the county in which the executor resides

86. Which of the following items are usually **NOT** designated on the plat for a new subdivision?

(A) Easements for sewer and water mains
(B) Land to be used for streets
(C) Numbered lots and blocks
(D) Prices of residential and commercial lots

87. A subdivision features spacious homes grouped on large cul-de-sac blocks connected to a central, winding road and surrounded by large, landscaped common areas. This is an example of which type of subdivision plan?

(A) Cluster plan
(B) Curvilinear system
(C) Rectangular street system
(D) Gridiron system

88. A subdivider can increase the amount of open or recreational space in a development by

(A) varying street patterns.
(B) meeting local housing standards.
(C) scattering housing units.
(D) eliminating multistory dwellings.

89. To protect the public from fraudulent interstate land sales, a developer involved in interstate land sales of 25 or more lots **MUST**

(A) provide each purchaser with a printed report disclosing details of the property.
(B) pay the prospective buyer's expenses to see the property involved.
(C) provide preferential financing.
(D) allow a 30-day cancellation period.

90. A woman grants a life estate to her son-in-law and stipulates that upon his death the title to the property will pass to her grandson. This second estate is known as

(A) a remainder.
(B) a reversion.
(C) an estate at sufferance.
(D) an estate for years.

■ ANSWER KEY WITH EXPLANATIONS

1. (B) Liens are monetary charges against the property. The lender records the mortgage as security for the loan. Easements, encroachments and deed restrictions are encumbrances on the property; they are not monetary.

2. (B) The broker is engaging in the illegal practice of blockbusting. The broker is trying to induce homeowners to sell their properties by making representations regarding the entry or prospective entry of persons of a particular race or national origin into the neighborhood.

3. (A) Depositing client money into the broker's personal checking account is the illegal practice of commingling funds. Brokers must deposit client funds into a special trust or escrow account.

4. (B) Brokers and salespeople must be cautious that they do not engage in the unauthorized practice of law. The salesperson should refer such questions as to how to take title to an appropriate attorney.

5. (C) The borrower's interest rate is 8.25%.
    [$412.50 × 12] ÷ $60,000 = .0825 or 8.25%

6. (B) The buyer has committed to working with only one broker/agent. However, the buyer has reserved the right to locate the property and thus not have to pay the agent.

7. (A) A general warranty deed contains the most covenants and offers the most protection to the grantee.

8. (A) The broker's policy is steering and violates the fair housing laws regardless of the motivation.

9. (C) A certificate of occupancy is issued after a new home has been constructed. The local government verifies that the building meets the requirements for kinds of materials and standards of workmanship.

10. (D) A salesperson or broker will compile a competitive market analysis (CMA) to assist the seller in determining an asking price. The CMA is a comparison of the prices of recently sold homes that are similar to a listing seller's home in terms of location, style and amenities.

11. (D) The IRS allows a real estate broker to treat his or her salespeople as independent contractors providing that all three conditions are met: The salesperson must hold a real estate license; a large percentage of the salesperson's income is directly related to sales made, not hours worked; and finally, a written agreement between the two parties states that the salesperson will be treated as an independent contractor for tax purposes.

12. (A) When evaluating an older home in an older neighborhood, the appraiser will give most weight to the sales comparison approach.

13. (B) Tenancy for years is a nonfreehold estate, i.e., a leasehold estate. It is characterized by a specific beginning and specific termination date. Neither the deaths of either landlord or tenant nor the sale of the property will terminate the lease.

14. (A) Outdated plumbing is an example of functional obsolescence because it no longer complies with current standards.

15. (A) When zoning changes in an area, generally, existing uses are permitted to remain as nonconforming uses. This is often called "grandfathering." Each local area has rules for how long and under what conditions the nonconforming use may remain.

16. (C) The property sold for $79,800.
[$2,593.50 × 2] ÷ 6.5% = $79,800

17. (D) Because the broker is working with both buyer and seller and is not an agent of either, the broker is acting as a transactional broker. Transactional brokerage is nonagency and is not recognized or permitted in every state.

18. (C) Reconciliation is the final step in the appraisal process in which the appraiser combines the estimates of value received from the sales comparison, cost, and income approaches to arrive at a final estimate of market value for the subject property.

19. (A) The selling salesperson received $1,139.78.
$95,900 × 7% × 50% × 35% − $35 = $1,139.78
(Remember to reread the problem to ensure that you have included all the variables, in this case, remembering to subtract the $35 for expenses.)

20. (B) Conspiring to fix prices is a violation of the antitrust laws and can cost the offender up to $100,000 in fines and up to three years' imprisonment.

21. (D) The seller's gross sales price has to be at least $69,149.
$65,000 ÷ .94 = $69,149

22. (A) Generally, the contract is voidable at the option of the party under duress. The contract is binding on the party who caused the duress. The party under duress may be able to terminate the contract.

23. (B) The buyer borrows money from the lender; thus, the buyer is the mortgagor, the lender is the mortgagee.

24. (B) The tax due is $960.
[$40,000 × 40%] × 1.5 = $24,000
$24,000 ÷ 100 × 4 = $960.

25. (C) The total cash needed is $6,540.
$60,000 × .90 = $54,000
[$54,000 × 1%] + $6,000 = $6,540

26. (C) The market value of the vacant land is $323,000.
$274,550 ÷ .85 = $323,000

27. (B) The capitalization rate is the rate of return a property will produce on the owner's investment. It is determined by dividing the net income by the value. The lower the cap rate, the higher the value, and vice versa.

28. (C) The broker will receive $14,000.
It is important to notice the word *and.*
640 ÷ 4 = 160 *and* 640 ÷ 4 = 160
[320 × $875] × 5% = $14,000

29. (C) The points are calculated on the amount of the loan and are $1,540.
$38,500 × 4% = $1,540

30. (B) $50,000 × 7.75% = $3,875
(Remember that the easy way to change fractions to decimals is to divide the top by the bottom: 3 ÷ 4 = .75)

31. (D) Another offer will **NOT** automatically terminate the first buyer's offer. However, an offer will automatically be terminated by the death of the offeror, a revocation, or a counteroffer (rejection) by the seller.

32. (D) The seller retains actual title but the buyer has an equitable ownership interest in the property.

33. (B) A novation is the process of substituting new parties to an existing obligation or substituting a new obligation for an old one.

34. (B) He borrowed $4,000. Read the question very carefully.

35. (B) Both parties, buyers and sellers, must sign to have a valid contract.

36. (A) Until the lender files the documentation stating that the note has been satisfied, a lien will remain on the property.

37. (D) The property has a value of $275,000.
$22,000 ÷ 8\% = \$275,000$

38. (B) The commission is based on the proceeds above the agreed-upon seller's net. This type of listing is illegal in many states.

39. (A) In a cooperative form of ownership, an owner is a shareholder in the corporation, receiving a proprietary lease to a specific apartment.

40. (A) A quitclaim deed would clear the cloud.

41. (D) Under an exclusive-agency buyer agency agreement with a licensee, if the buyer finds a property on his or her own, the buyer is not obligated to compensate the agent. The buyer may approach a for sale by owner.

42. (B) Under a net lease, the tenant is responsible for paying all or part of the taxes, insurance and maintenance. The building owner is responsible for the mortgage payment.

43. (C) The Civil Rights Act of 1866 prohibits racial discrimination. The law has been reaffirmed by *Jones v. Mayer* to prohibit all racial discrimination, private as well as public. There are no exemptions!

44. (C) In a balloon loan, the remaining balance "balloons" at a specific point in the future.

45. (D) A specific lien is a lien against only one parcel of real estate, while a general lien covers all of a debtor's property.

46. (D) The seller (optionor) would be required to sell but the buyer (optionee) has the choice (option) to buy or not to buy.

47. (C) The government has police powers that include taking private property for the public good. However, the government must pay a fair market value for the property it takes.

48. (D) The principle of substitution states that the maximum value of a property tends to be set by how much it would cost to purchase an equally desirable and valuable property. This concept is the principle on which the sales comparison approach is based.

49. (B) The value of a smaller home in an area of larger homes is enhanced (progresses) by the proximity and desirability of the larger properties.

50. (B) After a judgment has been entered and recorded with the county recorder, it generally becomes a general lien of the defendant and thus applies to all the property owned, both real and personal.

51. (B) If the property is destroyed, the contract to purchase is terminated. A meeting of the minds (a.k.a. mutual agreement) between the buyer and seller creates a legally binding and enforceable contract, which does not allow for changing one's mind without penalties. The contract is legally binding on the heirs and assigns.

52. (B) One can always sell what one owns. However, in doing so, the person who sold destroyed three of the unities required for joint tenancy: interest, time and title. Thus, the new owner is a tenant in common with the original owner.

53. (C) In most states, an oral lease for less than one year can be enforced.

54. (D) No valid agreement exists because the seller's counteroffer is a rejection of the buyer's offer and, once rejected, cannot be accepted later.

55. (B) Your property is the servient tenement; i.e., it "serves" the neighbor's property.

56. (C) The principal amount of the loan is $30,000.
[$562.50 × 4] ÷ 7.5% = $30,000

57. (A) The deed containing a clause that will determine its future use transfers a fee simple determinable estate.

58. (C) The appraised value of the house is $86,250.
[$460 × 12] ÷ 8% ÷ 80% = $86,250

59. (D) Zoning is not designed to establish price controls. Zoning ordinances may regulate building heights, population density and the appropriate use of buildings in the area.

60. (B) The listing is void because the court has already determined that the owner is incompetent to make a decision. A valid contract must be signed by competent parties.

61. (C) The lender can seek a deficiency judgment to recover the difference between the amount owed and the amount recovered at the sale.

62. (A) Under no circumstances are real estate licensees exempt from any portion of the fair housing law. Once the property is listed with a broker, the individual seller is no longer exempt from the act.

63. (D) The buyer will need to bring an additional $6,250 to settlement.
[$37,000 × 25%] – $3,000 = $6,250

64. (D) A contract signed under duress is voidable.

65. (B) Under a special warranty deed, the owner only warrants the property for the period of time he or she owned the property.

66. (D) Redlining is the illegal practice of refusing to make mortgage loans or issue insurance policies in specific areas because of the racial or religious makeup of the area.

67. (A) The buyer must bring $15,759 to the closing.
First, find the total debits for the buyer:
$84,500 + $1,250 = $85,750.
Then, find the total credits for the buyer:
$2,000 + $67,600 + [$1,880.96 ÷ 360 × 75] = $69,991.87.
Subtract the credits from the debits to arrive at the amount that the buyer must bring to closing: $85,750 – $69,991.87 = $15,758.13 or $15,759.
(Remember, there is no line reference to a down payment on a closing statement.)

68. (D) Federal fair housing laws prohibit changing terms and conditions based on any of the protected categories.

69. (A) The trustee signs a trustee's deed to transfer the property out of the trust.

70. (A) Although the property is unique, because it generates income, the appraiser will give the greatest weight to the income approach.

71. (D) A term loan is characterized by interest only payments during the term and by the entire principal being due at the end of the term.

72. (D) Each condominium unit owner has an undivided percentage interest in the common areas.

73. (A) The earnest money is a credit against the total amount that the buyer needs to bring to closing.

74. (D) When the buyer assumes the mortgage, the prepaid insurance and tax reserves are debit to the buyer, credit to the seller.

75. (B) The leaking roof is a material defect and must be disclosed to all prospective buyers. Federal fair housing laws prohibit discussion or disclosure of the AIDS-related death.

76. (C) HUD requires a fair housing poster with the equal housing logo prominently displayed in any place of business where real estate is offered for sale or rent.

77. (D) The cost is $3,505.
$[90 + 90 + 175 + 175] \times 6.5 = 3,445$ square feet of fence $\times \$.825 = \$2,842.125$ materials cost $[90 + 90 + 175 + 175] \times \$1.25 = \$662.50$ installation cost
$\$2,842.125 + \$662.50 = \$3,504.625$ or $\$3,505$

78. (B) In an open listing, the only agent who gets paid is the one who produces the buyer.

79. (D) A company can set its own commission structure.

80. (D) Failure to provide heat during the winter season constitutes constructive eviction. The landlord has an obligation to make the property habitable.

81. (D) A will is the instrument to transfer property at death.

82. (B) Title and possession pass to the niece by the probate court that validates the will and authenticates the transfer.

83. (C) Once a person has been declared legally incompetent, the person may not enter into any binding contracts, including writing a will. Thus, his or her property is distributed by the state laws of descent. The property does not escheat to the state because the owner died leaving heirs (spouse and children).

84. (D) The trustee conveys the property back to the trustor with a reconveyance deed.

85. (B) The probate will occur in the county in which the deceased lived or the location of the property.

86. (D) The plat would not address prices of residential and commercial lots.

87. (A) By clustering the housing units, the developer can increase the amount of open space.

88. (A) By slightly reducing lot sizes and clustering them around varying street plans, the development can increase the open space over traditional subdividing plans.

89. (A) The developer involved in interestate land sales of 25 or more lots must provide each purchaser with a printed report disclosing details of the property. This prevents developers from selling lots from a map to people who never get to see the lot they are actually buying.

90. (A) The son-in-law holds a life estate and the grandson holds a remainder estate, which he receives upon the death of the son-in-law.

■ BROKER EXAM #2

1. A tenant's landlord has sold the building in which the tenant lives to the state so that a freeway can be built. The tenant's lease has expired, but the landlord permits the tenant to stay in the apartment until the building is torn down. The tenant continues to pay the rent as prescribed in the lease. What kind of tenancy does this tenant have?

   (A) Holdover tenancy
   (B) Month-to-month tenancy
   (C) Tenancy at sufferance
   (D) Tenancy at will

2. The landlord of an apartment building neglected to repair the building's plumbing system. As a result, the apartments did not receive water, as provided by the leases. If a tenant's unit becomes uninhabitable, which of the following would **MOST** likely result?

   (A) Suit for possession
   (B) Claim of constructive eviction
   (C) Tenancy at sufferance
   (D) Suit for negligence

3. An owner is interested in selling his house as quickly as possible and believes that the best way to do this is to have several brokers compete against each other for the commission. The owner's listing agreements with four different brokers specifically promise that if one of them finds a buyer for his property, the owner will be obligated to pay a commission to that broker only. What type of agreement has the owner entered into?

   (A) Executed   (C) Unilateral
   (B) Discharged   (D) Bilateral

4. For each new tenant that the property manager signs, a building's owner pays an 8½ percent commission, based on the unit's annualized rent. Last year, the manager signed five new tenants. Three of the apartments rented for $795 per month; one rented for $1,200 per month; and one rented for $900 per month. What was the total amount of the manager's new-tenant commissions for that year?

   (A) $ 381.23   (C) $3,685.47
   (B) $2,952.90   (D) $4,574.70

5. The owner of a ranch enters into a sale-and-leaseback agreement with a buyer. Which of the following statements is **TRUE** of this arrangement?

   (A) The owner retains title to the ranch.
   (B) The buyer receives possession of the property.
   (C) The buyer is the lessor.
   (D) The owner is the lessor.

6. A real estate broker employed a buyer. When the broker finds a property the buyer might be interested in buying, he is careful to find out as much as possible about the property's owners and why their property is on the market. The broker's efforts to keep the buyer informed of all facts that could affect a transaction is the duty of

   (A) accounting.   (C) confidentiality.
   (B) loyalty.   (D) disclosure.

7. Which of the following are **NOT** violations of the Real Estate Settlement Procedures Act (RESPA)?

   (A) Providing a HUD-1 Uniform Settlement Statement to a borrower one day before the closing
   (B) Accepting a kickback on a loan subject to RESPA requirements
   (C) Requiring a particular title insurance company as a requirement of the sale
   (D) Accepting a fee or charging for services that were not performed

8. Which of the following situations does **NOT** violate the federal Fair Housing Act of 1968?

   (A) The refusal of a property manager to rent an apartment to a Catholic couple who are otherwise qualified
   (B) The general policy of a loan company to avoid granting home improvement loans to individuals living in transitional neighborhoods
   (C) The intentional neglect of a broker to show an Asian family any property listings in all-white neighborhoods
   (D) A widowed woman's insistence on renting her spare bedroom only to another widowed woman

9. If a storage tank that measures 12 feet by 9 feet by 8 feet is designed to store a gas that costs $1.82 per cubic foot, what does it cost to fill the tank to one-half of its capacity?

   (A) $685   (C) $ 864
   (B) $786   (D) $1,572

10. A buyer bought a house for $125,000. The house, which had originally sold for $118,250, appraised for $122,500. Based on these facts, if the buyer applies for an 80 percent mortgage, what will be the amount of the loan?

   (A) $94,600   (C) $100,000
   (B) $98,000   (D) $106,750

11. A purchaser offers to buy a seller's property by signing a purchase contract. The seller accepts the offer. What kind of title interest does the buyer have in the property at this point?

   (A) Legal
   (B) Equitable
   (C) Defeasible
   (D) The buyer has no title interest at this point.

12. Which of the following federal laws requires that finance charges be stated as an annual percentage rate?

   (A) Truth-in-Lending Act
   (B) Real Estate Settlement Procedures Act
   (C) Equal Credit Opportunity Act
   (D) Federal Fair Housing Act

13. A seller signed a 90-day listing agreement with a broker. Two weeks later, the seller was killed in an accident. What is the present status of the listing?

   (A) The listing agreement is binding on the seller's estate for the remainder of the 90 days.
   (B) Because the seller's intention to sell was clearly defined, the listing agreement is still in effect and the broker may proceed to market the property on behalf of the seller's estate.
   (C) The listing agreement is binding on the seller's estate only if the broker can produce an offer to purchase the property within the remainder of the listing period.
   (D) The listing agreement was terminated automatically when the seller died.

14. A woman conveys the ownership of an office building to a nursing home. The nursing home agrees that the rental income will pay for the expenses of caring for her parents. When her parents die, ownership of the office building will revert back to her. The estate held by the nursing home is a

   (A) remainder life estate.
   (B) legal life estate.
   (C) life estate pur autre vie.
   (D) temporary leasehold estate.

15. On a settlement statement, the cost of the lender's title insurance policy required for a new loan is usually shown as which of the following?

   (A) Credit to the seller
   (B) Credit to the buyer
   (C) Debit to the seller
   (D) Debit to the buyer

16. In a township of 36 sections, which of the following statements is **TRUE?**

   (A) Section 31 lies to the east of Section 32.
   (B) Section 18 is by law set aside for school purposes.
   (C) Section 6 lies in the northeast corner of the township.
   (D) Section 16 lies to the north of Section 21.

17. A licensee who is representing a seller is asked by the client to make sure that the deed does not reveal the actual sales price. In this case, the licensee

   (A) must inform the client that only the actual price of the real estate may appear on the deed.
   (B) may ask that a deed be prepared that shows only nominal consideration of $10.
   (C) should inform the seller that either the full price should be stated in the deed or all references to consideration should be removed from it.
   (D) may show a price on the deed other than the actual price, provided that the variance is not greater than 10% of the purchase price.

18. A broker obtained a listing agreement to act as the agent in the sale of a house. A buyer has been found for the property, and all agreements have been signed. As an agent for the seller, the broker is responsible for which of the following?

(A) Completing the buyer's loan application
(B) Making sure that the buyer receives copies of all documents the seller is required to deliver to the buyer
(C) Ensuring that the buyer is qualified for the new mortgage loan
(D) Scheduling the buyer's inspection of the property

19. A broker's office policy is that the salesperson's share of a commission is 65 percent. What is the salesperson's compensation if the sales price of a property is $195,000 and the broker is entitled to a 7½% commission?

(A) $ 950.63   (C) $ 9,506.25
(B) $8,872.50   (D) $95,062.50

20. Which of the following is one of the components an appraiser would use in preparing a cost-approach appraisal?

(A) Estimate the replacement cost of the improvements
(B) Deduct for the depreciation of the land and buildings
(C) Determine the original cost and adjust for depreciation
(D) Review the sales prices of comparable properties

21. When a mortgage lender provides the buyer and seller with statements of all fees and charges they will incur, the lender is complying with which of the following federal laws?

(A) Equal Credit Opportunity Act
(B) Truth-in-Lending Act (Regulation Z)
(C) Real Estate Settlement Procedures Act
(D) Fair Housing Act

22. The owner of a house wants to fence the yard for the family pet. When the fence is erected, the fencing materials become real estate through

(A) severance.   (C) annexation.
(B) subrogation.   (D) attachment.

23. A person conveys a life estate to his sister. Under the terms of the conveyance, the property will pass to his daughter on his sister's death. Which of the following BEST describes the daughter's interest in the property during the sister's lifetime?

(A) Remainder
(B) Reversion
(C) Life estate pur autre vie
(D) Redemption

24. On a settlement statement, prorations for real estate taxes paid in arrears are shown as a

(A) credit to the seller and a debit to the buyer.
(B) debit to the seller and a credit to the buyer.
(C) credit to both the seller and the buyer.
(D) debit to both the seller and the buyer.

25. A purchaser buys a house for $234,500 by making a $25,000 cash down payment and taking out a $209,500 mortgage for 30 years. The lot value is $80,000. If the purchaser wants to depreciate the property over a period of 27½ years, how much will be the annual depreciation amount using the straight-line method?

(A) $3,818.18   (C) $5,618.18
(B) $4,709.09   (D) $8,527.27

26. A conventional loan was closed on July 1 for $57,200 at 13.5% interest amortized over 25 years at $666.75 per month. Using a 360-day year, what would the principal amount be after the monthly payment was made August 1?

(A) $56,533.25   (C) $57,065.35
(B) $56,556.50   (D) $57,176.75

27. A conventional loan was closed on July 1 for $57,200 at 13.5% interest amortized over 25 years at $666.75 per month. Using a 360-day year, what would the interest portion of the August 1 payment?

(A) $610.65   (C) $643.50
(B) $620.25   (D) $666.75

28. A seller listed her home with a licensee for $90,000 but tells the licensee, who is acting as a seller's agent, "I've got to sell quickly because of a job transfer. If necessary, I can accept a price as low as $75,000." The licensee tells a prospective buyer to offer $80,000 "because the seller is desperate to sell." The seller accepts the buyer's offer. In this situation, which of the following statements is **TRUE?**

(A) The licensee's action did not violate any agency relationship with the seller because the licensee did not actually reveal the seller's lowest acceptable price.
(B) The licensee violated an established agency relationship with the seller.
(C) The licensee acted properly to obtain a quick offer on the seller's property, in accordance with the seller's instructions.
(D) The licensee violated established fiduciary duties toward the buyer by failing to disclose that the seller would accept a lower price than the buyer offered.

29. Which of the following **BEST** describes the capitalization rate under the income approach to estimating the value of real estate?

(A) Rate at which a property increases in value
(B) Rate of return a property earns as an investment
(C) Rate of capital required to keep a property operating most efficiently
(D) Maximum rate of return allowed by law on an investment

30. In the course of a day, two consumers walk into a broker's office. A buyer signs a buyer's brokerage agreement under which the broker will help the buyer find a three-bedroom house in the $85,000 to $100,000 price range. A seller signs a listing agreement to sell her two-bedroom condominium for $70,000. Based on these facts, which of the following statements is **TRUE?**

(A) The buyer is a client; the seller is a customer.
(B) The buyer is the customer; the seller is the broker's client.
(C) While both the buyer and the seller are clients, the broker owes the fiduciary duties of an agent only to the seller.
(D) Because both the seller and the buyer are the broker's clients; the broker owes the fiduciary duties of an agent to both.

31. An FHA-insured loan in the amount of $57,500 at 8½ percent for 30 years was closed on June 17. The first monthly payment is due on September 1. Using a 360-day year and assuming that interest is being paid for the day of closing, what was the amount of the interest adjustment the buyer had to make at the settlement?

(A) $ 0   (C) $230.80
(B) $190.12   (D) $407.29

32. If a home that originally cost $142,500 three years ago is now valued at 127% of its original cost, what is its current market value?

(A) $164,025   (C) $174,310
(B) $172,205   (D) $180,975

33. A buyer makes an offer on a property, and the seller accepts. Three weeks later, the buyer announces that "the deal's off" and refuses to go through with the sale. If the seller is entitled to keep the buyer's earnest money deposit, it is **MOST** likely because there is what kind of clause in the sales contract?

(A) Liquidated damages clause
(B) Contingent damages clause
(C) Actual damages clause
(D) Revocation clause

34. A search of the public record regarding title to a property is **MOST** likely to provide information about which of the following?

    (A) Encroachments
    (B) Rights of parties in possession
    (C) Inaccurate survey
    (D) Mechanics' liens

35. A rectangular lot is worth $193,600. This value is the equivalent of $4.40 per square foot. If one lot dimension is 200 feet, what is the other dimension?

    (A) 110 feet   (C) 400 feet
    (B) 220 feet   (D) 880 feet

36. A broker listed a property at an 8% commission rate. After the property was sold and the settlement had taken place, the seller discovered that the broker had been listing similar properties at 6% commission rates. Based on this information, which of the following statements is **TRUE?**

    (A) The broker has done nothing wrong because a commission rate is always negotiable between the parties.
    (B) If the broker inflated the usual commission rate for the area, the broker may be subject to discipline by the state real estate commission.
    (C) The seller is entitled to rescind the transaction based on the principle of lack of reality of consent.
    (D) The seller is entitled to a refund from the broker of 2% of the commission.

37. A tenant has six months remaining on her apartment lease. Her monthly rent is $875. The tenant moves out of the apartment, and another person moves in. This person pays the original tenant a monthly rental of $700, while the original tenant continues paying the full rental amount under her lease to the landlord. When the original tenant's lease term expires, the new occupant will either move out or sign a new lease with the landlord. This is an example of

    (A) assignment.
    (B) subletting.
    (C) rescission and renewal.
    (D) surrender.

38. One broker asked another, "Will I have to prove that I was the procuring cause in order to collect a commission if my seller sells the property without my help?" The other broker answered, "No, not if you have an

    (A) option listing."
    (B) open listing."
    (C) exclusive-agency listing."
    (D) exclusive-right-to-sell listing."

39. The capitalization rate on a property reflects (among other things) which of the following factors?

    (A) Rate of return
    (B) Replacement cost of the improvements
    (C) Real estate taxes
    (D) Debt service

40. An investment property worth $180,000 was purchased seven years ago for $142,000. At the time of the purchase, the land was valued at $18,000. Assuming a 31.5 economic year life for straight-line depreciation purposes, what is the present book value of the property?

    (A) $ 95,071   (C) $114,444
    (B) $113,071   (D) $126,000

41. After a buyer purchased a property from an owner, they both decided to rescind the recorded transfer. To do this, which of the following must happen?

    (A) The buyer must return the deed to the owner.
    (B) The parties must record a notice of rescission.
    (C) The parties must simply destroy the original deed in the presence of witnesses.
    (D) The owner must make a new deed to the buyer.

42. A farmer owns the W½ of the NW¼ of the NW¼ of a section. The adjoining property can be purchased for $300 per acre. Owning all of the NW¼ of the section would cost the farmer

    (A) $ 6,000.   (C) $42,000.
    (B) $12,000.   (D) $48,000.

43. A broker received a deposit, along with a written offer from a buyer. The offer stated: "The offeror will leave this offer open for the seller's acceptance for a period of ten days." On the fifth day, and before acceptance by the seller, the offeror notified the broker that the offer was withdrawn and demanded the return of the deposit. Which of the following statements is **TRUE** in this situation?

    (A) The offeror cannot withdraw the offer; it must be held open for the full ten-day period, as promised.
    (B) The offeror has the right to withdraw the offer and secure the return of the deposit any time before being notified of the seller's acceptance.
    (C) The offeror can withdraw the offer, and the seller and the broker will each retain one-half of the forfeited deposit.
    (D) While the offeror can withdraw the offer, the broker is legally entitled to declare the deposit forfeited and retain all of it in lieu of the lost commission.

44. In some states, by paying the debt after a foreclosure sale, a borrower has the right to regain the property under which of the following?

    (A) Novation   (C) Reversion
    (B) Redemption   (D) Recovery

45. The monthly rent on a warehouse was $1 per cubic yard. Assuming the warehouse was 36 feet by 200 feet by 12 feet high, what would the annual rent be?

    (A) $3,200   (C) $ 38,400
    (B) $9,600   (D) $115,200

46. If a veteran wishes to refinance a home by changing to a VA-guaranteed loan and the lender insists on 3½ discount points, which of the following options is available to the veteran?

    (A) Refinance with a VA loan, provided the lender charges no discount points
    (B) Refinance with a VA loan, provided the lender charges no more than two discount points
    (C) Be required to pay a maximum of 1 percent of the loan as an origination fee
    (D) Proceed with the refinance loan and pay the discount points

47. The owner conveys one property to his sister with no restrictions. He conveys another property to his brother "so long as no alcohol is consumed on the premise." Which of the following is **TRUE?**

    (A) The sister's interest has a determinable fee.
    (B) The brother has a fee simple estate.
    (C) The owner has retained a right to reenter the property conveyed to his sister.
    (D) The owner retains a right of reentry into the property conveyed to his brother.

48. A real estate transaction had a closing date of November 15. The seller, who was responsible for costs up to and including the date of settlement, had already paid the property taxes of $1,116 for the calendar year. Using a banker's year on the closing statement, the buyer would be

    (A) debited $139.50.
    (B) debited $976.50.
    (C) credited $139.50.
    (D) credited $976.50.

49. An agreement that ends all future lessor-lessee obligations under a lease is known as

    (A) an assumption.   (C) a novation.
    (B) a surrender.   (D) a breach.

50. What type of lease establishes a rental payment and requires the lessor to pay for the taxes, insurance and maintenance on the property?

    (A) Percentage   (C) Expense-only
    (B) Net   (D) Gross

51. A property manager leased a store for three years. The first year, the store's rent was $1,000 per month, and the rent was to increase 10% per year thereafter. The manager received a 7% commission for the first year, 5% for the second year and 3% for the balance of the lease. The total commission earned by the property manager was

    (A) $ 840.   (C) $1,936.
    (B) $1,613.   (D) $2,785.

52. Against a recorded deed from the owner of record, the party with the weakest position is a

    (A) person with a prior unrecorded deed who is not in possession.
    (B) person in possession with a prior unrecorded deed.
    (C) tenant in possession with nine months remaining on the lease.
    (D) painter who is half-finished painting the house at the time of the sale and who has not yet been paid.

53. A married couple files their income taxes jointly. Last year they sold their home for $340,000. Seven years ago when they were first married they bought the house for $250,000. Based on these facts, which of the following statements is **TRUE?**

    (A) Under current tax law, the couple will owe a capital gains tax this year on their $90,000 gain.
    (B) Current tax law permits the couple to exclude up to $250,000 in capital gain from their income tax.
    (C) Because their gain is less than $500,000, the couple will owe no capital gains tax this year.
    (D) Under current tax law, the couple is entitled to a penalty-free withdrawal of up to $10,000 from a 401(k) retirement account to use as a down payment.

54. A squatter moved into an abandoned home and installed new cabinets in the kitchen. When the owner discovered the occupancy, the owner had the squatter ejected. What is the status of the kitchen cabinets?

    (A) The squatter has no right to the cabinets or their value.
    (B) The cabinets remain because they are trade fixtures.
    (C) Although the cabinets stay, the squatter is entitled to the value of the improvements.
    (D) The squatter is entitled to keep the cabinets if they can be removed without damaging the real estate.

55. Three people are joint tenants. One owner sells her interest to a fourth person, and then one of the original owners dies. As a result, which of the following statements is **TRUE?**

    (A) The deceased heirs are joint tenants with the remaining owners.
    (B) The deceased heirs and the other joint tenant are joint tenants, but the new owner is a tenant in common.
    (C) The other joint tenant is a tenant in common with the new owner and the deceased heirs.
    (D) The remaining owner and the new owner are tenants in common.

56. In a settlement statement, the selling price *always* is

    (A) a debit to the buyer.
    (B) a debit to the seller.
    (C) a credit to the buyer.
    (D) greater than the loan amount.

57. The state wants to acquire a strip of farmland to build a highway. Does the state have the right to acquire this land for public use?

    (A) Yes; the state's right is called *condemnation.*
    (B) Yes; the state's right is called *eminent domain.*
    (C) Yes; the state's right is called *escheat.*
    (D) No; under the U.S. Constitution, private property never may be taken by state governments or the federal government.

58. A person died and his estate was distributed according to his will as follows: 54% to his wife; 18% to his children; 16% to his grandchildren; and the remainder to his college. The college received $79,000. How much did the children receive?

    (A) $105,333   (C) $355,500
    (B) $118,500   (D) $658,333

59. Which of the following is an example of external obsolescence?

    (A) Numerous pillars supporting the ceiling in a store
    (B) Leaks in the roof of a warehouse, making the premises unusable and therefore unrentable
    (C) Coal cellar in a house with central heating
    (D) Vacant, abandoned and run-down buildings in an area

60. Which of the following phrases, when placed in a print advertisement, would comply with the requirements of the Truth-in-Lending Act (Regulation Z)?

    (A) "12% interest"
    (B) "12% rate"
    (C) "12% annual interest"
    (D) "12% annual percentage rate"

61. Which of the following is **NOT TRUE** regarding a capitalization rate?

    (A) The rate increases when the risk increases.
    (B) An increase in rate means a decrease in value.
    (C) The net income is divided by the rate to estimate value.
    (D) A decrease in rate results in a decrease in value.

62. The Equal Credit Opportunity Act (ECOA) makes it illegal for lenders to refuse credit to or otherwise discriminate against which of the following applicants?

    (A) Parent of twins who receives public assistance and who cannot afford the monthly mortgage payments
    (B) New homebuyer who does not have a credit history
    (C) Single person who receives public assistance
    (D) Unemployed person with no job prospects and no identifiable source of income

63. When a person died, a deed was found in his desk drawer. While the deed had never been recorded, it was signed, dated and acknowledged. The deed gave the house to a local charity. His will, however, provided as follows: "I leave all of the real and personal property that I own to my beloved nephew." In this situation, the house **MOST** likely will go to the

    (A) charity because acknowledgment creates a presumption of delivery.
    (B) charity because his intent was clear from the deed.
    (C) nephew because the deceased still owned the house when he died.
    (D) nephew because the deed had not been recorded.

64. If a borrower takes out a $90,000 loan at 7½ percent interest to be repaid at the end of 15 years with interest paid annually, what is the total interest that the borrower will pay over the life of the loan?

    (A) $10,125   (C) $101,250
    (B) $80,000   (D) $180,000

65. After an offer is accepted, the seller finds that the broker was the undisclosed agent for the buyer as well as the agent for the seller. The seller may

    (A) withdraw from the listing agreement without obligation to broker.
    (B) withdraw but would be subject to liquidated damages.
    (C) withdraw but only with the concurrence of the buyer.
    (D) refuse to sell but would be subject to a suit for specific performance.

66. To net the owner $90,000 after a 6% commission is paid, the sale price would have to be

    (A) $95,400.   (C) $95,906.
    (B) $95,745.   (D) $96,000.

67. Which of the following would **MOST** likely be legal under the provisions of the Civil Rights Act of 1968?

   (A) A lender refuses to make loans in areas where more than 25% of the population is Hispanic.
   (B) A private country club development ties home ownership to club membership, but due to local demographics, all club members are white.
   (C) A church excludes African Americans from membership and rents its nonprofit housing to church members only.
   (D) A licensee directs prospective buyers away from areas where they are likely to feel uncomfortable because of their race.

68. It is discovered after a sale that the land parcel is 10% smaller than the owner represented it to be. The licensee who passed this information on to the buyer is

   (A) not liable as long as the licensee only repeated the seller's data.
   (B) not liable if the misrepresentation was unintentional.
   (C) not liable if the buyer actually inspected the parcel.
   (D) liable if the licensee knew or should have known of the discrepancy.

69. On a residential lot 70 feet square, the side yard building setbacks are 10 feet, the front yard setback is 25 feet, and the rear yard setback is 20 feet. The maximum possible size for a single-story structure would be how many square feet?

   (A) 1,000   (C) 1,250
   (B) 1,200   (D) 4,900

70. A parcel of vacant land 80 feet wide and 200 feet deep was sold for $200 per front foot. How much money would a salesperson receive as a 60% share in the 10% commission?

   (A) $640   (C) $1,600
   (B) $960   (D) $2,400

71. The rescission provisions of the Truth-in-Lending Act (Regulation Z) apply to which of the following transactions?

   (A) Home purchase loans
   (B) Construction lending
   (C) Business financing
   (D) Consumer credit

72. A property has a net income of $30,000. An appraiser decides to use a 12% capitalization rate rather than a 10% rate on this property. The use of the higher rate results in

   (A) a 2% increase in the appraised value.
   (B) a $50,000 increase in the appraised value.
   (C) a $50,000 decrease in the appraised value.
   (D) no change in the appraised value.

73. The section in a purchase contract that would provide for the buyer to forfeit any earnest money if the buyer fails to complete the purchase is known as a provision for

   (A) liquidated damages.
   (B) punitive damages.
   (C) hypothecation.
   (D) subordination.

74. In one commercial building, the tenant intends to start a small health food shop. In an identical adjacent building is a showroom leased to a major national retailing chain. Both tenants have long-term leases with identical rents. Which of the following statements is **TRUE?**

   (A) If the values of the buildings were the same before the leases, the values will be the same after the leases.
   (B) An appraiser would most likely use a higher capitalization rate for the store leased to the national retailing chain.
   (C) The most accurate appraisal method an appraiser could use would be the sales comparison approach to value.
   (D) The building with the health food shop will probably appraise for less than the other building.

75. An insurance company agreed to provide a developer with financing for a shopping center at 11% interest plus an equity position. What type of loan is this?

(A) Package   (C) Open end
(B) Participation   (D) Blanket

76. A $100,000 loan at 12% could be amortized with monthly payments of $1,200.22 on a 15-year basis or payments of $1,028.63 on a 30-year basis. The 30-year loan results in total payments of what percent of the 15-year total payments?

(A) 146 percent   (C) 171 percent
(B) 158 percent   (D) 228 percent

77. According to a broker's CMA, a property is worth $125,000. The homeowner bought the property for $90,000 and added $50,000 in improvements, for a total of $140,000. The property sold for $122,500. Which of these amounts represents the property's market value?

(A) $ 90,000   (C) $125,500
(B) $122,500   (D) $140,000

78. What will be the amount of tax payable where the property's assessed value is $85,000 and the tax rate is 40 mills in a community in which an equalization factor of 110% is used?

(A) $2,337.50   (C) $3,700.40
(B) $3,090.91   (D) $3,740.00

79. In a settlement statement, how will a proration of prepaid water, gas and electric charges be reflected?

(A) Debit to the seller, credit to the buyer
(B) Debit to the buyer, credit to the seller
(C) Debit to the buyer only
(D) Credit to the seller only

80. An apartment manager decides not to purchase flood insurance. Instead, the manager installs raised platforms in the basement storage areas and has the furnace placed on eight-inch legs. This form of risk management is known as

(A) avoiding the risk.
(B) controlling the risk.
(C) retaining the risk.
(D) transferring the risk.

81. Public land-use controls do **NOT** include which of the following?

(A) Subdivision regulations
(B) Restrictive covenants
(C) Environmental protection laws
(D) Comprehensive plan specifications

82. Under its police powers, a town may **NOT** legally regulate which of the following?

(A) The number of buildings
(B) The size of buildings
(C) The type of building materials
(D) What kind of people may live in a building

83. The purpose of a building permit is to

(A) assert a deed's restrictive covenant.
(B) maintain municipal control over the volume of building.
(C) provide evidence of compliance with municipal regulations.
(D) show compliance with restrictive covenants.

84. Zoning powers are conferred on municipal governments in which of the following ways?

(A) By state enabling acts
(B) Through the master plan
(C) By popular local vote
(D) Through city charters

85. The town of East Westchester enacts a new zoning code. Under the new code, commercial buildings are not permitted within 1,000 feet of Lake Westchester. A commercial building that is permitted to continue in its former use even though it is built on the lakeshore is an example of

    (A) a nonconforming use.
    (B) a variance.
    (C) a special use.
    (D) adverse possession.

86. A licensed real estate salesperson has a written contract with her broker. It specifies that the salesperson is not an employee. In the last year, just less than half of *the salesperson's* income from real estate transactions came from sales commissions. The remainder was based on an hourly wage paid by *the broker.* Using these facts, it is likely that the IRS would classify *the salesperson* as which of the following for federal income tax purposes?

    (A) Self-employed
    (B) Employee
    (C) Independent contractor
    (D) Part-time real estate salesperson

87. When acting as an employee rather than an independent contractor, a salesperson is obligated to

    (A) list properties in his or her own name.
    (B) assume responsibilities assigned by the broker.
    (C) accept a commission from another broker.
    (D) advertise property on his or her own behalf.

88. A real estate broker learns that her neighbor wishes to sell his house. The broker knows the property well and is able to persuade a buyer to make an offer for the property. The broker then asks the neighbor if the broker can present an offer from the prospective buyer, and the neighbor agrees. At this point, which of the following statements is **TRUE?**

    (A) The neighbor is not obligated to pay the broker a commission.
    (B) The buyer is obligated to pay the broker for locating the property.
    (C) The neighbor is obligated to pay the broker a commission.
    (D) The broker may not be considered the procuring cause without a written contract.

89. A broker would have the right to dictate which of the following to an independent contractor?

    (A) Number of hours the person would have to work
    (B) Work schedule the person would have to follow
    (C) Minimum acceptable dress code for the office
    (D) Compensation the person would receive

90. Two salespersons work for a broker. One afternoon, they agree to divide their town into a northern region and a southern region. One will handle listings in the northern region, and the other will handle listings in the southern region. Which of the following statements is **TRUE** regarding this agreement?

    (A) The agreement between the salespersons does not violate antitrust laws.
    (B) The agreement between the salesperson constitutes illegal price-fixing.
    (C) The salespersons have violated the Sherman Antitrust Act and are liable for triple damages.
    (D) The salespersons are guilty of group boycotting with regard to other salespersons in their office.

■ ANSWER KEY WITH EXPLANATIONS

1. (D) The tenant is a tenant at will. Either the landlord or tenant may terminate the lease with little or no notice. Although historically no notice is required, many states have mandated a limited amount of notice.

2. (B) Constructive eviction occurs when the landlord's actions or inaction makes the property uninhabitable.

3. (C) An open listing, of which this is an example, is a unilateral contract. No broker is obligated to sell the property, but if one of them does, the owner is obligated to pay the commission.

4. (D) The manager has earned $4,574.70 in commissions.
$795 \times 12 \times 3 = \$28,620$
$\$1,200 \times 12 = \$14,400$
$\$900 \times 12 = \$10,800$
$[\$28,620 + \$14,400 + \$10,800] \times 8.5\% = \$4,574.70$

5. (C) The buyer now becomes the lessor. The original owner is the lessee.

6. (D) Agents are to disclose facts that may affect their clients' decision to buy or sell.

7. (A) Under RESPA, the buyer has the right to see the closing statement (HUD-1) one business day before closing.

8. (D) The fair housing laws do permit a person to specify a sexual preference when renting a room in a house, i.e., sharing living space.

9. (B) It will cost $786 to fill the tank half full.
$12 \times 9 \times 8 = 864$
$[864 \times \$1.82] \div 2 = \$786$

10. (B) The amount of the loan, $98,000, is based on a percentage of the sale price or appraised price, whichever is less. In this case, the LTV is based on the appraised value.
$\$122,500 \times .80 = \$98,000$

11. (B) Once the seller promises to sell to the buyer, the buyer holds an equitable interest in the property. The seller still holds legal title, but the buyer's interest is so strong that the seller cannot sell to another buyer without written permission of the first buyer.

12. (A) The Truth-in-Lending Act requires that lenders state the true cost of borrowing money as stated in the APR, annual percentage rate. RESPA requires that a buyer receive a good-faith estimate within three business days of completed loan application.

13. (D) The listing agreement is terminated automatically upon the seller's death. At that moment, the heirs or whoever is named in the will become the owners (after probate, of course), so they will decide about selling the house.

14. (C) The woman conveys a life estate pur autre vie to the nursing home, based on the life of another, in this case, the mother.

15. (D) The cost of the mortgagee's title insurance policy is a debit to the buyer.

16. (D) Township sections are numbered by six from right to left, by six left to right. Thus, section 16 is directly north of section 21.

17. (B) Consideration must be made in a formal document, such as a deed, but any amount may be stated. In fact, many deeds contain the phrase, "in consideration of $10 and other good sums. . . ."

18. (B) The agent does have the duty to see that the buyer receives a true copy of what the buyer and seller have agreed to. This agent is the agent of the seller and holds a duty to perform for the seller, not the buyer.

19. (C) The broker is entitled to $9,506.25.
$195,000 \times 7.5\% \times 65\% = \$9,506.25$

20. (A) The cost approach requires that the appraiser estimate the replacement cost of the improvements. The appraiser will depreciate the value of the buildings, but in real estate, land is never depreciated.

21. (C) RESPA requires that the buyer be given a good-faith estimate of closing costs within three business days of the completed loan application and that the buyer has the right to see the HUD-1 form the business day before closing.

22. (C) Personal property becomes real property by annexation.

23. (A) The daughter holds a remainder interest during the sister's lifetime. The sister holds a life interest.

24. (B) Because the taxes are due at the end of the year, the seller must pay for the time that the seller owned the property. Thus, the prorated taxes are a debit to the seller and a credit to the buyer.

25. (C) If the buyer uses a straight-line method to depreciate the house over 27.5 years, the annual depreciation is $5,618.18.
$\$234,500 - \$80,000 = \$154,500$
$\$154,500 \div 27.5 = \$5,618.18$

26. (D) The amount owed on principal after the first monthly payment is $57,176.75.
$\$57,200 \times 13.5\% = \$7,722$
$\$7,722 \div 12 = \$643.50$
$\$666.75 - \$643.50 \text{ interest} = \$23.25 \text{ toward principal}$
$\$57,200 - \$23.25 = \$57,176.75$

27. (C) The interest portion would be $643.50
$\$57,200 \times 13.5\% = \$7,722$
$\$7,722 \div 12 = \$643.50$

28. (B) The agent may not disclose the seller's motivation. Doing so is a violation of the agent's fiduciary duty. The only way that an agent may disclose the seller's motivation is with written permission from the seller.

29. (B) The capitalization rate may be considered as a rate of return a property earns as an investment.

30. (D) As described the broker has two clients: a seller and a buyer. There may be a problem if the buyer decides to buy the seller's condo. At that point, the broker will ask if the two will agree to dual representation, if dual agency is permitted in that state. In some states, dual agency is prohibited; in that case, the broker might act as a transactional broker.

31. (B) Interest must be paid on the day of closing. Thus, the buyer must pay for 14 days of interim interest.
$\$57,500 \times 8.5\% = \$4,887.50$
$\$4,887.50 \div 360 \times 14 = \$190.12$

32. (D) The current value of the home is $180,975.
$\$142,500 \times 127\% = \$180,975$

33. (A) The earnest money is a good-faith deposit. If the buyer defaults, then the seller is able to keep the earnest money as liquidated damages.

34. (D) A title search will discover a properly recorded mechanic's lien. Survey will uncover encroachments and perhaps an earlier inaccurate survey as well. A physical inspection of the property is necessary to learn about parties in possession and their possible rights.

35. (B) The lot measures 220 feet by 200 feet.
$$\$193,600 \div 4.4 \div 200 = 220$$

36. (A) A broker is free to negotiate any commission rate. There is no standard rate.

37. (B) When the tenant sublet her apartment, she gave up some of her rights. An assignment is giving up all of the tenant's remaining rights. Although a tenant can give up rights, a tenant can never give up responsibility, i.e., if the subletting tenant fails to pay rent, the original tenant is responsible.

38. (D) Under an exclusive right to sell, a broker is entitled to a commission if the property is sold, whether by the owner, the broker or anyone else.

39. (A) The capitalization rate is based on a rate of return.

40. (C) The present book value of the property is $114,444.
$$\$142,000 - \$18,000 = \$124,000$$
$$\$124,000 - [\$124,000 \div 31.5 \times 7] + \$18,000 = \$114,444$$

41. (B) The rescission is recorded to have public notice terminating the previous action. Another method would have the buyer file a new transfer back to the seller.

42. (C) Buying the adjoining property will cost the farmer $42,000.
$$640 \div 2 \div 4 \div 4 = 20 \text{ acres}$$
$$640 \div 4 = 160 \text{ (quarter section)}$$
$$160 - 20 = 140 \text{ acres to purchase}$$
$$140 \times \$300 = \$42,000$$

43. (B) An offer is not an agreement and can be withdrawn at anytime before the offeror is notified that the offer has been accepted.

44. (B) Under a statutory right of redemption, offered in some states, the delinquent debtor has the right to "redeem" the property up to a certain time after the foreclosure sale.

45. (C) The annual rent is $38,400.
$$[36 \times 200 \times 12] \div 27 \times [\$1 \times 12] = \$38,400$$

46. (D) A veteran may pay discount points on a refinance.

47. (A) The brother's property has a clause that allows his brother the right to reenter the property to inspect that no alcohol is being used. The brother's fee is determinable; the sister's is fee simple.

48. (A) The taxes for 45 days are debited to the buyer, a credit to the seller.
$$\$1,116 \div 360 \times 45 = \$139.50.$$

49. (B) Once the lease has been surrendered and accepted, the lease is terminated.

50. (D) Under the gross lease, the tenant makes one payment and the lessor pays for the upkeep of the property including taxes.

51. (C) The property manager earns $1,936 over a period of three years.
$1,000 × 12 = $12,000 × 7% = $840
$12,000 × 110% = $13,200 × 5% = $660
$13,200 × 110% = $14,520 × 3% = $435.60
$840 + $660 + $435.60 = $1,935.60 or rounded $1,936

52. (A) Recording the deed and/or possessing the property both establish rights. Failure to do either places this party in the weakest position. A house painter only has the right to file a lien for payment of his work; a tenant has possession to the end of the lease.

53. (C) The couple owes no tax on this capital gain. Taxpayers who file singly are entitled to a $250,000 exclusion. Taxpayers who are married and who file jointly are entitled to a $500,000 exclusion.

54. (A) The squatter occupied the property illegally. The cabinets become part of the real property by annexation.

55. (D) One can always sell what one owns. When the first owner sold to the fourth person, the owner destroyed three of the essential unities required for joint tenancy: interest, time and title. After the death of the second original owner, the two remaining owners are tenants in common.

56. (A) The sales price is always a debit to the buyer, a credit to the seller.

57. (B) Eminent domain is the state's right to acquire private property for public use after paying fair and just compensation. The legal action is condemnation.

58. (B) The children receive $118,500.
100% − 54% − 18% − 16% = 12%
$79,000 ÷ 12% = $658,333
$658,333 × 18% = $118,500

59. (D) External obsolescence is always incurable because the property in the area is out of the control of the subject property owner.

60. (D) The Truth-in-Lending Act requires that lenders reveal the true cost of borrowing money by publishing the annual percentage rate (APR).

61. (B) If the net income stays the same, changing the cap rate will change the indicated value. Example: $10,000 net income divided by 8% = $125,000 versus $10,000 divided by 10% = $100,000.
The lower the cap rate, the higher the value, and vice versa.

62. (C) ECOA prohibits lenders from discriminating against borrowers because their income comes from public assistance.

63. (C) The deed must be delivered and accepted during the grantor's lifetime. The grantor did not deliver the deed. Because the charity never accepted the deed, the house will most likely go to the nephew.

64. (C) The total interest paid over the life of the loan is $101,250.
$90,000 × 7.5% × 15 = $101,250

65. (A) The seller would have recourse against the agent and depending on the extent of the breech of fiduciary duty could terminate the listing. The contract with the buyer may also be voidable.

66. (B) The sale price must be at least $95,745 in order to net the owner $90,000.
$90,000 ÷ 94% = $95,745

67. (B) Private clubs are exempt under the 1968 fair housing laws, so long as membership is not restricted.

68. (D) A misrepresentation of the size of the lot is an example of a material fact. The agent may be liable if the agent knew or should have known of the misrepresentation.

69. (C) The maximum possible size would be 1,250 square feet.
$$[70 - 20 - 25] \times [70 - 10 - 10] = 1,250$$

70. (B) The salesperson receives $960.
$$80 \times \$200 \times 10\% \times 60\% = \$960$$

71. (D) While the right of rescission applies to most consumer credit transactions, it does not apply to residential purchase-money, first mortgage or deed of trust loans.

72. (C) It results in a $50,000 decrease because the lower the cap rate, the higher the value.
$$\$30,000 \div 12\% = \$250,000$$
$$\$30,000 \div 10\% = \$300,000$$
$$\$300,000 - \$250,000 = \$50,000$$

73. (A) Earnest money is an excellent example of liquidated damages.

74. (D) A lease with a national retailing change would be considered a more secure source of income; therefore, that building will probably appraise for more.

75. (B) In a participation loan, the lender gives a concession and also becomes a "participant" in the project. The lender shares in both the risk and the rewards. The lender becomes a participant in the property.

76. (C) The 30-year loan payments are 171% of the 15-year payments.
$$\$1,200.22 \times 12 \times 15 = \$216,039.60$$
$$\$1,028.63 \times 12 \times 30 = \$370,306.80$$
$$\$370,306.80 \div \$216,039.60 = 1.71 \text{ or } 171\%$$

77. (B) The market value is $122,500 because the market value for this property would be what a person would pay for the property.

78. (D) The property tax is $3,740.
$$\$85,000 \times 110\% \times .04 = \$3,740$$

79. (B) At closing, items paid for but not used are a credit to the seller, debit to the buyer. The buyer reimburses the seller for the rest of the timeframe.

80. (B) An example of "controlling the risk" is when the manager takes action to limit the chances of flood damage.

81. (B) Deed restrictions are private land-use controls, not public. The property owners enforce restrictive covenants. Examples of public land-use controls include zoning, building permits and certificates of occupancy.

82. (D) Police powers do not allow the government to select what kind of people may live in a building.

83. (C) Cities require the use of building permits in order to monitor and provide evidence that the builder has complied with municipal regulations.

84. (A) State enabling acts grant zoning powers to the local community

85. (A) When new zoning rules are applied, properties previously used for a purpose that is now prohibited are permitted to stay, with certain conditions, and are called "nonconforming."

86. (B) The real estate salesperson who earned more than half of his or her income from hourly work paid for by his or her broker will be considered an employee.

87. (B) The broker can assign any legal task in relation to the employment.

88. (A) The broker is unlikely to receive a commission. The broker apparently volunteered services without expressly being hired. Also, most states require that an enforceable listing agreement be in writing.

89. (D) A real estate broker is permitted to dictate compensation to the independent contractor.

90. (A) Companies can allocate regions and set commissions within their own company.

Glossary

abstract of title The condensed history of a title to a particular parcel of real estate, consisting of a summary of the original grant and all subsequent conveyances and encumbrances affecting the property and a certification by the abstractor that the history is complete and accurate.

acceleration clause The clause in a mortgage or deed of trust that can be enforced to make the entire debt due immediately if the borrower defaults on an installment payment or other covenant.

accession Acquiring title to additions or improvements to real property as a result of the annexation of fixtures or the accretion of alluvial deposits along the banks of streams.

accretion The increase or addition of land by the deposit of sand or soil washed up naturally from a river, lake or sea.

accrued items On a closing statement, items of expense that are incurred but not yet payable, such as interest on a mortgage loan or taxes on real property.

acknowledgment A formal declaration made before a duly authorized officer, usually a notary public, by a person who has signed a document.

acre A measure of land equal to 43,560 square feet, 4,840 square yards, 4,047 square meters, 160 square rods or 0.4047 hectares.

actual eviction The legal process that results in the tenant's being physically removed from the leased premises.

actual notice Express information or fact; that which is known; direct knowledge.

adjustable-rate mortgage (ARM) A loan characterized by a fluctuating interest rate, usually one tied to a bank or savings and loan association cost-of-funds index.

adjusted basis *See* basis.

ad valorem tax A tax levied according to value, generally used to refer to real estate tax. Also called the *general tax.*

adverse possession The actual, open, notorious, hostile and continuous possession of another's land under a claim of title. Possession for a statutory period may be a means of acquiring title.

affidavit of title A written statement, made under oath by a seller or grantor of real property and acknowledged by a notary public, in which the grantor (1) identifies himself or herself and indicates marital status, (2) certifies that since the examination of the title on the date of the contracts no defects have occurred in the title and (3) certifies that he or she is in possession of the property (if applicable).

agency The relationship between a principal and an agent wherein the agent is authorized to represent the principal in certain transactions.

agency coupled with an interest An agency relationship in which the agent is given an estate or interest in the subject of the agency (the property).

agent One who acts or has the power to act for another. A fiduciary relationship is created under the law of agency when a property owner, as the principal, executes a listing agreement or management contract authorizing a licensed real estate broker to be his or her agent.

air lot A designated airspace over a piece of land. An air lot, like surface property, may be transferred.

air rights The right to use the open space above a property, usually allowing the surface to be used for another purpose.

alienation The act of transferring property to another. Alienation may be voluntary, such as by gift or sale, or involuntary, as through eminent domain or adverse possession.

alienation clause The clause in a mortgage or deed of trust that states that the balance of the secured debt becomes immediately due and payable at the lender's option if the property is sold by the borrower. In effect this clause prevents the borrower from assigning the debt without the lender's approval.

allodial system A system of land ownership in which land is held free and clear of any rent or service due to the government; commonly contrasted to the feudal system. Land is held under the allodial system in the United States.

American Land Title Association (ALTA) policy A title insurance policy that protects the interest in a collateral property of a mortgage lender who originates a new real estate loan.

amortized loan A loan in which the principal as well as the interest is payable in monthly or other periodic installments over the term of the loan.

annual percentage rate (APR) The relationship of the total finance charges associated with a loan. This must be disclosed to borrowers by lenders under the Truth-in-Lending Act.

anticipation The appraisal principle that holds that value can increase or decrease based on the expectation of some future benefit or detriment produced by the property.

antitrust laws Laws designed to preserve the free enterprise of the open marketplace by making illegal certain private conspiracies and combinations formed to minimize competition. Most violations of antitrust laws in the real estate business involve either price-fixing (brokers conspiring to set fixed compensation rates) or allocation of customers or markets (brokers agreeing to limit their areas of trade or dealing to certain areas or properties).

appraisal An estimate of the quantity, quality or value of something. The process through which conclusions of property value are obtained; also refers to the report that sets forth the process of estimation and conclusion of value.

appreciation An increase in the worth or value of a property due to economic or related causes, which may prove to be either temporary or permanent; opposite of depreciation.

appurtenance A right, privilege or improvement belonging to, and passing with, the land.

appurtenant easement An easement that is annexed to the ownership of one parcel and allows the owner the use of the neighbor's land.

APR *See* annual percentage rate.

ARM *See* adjustable-rate mortgage.

articles of agreement for warranty deed *See* installment contract.

asbestos A mineral once used in insulation and other materials that can cause respiratory diseases.

assemblage The combining of two or more adjoining lots into one larger tract to increase their total value. *See* plottage.

assessment The imposition of a tax, charge or levy, usually according to established rates.

assignment The transfer in writing of interest in a bond, mortgage, lease or other instrument.

assumption of mortgage Acquiring title to property on which there is an existing mortgage and agreeing to be personally liable for the terms and conditions of the mortgage, including payments.

attachment The act of taking a person's property into legal custody by writ or other judicial order to hold it available for application to that person's debt to a creditor.

attorney-in-fact *See* power of attorney.

attorney's opinion of title An abstract of title that an attorney has examined and has certified to be, in his or her opinion, an accurate statement of the facts concerning the property ownership.

automated underwriting Computer systems that permit lenders to expedite the loan approval process and reduce lending costs.

automatic extension A clause in a listing agreement that states that the agreement will continue automatically for a certain period of time after its expiration date. In many states, use of this clause is discouraged or prohibited.

avulsion The sudden tearing away of land, as by earthquake, flood, volcanic action or the sudden change in the course of a stream.

balance The appraisal principle that states that the greatest value in a property will occur when the type and size of the improvements are proportional to each other as well as the land.

balloon payment A final payment of a mortgage loan that is considerably larger than the required periodic payments because the loan amount was not fully amortized.

bargain and sale deed A deed that carries with it no warranties against liens or other encumbrances but that does imply that the grantor has the right to convey title. The grantor may add warranties to the deed at his or her discretion.

base line The main imaginary line running east and west and crossing a principal meridian at a definite point, used by surveyors for reference in locating and describing land under the rectangular (government) survey system of legal description.

basis The financial interest that the Internal Revenue Service attributes to an owner of an investment property for the purpose of determining annual depreciation and gain or loss on the sale of the asset. If a property was acquired by purchase, the owner's basis is the cost of the property plus the value of any capital expenditures for improvements to the property, minus any depreciation allowable or actually taken. This new basis is called the *adjusted basis*.

bench mark A permanent reference mark or point established for use by surveyors in measuring differences in elevation.

beneficiary (1) The person for whom a trust operates or in whose behalf the income from a trust estate is drawn. (2) A lender in a deed of trust loan transaction.

bilateral contract *See* contract.

binder An agreement that may accompany an earnest money deposit for the purchase of real property as evidence of the purchaser's good faith and intent to complete the transaction.

blanket loan A mortgage covering more than one parcel of real estate, providing for each parcel's partial release from the mortgage lien upon repayment of a definite portion of the debt.

blockbusting The illegal practice of inducing homeowners to sell their properties by making representations regarding the entry or prospective entry of persons of a particular race or national origin into the neighborhood.

blue-sky laws Common name for those state and federal laws that regulate the registration and sale of investment securities.

boot Money or property given to make up any difference in value or equity between two properties in an *exchange*.

branch office A secondary place of business apart from the principal or main office from which real estate business is conducted. A branch office usually must be run by a licensed real estate broker working on behalf of the broker.

breach of contract Violation of any terms or conditions in a contract without legal excuse; for example, failure to make a payment when it is due.

broker One who acts as an intermediary on behalf of others for a fee or commission.

brokerage The bringing together of parties interested in making a real estate transaction.

buffer zone A strip of land, usually used as a park or designated for a similar use, separating land dedicated to one use from land dedicated to another use (e.g., residential from commercial).

building code An ordinance that specifies minimum standards of construction for buildings to protect public safety and health.

building permit Written governmental permission for the construction, alteration or demolition of an improvement, showing compliance with building codes and zoning ordinances.

bulk transfer See Uniform Commercial Code.

bundle of legal rights The concept of land ownership that includes ownership of all legal rights to the land—for example, possession, control within the law and enjoyment.

buydown A financing technique used to reduce the monthly payments for the first few years of a loan. Funds in the form of discount points are given to the lender by the builder or seller to buy down or lower the effective interest rate paid by the buyer, thus reducing the monthly payments for a set time.

buyer's agent A residential real estate broker or salesperson who represents the prospective purchaser in a transaction. The buyer's agent owes the buyer/principal the common-law or statutory agency duties.

buyer's broker A residential real estate broker who represents prospective buyers exclusively. As the buyer's agent, the broker owes the buyer/principal the common-law or statutory agency duties.

buyer-agency agreement A principal-agent relationship in which the broker is the agent for the buyer, with fiduciary responsibilities to the buyer. The broker represents the buyer under the law of agency.

capital gain Profit earned from the sale of an asset.

capitalization A mathematical process for estimating the value of a property using a proper rate of return on the investment and the annual net operating income expected to be produced by the property. The formula is expressed as Income ÷ Rate = Value

capitalization rate The rate of return a property will produce on the owner's investment.

cash flow The net spendable income from an investment, determined by deducting all operating and fixed expenses from the gross income. When expenses exceed income, a negative cash flow results.

cash rent In an agricultural lease, the amount of money given as rent to the landowner at the outset of the lease, as opposed to sharecropping.

caveat emptor A Latin phrase meaning "Let the buyer beware."

CERCLA *See* Comprehensive Environmental Response, Compensation and Liability Act.

certificate of reasonable value (CRV) A form indicating the appraised value of a property being financed with a VA loan.

certificate of sale The document generally given to the purchaser at a tax foreclosure sale. A certificate of sale does not convey title; normally it is an instrument certifying that the holder received title to the property after the redemption period passed and that the holder paid the property taxes for that interim period.

certificate of title A statement of opinion on the status of the title to a parcel of real property based on an examination of specified public records.

chain of title The succession of conveyances, from some accepted starting point, whereby the present holder of real property derives title.

change The appraisal principle that holds that no physical or economic condition remains constant.

chattel *See* personal property.

Civil Rights Act of 1866 An act that prohibits racial discrimination in the sale and rental of housing.

CLO *See* computerized loan organization system.

closing statement A detailed cash accounting of a real estate transaction showing all cash received, all charges and credits made and all cash paid out in the transaction.

cloud on title Any document, claim, unreleased lien or encumbrance that may impair the title to real property or make the title doubtful; usually revealed by a title search and removed by either a quitclaim deed or suit to quiet title.

clustering The grouping of homesites within a subdivision on smaller lots than normal, with the remaining land used as common areas.

CMA *See* competitive market analysis.

code of ethics A written system of standards for ethical conduct.

codicil A supplement or an addition to a will, executed with the same formalities as a will, that normally does not revoke the entire will.

coinsurance clause A clause in insurance policies covering real property that requires the policyholder to maintain fire insurance coverage generally equal to at least 80 percent of the property's actual replacement cost.

commingling The illegal act by a real estate broker of placing client or customer funds with personal funds. By law, brokers are required to maintain a separate *trust account* or *escrow account* for other parties' funds held temporarily by the broker.

commission Payment to a broker for services rendered, such as in the sale or purchase of real property; usually a percentage of the selling price of the property.

common elements Parts of a property that are necessary or convenient to the existence, maintenance and safety of a condominium or are normally in common use by all of the condominium residents. Each condominium owner has an undivided ownership interest in the common elements.

common law The body of law based on custom, usage and court decisions.

community property A system of property ownership based on the theory that each spouse has an equal interest in the property acquired by the efforts of either spouse during marriage. A holdover of Spanish law found predominantly in western states; the system was unknown under English common law.

comparables Properties used in an appraisal report that are substantially equivalent to the subject property.

competition The appraisal principle that states that excess profits generate competition.

competitive market analysis (CMA) A comparison of the prices of recently sold homes that are similar to a listing seller's home in terms of location, style and amenities.

Comprehensive Environmental Response, Compensation and Liability Act (CERCLA) A federal law administered by the Environmental Protection Agency that establishes a process for identifying parties responsible for creating hazardous waste sites, forcing liable parties to clean up toxic sites, bringing legal action against responsible parties and funding the abatement of toxic sites. See Superfund.

comprehensive plan See master plan.

computerized loan origination (CLO) system An electronic network for handling loan applications through remote computer terminals linked to various lenders' computers.

condemnation A judicial or administrative proceeding to exercise the power of eminent domain, through which a government agency takes private property for public use and compensates the owner.

conditional-use permit Written governmental permission allowing a use inconsistent with zoning but necessary for the common good, such as locating an emergency medical facility in a predominantly residential area.

condominium The absolute ownership of a unit in a multiunit building based on a legal description of the airspace the unit actually occupies, plus an undivided interest in the ownership of the common elements, which are owned jointly with the other condominium unit owners.

confession of judgment clause Permits judgment to be entered against a debtor without the creditors having to institute legal proceedings.

conformity The appraisal principle that holds that the greater the similarity among properties in an area, the better they will hold their value.

consideration (1) That received by the grantor in exchange for his or her deed. (2) Something of value that induces a person to enter into a contract.

construction loan *See* interim financing.

constructive eviction Actions of a landlord that so materially disturb or impair a tenant's enjoyment of the leased premises that the tenant is effectively forced to move out and terminate the lease without liability for any further rent.

constructive notice Notice given to the world by recorded documents. All people are charged with knowledge of such documents and their contents, whether or not they have actually examined them. Possession of property is also considered constructive notice that the person in possession has an interest in the property.

construction loan *See* interim financing.

contingency A provision in a contract that requires a certain act to be done or a certain event to occur before the contract becomes binding.

contract A legally enforceable promise or set of promises that must be performed and for which, if a breach of the promise occurs, the law provides a remedy. A contract may be either unilateral, by which only one party is bound to act, or bilateral, by which all parties to the instrument are legally bound to act as prescribed.

contract broker *See* nonagent.

contract for deed *See* installment contract.

contribution The appraisal principle that states that the value of any component of a property is what it gives to the value of the whole or what its absence detracts from that value.

conventional loan A loan that requires no insurance or guarantee.

conveyance A term used to refer to any document that transfers title to real property. The term is also used in describing the act of transferring.

cooperating broker *See* listing broker.

cooperative A residential multiunit building whose title is held by a trust or corporation that is owned by and operated for the benefit of persons living within the building, who are the beneficial owners of the trust or stockholders of the corporation, each possessing a proprietary lease.

co-ownership Title ownership held by two or more persons.

corporation An entity or organization, created by operation of law, whose rights of doing business are essentially the same as those of an individual. The entity has continuous existence until it is dissolved according to legal procedures.

correction lines Provisions in the rectangular survey (government survey) system made to compensate for the curvature of the earth's surface. Every fourth township line (at 24-mile intervals) is used as a correction line on which the intervals between the north and south range lines are remeasured and corrected to a full six miles.

cost approach The process of estimating the value of a property by adding to the estimated land value the appraiser's estimate of the reproduction or replacement cost of the building, less *depreciation.*

cost recovery An Internal Revenue Service term for depreciation.

counteroffer A new offer made in response to an offer received. It has the effect of rejecting the original offer, which cannot be accepted thereafter unless revived by the offeror.

covenant A written agreement between two or more parties in which a party or parties pledge to perform or not perform specified acts with regard to property; usually found in such real estate documents as deeds, mortgages, leases and contracts for deed.

covenant of quiet enjoyment The covenant implied by law by which a landlord guarantees that a tenant may take possession of leased premises and that the landlord will not interfere in the tenant's possession or use of the property.

credit On a closing statement, an amount entered in a person's favor—either an amount the party has paid or an amount for which the party must be reimbursed.

CRV *See* certificate of reasonable value.

curtesy A life estate, usually a fractional interest, given by some states to the surviving husband in real estate owned by his deceased wife. Most states have abolished curtesy.

datum A horizontal plane from which heights and depths are measured.

debit On a closing statement, an amount charged; that is, an amount that the debited party must pay.

decedent A person who has died.

dedication The voluntary transfer of private property by its owner to the public for some public use, such as for streets or schools.

deed A written instrument that, when executed and delivered, conveys title to or an interest in real estate.

deed in lieu of foreclosure A deed given by the mortgagor to the mortgagee when the mortgagor is in default under the terms of the mortgage. This is a way for the mortgagor to avoid foreclosure.

deed in trust An instrument that grants a trustee under a land trust full power to sell, mortgage and subdivide a parcel of real estate. The beneficiary controls the trustee's use of these powers under the provisions of the trust agreement.

deed of reconveyance *See* realease deed.

deed of trust *See* trust deed.

deed of trust lien *See* trust deed lien.

deed restrictions Clauses in a deed limiting the future uses of the property. Deed restrictions may impose a vast variety of limitations and conditions—for example, they may limit the density of buildings, dictate the types of structures that can be erected or prevent buildings from being used for specific purposes or even from being used at all.

default The nonperformance of a duty, whether arising under a contract or otherwise; failure to meet an obligation when due.

defeasance clause A clause used in leases and mortgages that cancels a specified right upon the occurrence of a certain condition, such as cancellation of a mortgage upon repayment of the mortgage loan.

defeasible fee estate An estate in which the holder has a fee simple title that may be divested upon the occurrence or nonoccurrence of a specified event. There are two categories of defeasible fee estates: (1) fee simple on condition precedent (fee simple determinable) and (2) fee simple on condition subsequent.

deficiency judgment A personal judgment levied against the borrower when a foreclosure sale does not produce sufficient funds to pay the mortgage debt in full.

demand The amount of goods people are willing and able to buy at a given price; often coupled with supply.

density zoning Zoning ordinances that restrict the maximum average number of houses per acre that may be built within a particular area, generally a subdivision.

depreciation (1) In appraisal, a loss of value in property due to any cause, including *physical deterioration, functional obsolescence* and *external obsolescence*. (2) In real estate investment, an expense deduction for tax purposes taken over the period of ownership of income property. *See* cost recovery.

descent Acquisition of an estate by inheritance in which an heir succeeds to the property by operation of law.

designated agent A licensee authorized by a broker to act as the agent for a specific principal in a particular transaction.

developer One who attempts to put land to its most profitable use through the construction of improvements.

devise A gift of real property by will. The donor is the devisor, and the recipient is the devisee.

discount point A unit of measurement used for various loan charges; one point equals one percent of the amount of the loan.

dominant tenement A property that includes in its ownership the appurtenant right to use an easement over another person's property for a specific purpose.

dower The legal right or interest, recognized in some states, that a wife acquires in the property her husband held or acquired during their marriage. During the husband's lifetime the right is only a possibility of an interest; upon his death it can become an interest in land.

dual agency Representing both parties to a transaction. This is unethical unless both parties agree to it, and it is illegal in many states.

due-on-sale clause A provision in the mortgage that states that the entire balance of the note is immediately due and payable if the mortgagor transfers (sells) the property.

duress Unlawful constraint or action exercised upon a person whereby the person is forced to perform an act against his or her will. A contract entered into under duress is voidable.

earnest money Money deposited by a buyer under the terms of a contract, to be forfeited if the buyer defaults but applied to the purchase price if the sale is closed.

easement A right to use the land of another for a specific purpose, such as for a right-of-way or utilities; an incorporeal interest in land.

easement by condemnation An easement created by the government or government agency that has exercised its right under eminent domain.

easement by necessity An easement allowed by law as necessary for the full enjoyment of a parcel of real estate; for example, a right of ingress and egress over a grantor's land.

easement by prescription An easement acquired by continuous, open and hostile use of the property for the period of time prescribed by state law.

easement in gross An easement that is not created for the benefit of any *land* owned by the owner of the easement but that attaches *personally to the easement owner.* For example, a right granted by Eleanor Franks to Joe Fish to use a portion of her property for the rest of his life would be an easement in gross.

ECOA *See* Equal Credit Opportunity Act.

economic life The number of years during which an improvement will add value to the land.

emblements Growing crops, such as grapes and corn, that are produced annually through labor and industry; also called *fructus industriales.*

eminent domain The right of a government or municipal quasi-public body to acquire property for public use through a court action called *condemnation,* in which the court decides that the use is a public use and determines the compensation to be paid to the owner.

employee Someone who works as a direct employee of an employer and has employee status. The employer is obligated to withhold income taxes and Social Security taxes from the compensation of employees. *See also* independent contractor.

employment contract A document evidencing formal employment between employer and employee or between principal and agent. In the real estate business this generally takes the form of a listing agreement or management agreement.

enabling acts State legislation that confers zoning powers on municipal governments.

encapsulation A method of controlling environmental contamination by sealing off a dangerous substance.

encroachment A building or some portion of it—a wall or fence, for instance—that extends beyond the land of the owner and illegally intrudes on some land of an adjoining owner or a street or alley.

encumbrance Anything—such as a mortgage, tax, or judgment lien, an easement, a restriction on the use of the land or an outstanding dower right—that may diminish the value or use and enjoyment of a property.

Equal Credit Opportunity Act (ECOA) The federal law that prohibits discrimination in the extension of credit because of race, color, religion, national origin, sex, age or marital status.

equalization The raising or lowering of assessed values for tax purposes in a particular county or taxing district to make them equal to assessments in other counties or districts.

equalization factor A factor (number) by which the assessed value of a property is multiplied to arrive at a value for the property that is in line with statewide tax assessments. The *ad valorem tax* would be based on this adjusted value.

equitable lien *See* statutory lien.

equitable right of redemption The right of a defaulted property owner to recover the property prior to its sale by paying the appropriate fees and charges.

equitable title The interest held by a vendee under a contract for deed or an installment contract; the equitable right to obtain absolute ownership to property when legal title is held in another's name.

equity The interest or value that an owner has in property over and above any indebtedness.

erosion The gradual wearing away of land by water, wind and general weather conditions; the diminishing of property by the elements.

escheat The reversion of property to the state or county, as provided by state law, in cases where a decedent dies intestate without heirs capable of inheriting, or when the property is abandoned.

escrow The closing of a transaction through a third party called an *escrow agent,* or *escrowee,* who receives certain funds and documents to be delivered upon the performance of certain conditions outlined in the escrow instructions.

escrow account The trust account established by a broker under the provisions of the license law for the purpose of holding funds on behalf of the broker's principal or some other person until the consummation or termination of a transaction.

escrow instructions A document that sets forth the duties of the escrow agent, as well as the requirements and obligations of the parties, when a transaction is closed through an escrow.

estate (tenancy) at sufferance The tenancy of a lessee who lawfully comes into possession of a landlord's real estate but who continues to occupy the premises improperly after his or her lease rights have expired.

estate (tenancy) at will An estate that gives the lessee the right to possession until the estate is terminated by either party; the term of this estate is indefinite.

estate (tenancy) for years An interest for a certain, exact period of time in property leased for a specified consideration.

estate (tenancy) from period to period An interest in leased property that continues from period to period— week to week, month to month or year to year.

estate in land The degree, quantity, nature and extent of interest a person has in real property.

estate taxes Federal taxes on a decedent's real and personal property.

estoppel Method of creating an agency relationship in which someone states incorrectly that another person is his or her agent and a third person relies on that representation.

estoppel certificate A document in which a borrower certifies the amount owed on a mortgage loan and the rate of interest.

ethics The system of moral principles and rules that becomes standards for professional conduct.

eviction A legal process to oust a person from possession of real estate.

evidence of title Proof of ownership of property; commonly a certificate of title, an abstract of title with lawyer's opinion, title insurance or a Torrens registration certificate.

exchange A transaction in which all or part of the consideration is the transfer of like-kind property (such as real estate for real estate). *See* boot.

exclusive-agency listing A listing contract under which the owner appoints a real estate broker as his or her exclusive agent for a designated period of time to sell the property, on the owner's stated terms, for a commission. The owner reserves the right to sell without paying anyone a commission if he or she sells to a prospect who has not been introduced or claimed by the broker.

exclusive-right-to-sell listing A listing contract under which the owner appoints a real estate broker as his or her exclusive agent for a designated period of time, to sell the property on the owner's stated terms, and agrees to pay the broker a commission when the property is sold, whether by the broker, the owner or another broker.

executed contract A contract in which all parties have fulfilled their promises and thus performed the contract.

execution The signing and delivery of an instrument. Also, a legal order directing an official to enforce a judgment against the property of a debtor.

executory contract A contract under which something remains to be done by one or more of the parties.

express agreement An oral or written contract in which the parties state the contract's terms and express their intentions in words.

express contract *See* express agreement.

external depreciation Reduction in a property's value caused by outside factors (those that are off the property).

facilitator *See* nonagent.

Fair Housing Act The federal law that prohibits discrimination in housing based on race, color, religion, sex, handicap, familial status and national origin.

Fannie Mae A quasi-government agency established to purchase any kind of mortgage loans in the secondary mortgage market from the primary lenders.

Farmer's Home Administration (FmHA) An agency of the federal government that provides credit assistance to farmers and other individuals who live in rural areas.

Federal Deposit Insurance Corporation (FDIC) An independent federal agency that insures the deposits in commercial banks.

Federal Home Loan Mortgage Corporation (FHLMC) *See* Freddie Mac.

Federal National Mortgage Association (FNMA) *See* Fannie Mae.

Federal Reserve System The country's central banking system, which is responsible for the nation's monetary policy by regulating the supply of money and interest rates.

fee simple absolute The maximum possible estate or right of ownership of real property, continuing forever.

fee simple defeasible *See* defeasible fee estate.

feudal system A system of ownership usually associated with precolonial England, in which the king or other sovereign is the source of all rights. The right to possess real property was granted by the sovereign to an individual as a life estate only. Upon the death of the individual, title passed back to the sovereign, not to the decedent's heirs.

FHA loan A loan insured by the Federal Housing Administration and made by an approved lender in accordance with the FHA's regulations.

fiduciary One in whom trust and confidence is placed; a reference to a broker employed under the terms of a listing contract or buyer agency agreement.

fiduciary relationship A relationship of trust and confidence, as between trustee and beneficiary, attorney and client or principal and agent.

Financial Institutions Reform, Recovery and Enforcement Act (FIRREA) This act restructured the savings and loan association regulatory system; enacted in response to the savings and loan crisis of the 1980s.

financing statement *See* Uniform Commercial Code.

FIRREA *See* Financial Instituitions Reform, Recovery and Enforcement Act.

fiscal policy The government's policy in regard to taxation and spending programs. The balance between these two areas determines the amount of money the government will withdraw from or feed into the economy, which can counter economic peaks and slumps.

fixture An item of personal property that has been converted to real property by being permanently affixed to the realty.

foreclosure A legal procedure whereby property used as security for a debt is sold to satisfy the debt in the event of default in payment of the mortgage note or default of other terms in the mortgage document. The foreclosure procedure brings the rights of all parties to a conclusion and passes the title in the mortgaged property to either the holder of the mortgage or a third party who may purchase the realty at the foreclosure sale, free of all encumbrances affecting the property subsequent to the mortgage.

fractional section A parcel of land less than 160 acres, usually found at the edge of a rectangular survey.

fraud Deception intended to cause a person to give up property or a lawful right.

Freddie Mac A corporation established to purchase primarily conventional mortgage loans in the secondary mortgage market.

freehold estate An estate in land in which ownership is for an indeterminate length of time, in contrast to a *leasehold estate.*

front footage The measurement of a parcel of land by the number of feet of street or road frontage.

fructus industries *See* emblements.

functional obsolescence A loss of value to an improvement to real estate arising from functional problems, often caused by age or poor design.

future interest A person's present right to an interest in real property that will not result in possession or enjoyment until some time in the future, such as a reversion or right of reentry.

gap A defect in the chain of title of a particular parcel of real estate; a missing document or conveyance that raises doubt as to the present ownership of the land.

general agent One who is authorized by a principal to represent the principal in a specific range of matters.

general lien The right of a creditor to have all of a debtor's property—both real and personal—sold to satisfy a debt.

general partnership *See* partnership.

general tax *See* ad valorem tax.

general warranty deed A deed in which the grantor fully warrants good clear title to the premises. Used in most real estate deed transfers, a general warranty deed offers the greatest protection of any deed.

Ginnie Mae A government agency that plays an important role in the secondary mortgage market. It sells mortgage-backed securities that are backed by pools of FHA and VA loans.

government check The 24-mile-square parcels composed of 16 townships in the rectangular (government) survey system of legal description.

government lot Fractional sections in the rectangular (government) survey system that are less than one quarter-section in area.

Government National Mortgage Association (GNMA) *See* Ginnie Mae.

government survey system *See* rectangular (government) survey system.

graduated-payment mortgage (GPM) A loan in which the monthly principal and interest payments increase by a certain percentage each year for a certain number of years and then level off for the remaining loan term.

grantee A person who receives a conveyance of real property from a grantor.

granting clause Words in a deed of conveyance that state the grantor's intention to convey the property at the present time. This clause is generally worded as "convey and warrant," "grant," "grant, bargain and sell" or the like.

grantor The person transferring title to or an interest in real property to a grantee.

gross income multiplier A figure used as a multiplier of the gross annual income of a property to produce an estimate of the property's value.

gross lease A lease of property according to which a landlord pays all property charges regularly incurred through ownership, such as repairs, taxes, insurance and operating expenses. Most residential leases are gross leases.

gross rent multiplier (GRM) The figure used as a multiplier of the gross monthly income of a property to produce an estimate of the property's value.

ground lease A lease of land only, on which the tenant usually owns a building or is required to build as specified in the lease. Such leases are usually long-term net leases; the tenant's rights and obligations continue until the lease expires or is terminated through default.

growing-equity mortgage (GEM) A loan in which the monthly payments increase annually, with the increased amount being used to reduce directly the principal balance outstanding and thus shorten the overall term of the loan.

habendum clause That part of a deed beginning with the words "to have and to hold," following the granting clause and defining the extent of ownership the grantor is conveying.

heir One who might inherit or succeed to an interest in land under the state law of descent when the owner dies without leaving a valid will.

highest and best use The possible use of a property that would produce the greatest net income and thereby develop the highest value.

holdover tenancy A tenancy whereby a lessee retains possession of leased property after the lease has expired and the landlord, by continuing to accept rent, agrees to the tenant's continued occupancy as defined by state law.

holographic will A will that is written, dated and signed in the testator's handwriting.

home equity loan A loan (sometimes called a *line of credit*) under which a property owner uses his or her residence as collateral and can then draw funds up to a prearranged amount against the property.

homeowner's insurance policy A standardized package insurance policy that covers a residential real estate owner against financial loss from fire, theft, public liability and other common risks.

homestead Land that is owned and occupied as the family home. In many states, a portion of the area or value of this land is protected or exempt from judgments for debts.

hypothecate To pledge property as security for an obligation or loan without giving up possession of it.

implied agreement A contract under which the agreement of the parties is demonstrated by their acts and conduct.

implied contract *See* implied agreement.

implied warranty of habitability A theory in landlord/tenant law in which the landlord renting residential property implies that the property is habitable and fit for its intended use.

improvement (1) Any structure, usually privately owned, erected on a site to enhance the value of the property—for example, building a fence or a driveway. (2) A publicly owned structure added to or benefiting land, such as a curb, sidewalk, street or sewer.

income approach The process of estimating the value of an income-producing property through capitalization of the annual net income expected to be produced by the property during its remaining useful life.

incorporeal right A nonpossessory right in real estate; for example, an easement or a right-of-way.

independent contractor Someone who is retained to perform a certain act but who is subject to the control and direction of another only as to the end result and not as to the way in which the act is performed. Unlike an employee, an independent contractor pays for all expenses and Social Security and income taxes and receives no employee benefits. Most real estate salespeople are independent contractors. *See also* employee.

index method The appraisal method of estimating building costs by multiplying the original cost of the property by a percentage factor to adjust for current construction costs.

inflation The gradual reduction of the purchasing power of the dollar, usually related directly to the increases in the money supply by the federal government.

inheritance taxes State-imposed taxes on a decedent's real and personal property.

installment contract A contract for the sale of real estate whereby the purchase price is paid in periodic installments by the purchaser, who is in possession of the property even though title is retained by the seller until a future date, which may not be until final payment. Also called a *contract for deed* or *articles of agreement for warranty deed*.

installment sale A transaction in which the sales price is paid in two or more installments over two or more years. If the sale meets certain requirements, a taxpayer can postpone reporting such income until future years by paying tax each year only on the proceeds received that year.

interest A charge made by a lender for the use of money.

interim financing A short-term loan usually made during the construction phase of a building project (in this case often referred to as a *construction loan*).

Interstate Land Sales Full Disclosure Act A federal law that regulates the sale of certain real estate in interstate commerce.

intestate The condition of a property owner who dies without leaving a valid will. Title to the property will pass to the decedent's heirs as provided in the state law of descent.

intrinsic value An appraisal term referring to the value created by a person's personal preferences for a particular type of property.

investment Money directed toward the purchase, improvement and development of an asset in expectation of income or profits.

involuntary alienation *See* alienation.

involuntary lien A lien placed on property without the consent of the property owner.

joint tenancy Ownership of real estate between two or more parties who have been named in one conveyance as joint tenants. Upon the death of a joint tenant, the decedent's interest passes to the surviving joint tenant or tenants by the *right of survivorship*.

joint venture The joining of two or more people to conduct a specific business enterprise. A joint venture is similar to a partnership in that it must be created by agreement between the parties to share in the losses and profits of the venture. It is unlike a partnership in that the venture is for one specific project only, rather than for a continuing business relationship.

judgment The formal decision of a court upon the respective rights and claims of the parties to an action or suit. After a judgment has been entered and recorded with the county recorder, it usually becomes a general lien on the property of the defendant.

judicial precedent In law, the requirements established by prior court decisions.

junior lien An obligation, such as a second mortgage, that is subordinate in right or lien priority to an existing lien on the same realty.

laches An equitable doctrine used by courts to bar a legal claim or prevent the assertion of a right because of undue delay or failure to assert the claim or right.

land The earth's surface, extending downward to the center of the earth and upward infinitely into space, including things permanently attached by nature, such as trees and water.

land contract *See* installment contract.

latent defect A hidden structural defect that could not be discovered by ordinary inspection and that threatens the property's soundness or the safety of its inhabitants. Some states impose on sellers and licensees a duty to inspect for and disclose latent defects.

law of agency *See* agency.

lease A written or oral contract between a landlord (the lessor) and a tenant (the lessee) that transfers the right to exclusive possession and use of the landlord's real property to the lessee for a specified period of time and for a stated consideration (rent). By state law leases for longer than a certain period of time (generally one year) must be in writing to be enforceable.

leasehold estate A tenant's right to occupy real estate during the term of a lease, generally considered to be a personal property interest.

lease option A lease under which the tenant has the right to purchase the property either during the lease term or at its end.

lease purchase The purchase of real property, the consummation of which is preceded by a lease, usually long-term. Typically done for tax or financing purposes.

legacy A disposition of money or personal property by will.

legal description A description of a specific parcel of real estate complete enough for an independent surveyor to locate and identify it.

legally competent parties People who are recognized by law as being able to contract with others; those of legal age and sound mind.

lessee *See* lease.

lessor *See* lease.

leverage The use of borrowed money to finance an investment.

levy To assess; to seize or collect. To levy a tax is to assess a property and set the rate of taxation. To levy an execution is to officially seize the property of a person in order to satisfy an obligation.

license (1) A privilege or right granted to a person by a state to operate as a real estate broker or salesperson. (2) The revocable permission for a temporary use of land—a personal right that cannot be sold.

lien A right given by law to certain creditors to have their debts paid out of the property of a defaulting debtor, usually by means of a court sale.

lien theory Some states interpret a mortgage as being purely a lien on real property. The mortgagee thus has no right of possession but must foreclose the lien and sell the property if the mortgagor defaults.

life cycle costing In property management, comparing one type of equipment with another based on both purchase cost and operating cost over its expected useful lifetime.

life estate An interest in real or personal property that is limited in duration to the lifetime of its owner or some other designated person or persons.

life tenant A person in possession of a life estate.

like-kind *See* exchange.

limited partnership *See* partnership.

line of credit See see home equity loan.

liquidated damages An amount predetermined by the parties to a contract as the total compensation to an injured party should the other party breach the contract.

liquidity The ability to sell an asset and convert it into cash, at a price close to its true value, in a short period of time.

lis pendens A recorded legal document giving constructive notice that an action affecting a particular property has been filed in either a state or a federal court.

listing agreement A contract between an owner (as principal) and a real estate broker (as agent) by which the broker is employed as agent to find a buyer for the owner's real estate on the owner's terms, for which service the owner agrees to pay a commission.

listing broker The broker in a multiple-listing situation from whose office a listing agreement is initiated, as opposed to the cooperating broker, from whose office negotiations leading up to a sale are initiated. The listing broker and the *cooperating broker* may be the same person.

littoral rights (1) A landowner's claim to use water in large navigable lakes and oceans adjacent to his or her property. (2) The ownership rights to land bordering these bodies of water up to the high-water mark.

loan origination fee A fee charged to the borrower by the lender for making a mortgage loan. The fee is usually computed as a percentage of the loan amount.

loan-to-value ratio The relationship between the amount of the mortgage loan and the value of the real estate being pledged as collateral.

lot-and-block (recorded plat) system A method of describing real property that identifies a parcel of land by reference to lot and block numbers within a subdivision, as specified on a recorded subdivision plat.

management agreement A contract between the owner of income property and a management firm or individual property manager that outlines the scope of the manager's authority.

market A place where goods can be bought and sold and a price established.

marketable title Good or clear title, reasonably free from the risk of litigation over possible defects.

market value The most probable price property would bring in an arm's-length transaction under normal conditions on the open market.

master plan A comprehensive plan to guide the long-term physical development of a particular area.

mechanic's lien A statutory lien created in favor of contractors, laborers and materialmen who have performed work or furnished materials in the erection or repair of a building.

meridian One of a set of imaginary lines running north and south and crossing a base line at a definite point, used in the rectangular (government) survey system of property description.

metes-and-bounds description A legal description of a parcel of land that begins at a well-marked point and follows the boundaries, using directions and distances around the tract, back to the place of beginning.

mill One-tenth of one cent. Some states use a mill rate to compute real estate taxes; for example, a rate of 52 mills would be $0.052 tax for each dollar of assessed valuation of a property.

minor Someone who has not reached the age of majority and therefore does not have legal capacity to transfer title to real property.

MLS *See* multiple-listing service.

monetary policy Governmental regulation of the amount of money in circulation through such institutions as the Federal Reserve Board.

month-to-month tenancy A periodic tenancy under which the tenant rents for one month at a time. In the absence of a rental agreement (oral or written) a tenancy is generally considered to be month to month.

monument A fixed natural or artificial object used to establish real estate boundaries for a metes-and-bounds description.

mortgage A conditional transfer or pledge of real estate as security for the payment of a debt. Also, the document creating a mortgage lien.

mortgage banker Mortgage loan companies that originate, service and sell loans to investors.

mortgage broker An agent of a lender who brings the lender and borrower together. The broker receives a fee for this service.

mortgagee A lender in a mortgage loan transaction.

mortgage lien A lien or charge on the property of a mortgagor that secures the underlying debt obligations.

mortgagor A borrower in a mortgage loan transaction.

multiperil policies Insurance policies that offer protection from a range of potential perils, such as those of a fire, hazard, public liability and casualty.

multiple-listing clause A provision in an exclusive listing for the authority and obligation on the part of the listing broker to distribute the listing to other brokers in the multiple-listing organization.

multiple-listing service (MLS) A marketing organization composed of member brokers who agree to share their listing agreements with one another in the hope of procuring ready, willing and able buyers for their properties more quickly than they could on their own. Most multiple-listing services accept exclusive-right-to-sell or exclusive-agency listings from their member brokers.

negotiable instrument A written promise or order to pay a specific sum of money that may be transferred by endorsement or delivery. The transferee then has the original payee's right to payment.

net lease A lease requiring the tenant to pay not only rent but also costs incurred in maintaining the property, including taxes, insurance, utilities and repairs.

net listing A listing based on the net price the seller will receive if the property is sold. Under a net listing the broker can offer the property for sale at the highest price obtainable to increase the commission. This type of listing is illegal in many states.

net operating income (NOI) The income projected for an income-producing property after deducting losses for vacancy and collection and operating expenses.

nonagent An intermediary between a buyer and seller, or landlord and tenant, who assists both parties with a transaction without representing either. Also known as a *facilitator, transaction broker, transaction coordinator* and *contract broker.*

nonconforming use A use of property that is permitted to continue after a zoning ordinance prohibiting it has been established for the area.

nonhomogeneity A lack of uniformity; dissimilarity. Because no two parcels of land are exactly alike, real estate is said to be nonhomogeneous.

note *See* promissory note.

novation Substituting a new obligation for an old one or substituting new parties to an existing obligation.

nuncupative will An oral will declared by the testator in his or her final illness, made before witnesses and afterward reduced to writing.

obsolescence The loss of value due to factors that are outmoded or less useful. Obsolescence may be functional or economic.

occupancy permit A permit issued by the appropriate local governing body to establish that the property is suitable for habitation by meeting certain safety and health standards.

offer and acceptance Two essential components of a valid contract; a "meeting of the minds."

offeror/offeree The person who makes the offer is the offeror. The person to whom the offer is made is the offeree.

Office of Thrift Supervision (OTS) Monitors and regulates the savings and loan industry. OTS was created by *FIRREA.*

open-end loan A mortgage loan that is expandable by increments up to a maximum dollar amount, the full loan being secured by the same original mortgage.

open listing A listing contract under which the broker's commission is contingent on the broker's producing a ready, willing and able buyer before the property is sold by the seller or another broker.

option An agreement to keep open for a set period an offer to sell or purchase property.

option listing Listing with a provision that gives the listing broker the right to purchase the listed property.

ostensible agency A form of implied agency relationship created by the actions of the parties involved rather than by written agreement or document.

package loan A real estate loan used to finance the purchase of both real property and personal property, such as in the purchase of a new home that includes carpeting, window coverings and major appliances.

parol evidence rule A rule of evidence providing that a written agreement is the final expression of the agreement of the parties, not to be varied or contradicted by prior or contemporaneous oral or written negotiations.

participation mortgage A mortgage loan wherein the lender has a partial equity interest in the property or receives a portion of the income from the property.

partition The division of cotenants' interests in real property when the parties do not all voluntarily agree to terminate the co-ownership; takes place through court procedures.

partnership An association of two or more individuals who carry on a continuing business for profit as co-owners. Under the law a partnership is regarded as a group of individuals rather than as a single entity. A *general partnership* is a typical form of joint venture in which each general partner shares in the administration, profits and losses of the operation. A *limited partnership* is a business arrangement whereby the operation is administered by one or more general partners and funded, by and large, by limited or silent partners, who are by law responsible for losses only to the extent of their investments.

party wall A wall that is located on or at a boundary line between two adjoining parcels of land and is used or is intended to be used by the owners of both properties.

patent A grant or franchise of land from the United States government.

payment cap The limit on the amount the monthly payment can be increased on an adjustable-rate mortgage when the interest rate is adjusted.

payoff statement *See* reduction certificate.

percentage lease A lease, commonly used for commercial property, whose rental is based on the tenant's gross sales at the premises; it usually stipulates a base monthly rental plus a percentage of any gross sales above a certain amount.

percolation test A test of the soil to determine if it will absorb and drain water adequately to use a septic system for sewage disposal.

periodic estate (tenancy) *See* estate from period to period.

personal property Items, called *chattels,* that do not fit into the definition of real property; movable objects.

physical deterioration A reduction in a property's value resulting from a decline in physical condition; can be caused by action of the elements or by ordinary wear and tear.

planned unit development (PUD) A planned combination of diverse land uses, such as housing, recreation and shopping, in one contained development or subdivision.

plat map A map of a town, section or subdivision indicating the location and boundaries of individual properties.

plottage The increase in value or utility resulting from the consolidation (assemblage) of two or more adjacent lots into one larger lot.

PMI *See* private mortgage insurance.

point of beginning (POB) In a metes-and-bounds legal description, the starting point of the survey, situated in one corner of the parcel; all metes-and-bounds descriptions must follow the boundaries of the parcel back to the point of beginning.

police power The government's right to impose laws, statutes and ordinances, including zoning ordinances and building codes, to protect the public health, safety and welfare.

power of attorney A written instrument authorizing a person, the *attorney-in-fact,* to act as agent for another person to the extent indicated in the instrument.

prepaid items On a closing statement, items that have been paid in advance by the seller, such as insurance premiums and some real estate taxes, for which he or she must be reimbursed by the buyer.

prepayment penalty A charge imposed on a borrower who pays off the loan principal early. This penalty compensates the lender for interest and other charges that would otherwise be lost.

price-fixing *See* antitrust laws.

primary mortgage market The mortgage market in which loans are originated and consisting of lenders such as commercial banks, savings and loan associations and mutual savings banks.

principal (1) A sum loaned or employed as a fund or an investment, as distinguished from its income or profits. (2) The original amount (as in a loan) of the total due and payable at a certain date. (3) A main party to a transaction—the person for whom the agent works.

principal meridian The main imaginary line running north and south and crossing a base line at a definite point, used by surveyors for reference in locating and describing land under the rectangular (government) survey system of legal description.

prior appropriation A concept of water ownership in which the landowner's right to use available water is based on a government-administered permit system.

priority The order of position or time. The priority of liens is generally determined by the chronological order in which the lien documents are recorded; tax liens, however, have priority even over previously recorded liens.

private mortgage insurance (PMI) Insurance provided by private carrier that protects a lender against a loss in the event of a foreclosure and deficiency.

probate A legal process by which a court determines who will inherit a decedent's property and what the estate's assets are.

procuring cause The effort that brings about the desired result. Under an open listing the broker who is the procuring cause of the sale receives the commission.

progression An appraisal principle that states that, between dissimilar properties. the value of the lesser-quality property is favorably affected by the presence of the better-quality property.

promissory note A financing instrument that states the terms of the underlying obligation, is signed by its maker and is negotiable (transferable to a third party).

property manager Someone who manages real estate for another person for compensation. Duties include collecting rents, maintaining the property and keeping up all accounting.

property reports The mandatory federal and state documents compiled by subdividers and developers to provide potential purchasers with facts about a property prior to their purchase.

proprietary lease A lease given by the corporation that owns a cooperative apartment building to the shareholder for the shareholder's right as a tenant to an individual apartment.

prorations Expenses, either prepaid or paid in arrears, that are divided or distributed between buyer and seller at the closing.

protected class Any group of people designated as such by the Department of Housing and Urban Development (HUD) in consideration of federal and state civil rights legislation. Currently includes ethnic minorities, women, religious groups, the handicapped and others.

PUD *See* planned unit development.

puffing Exaggerated or superlative comments or opinions.

pur autre vie "For the life of another." A life estate pur autre vie is a life estate that is measured by the life of a person other than the grantee.

purchase-money mortgage (PMM) A note secured by a mortgage or deed of trust given by a buyer, as borrower, to a seller, as lender, as part of the purchase price of the real estate.

pyramiding The process of acquiring additional properties by refinancing properties already owned and investing the loan proceeds in additional properties.

quantity-survey method The appraisal method of estimating building costs by calculating the cost of all of the physical components in the improvements, adding the cost to assemble them and then including the indirect costs associated with such construction.

quiet title A court action to remove a cloud on the title.

quitclaim deed A conveyance by which the grantor transfers whatever interest he or she has in the real estate, without warranties or obligations.

radon A naturally occurring gas that is suspected of causing lung cancer.

range A strip of land six miles wide, extending north and south and numbered east and west according to its distance from the principal meridian in the rectangular (government) survey system of legal description.

rate cap The limit on the amount the interest rate can be increased at each adjustment period in an adjustable-rate loan. The cap may also set the maximum interest rate that can be charged during the life of the loan.

ratification Method of creating an agency relationship in which the principal accepts the conduct of someone who acted without prior authorization as the principal's agent.

ready, **willing and able buyer** One who is prepared to buy property on the seller's terms and is ready to take positive steps to consummate the transaction.

real estate Land; a portion of the earth's surface extending downward to the center of the earth and upward infinitely into space, including all things permanently attached to it, whether naturally or artificially.

real estate investment syndicate *See* syndicate.

real estate investment trust (REIT) Trust ownership of real estate by a group of individuals who purchase certificates of ownership in the trust, which in turn invests the money in real property and distributes the profits back to the investors free of corporate income tax.

real estate license law State law enacted to protect the public from fraud, dishonesty and incompetence in the purchase and sale of real estate.

real estate mortgage investment conduit (REMIC) A tax entity that issues multiple classes of investor interests (securities) backed by a pool of mortgages.

real estate recovery fund A fund established in some states from real estate license revenues to cover claims of aggrieved parties who have suffered monetary damage through the actions of a real estate licensee.

Real Estate Settlement Procedures Act (RESPA) The federal law that requires certain disclosures to consumers about mortgage loan settlements. The law also prohibits the payment or receipt of kickbacks and certain kinds of referral fees.

real property The interests, benefits and rights inherent in real estate ownership.

REALTOR® A registered trademark term reserved for the sole use of active members of local REALTOR® boards affiliated with the National Association of REALTOR®.

reconciliation The final step in the appraisal process, in which the appraiser combines the estimates of value received from the sales comparison, cost and income approaches to arrive at a final estimate of market value for the subject property.

reconveyance deed A deed used by a trustee under a deed of trust to return title to the trustor.

recording The act of entering or recording documents affecting or conveying interests in real estate in the recorder's office established in each county. Until it is recorded, a deed or mortgage ordinarily is not effective against subsequent purchasers or mortgagees.

rectangular (government) survey system A system established in 1785 by the federal government, providing for surveying and describing land by reference to principal meridians and base lines.

redemption The right of a defaulted property owner to recover his or her property by curing the default.

redemption period A period of time established by state law during which a property owner has the right to redeem his or her real estate from a foreclosure or tax sale by paying the sales price, interest and costs. Many states do not have mortgage redemption laws.

redlining The illegal practice of a lending institution denying loans or restricting their number for certain areas of a community.

reduction certificate (payoff statement) The document signed by a lender indicating the amount required to pay a loan balance in full and satisfy the debt; used in the settlement process to protect both the seller's and the buyer's interests.

registrar *See* Torrens system.

regression An appraisal principle that states that, between dissimilar properties, the value of the better-quality property is affected adversely by the presence of the lesser-quality property.

Regulation Z Implements the Truth-in-Lending Act requiring credit institutions to inform borrowers of the true cost of obtaining credit.

release deed A document, also known as a *deed of reconveyance,* that transfers all rights given a trustee under a deed of trust loan back to the grantor after the loan has been fully repaid.

remainder interest The remnant of an estate that has been conveyed to take effect and be enjoyed after the termination of a prior estate, such as when an owner conveys a life estate to one party and the remainder to another.

rent A fixed, periodic payment made by a tenant of a property to the owner for possession and use, usually by prior agreement of the parties.

rent schedule A statement of proposed rental rates, determined by the owner or the property manager or both, based on a building's estimated expenses, market supply and demand and the owner's long-range goals for the property.

replacement cost The construction cost at current prices of a property that is not necessarily an exact duplicate of the subject property but serves the same purpose or function as the original.

reproduction cost The construction cost at current prices of an exact duplicate of the subject property.

Resolution Trust Corporation The organization created by *FIRREA* to liquidate the assets of failed savings and loan associations.

RESPA *See* Real Estate Sttlement Procedures Act.

restrictive covenants A clause in a deed that limits the way that the real estate ownership may be used.

reverse-annuity mortgage (RAM) A loan under which the homeowner receives monthly payments based on his or her accumulated equity rather than a lump sum. The loan must be repaid at a prearranged date or upon the death of the owner or the sale of the property.

reversionary interest The remnant of an estate that the grantor holds after granting a life estate to another person.

reversionary right The return of the rights of possession and quiet enjoyment to the lessor at the expiration of a lease.

right of survivorship *See* joint tenancy.

right-of-way The right given by one landowner to another to pass over the land, construct a roadway or use as a pathway, without actually transferring ownership.

riparian rights An owner's rights in land that borders on or includes a stream, river or lake. These rights include access to and use of the water.

risk management Evaluation and selection of appropriate property and other insurance.

rules and regulations Real estate licensing authority orders that govern licensees' activities; they usually have the same force and effect as statutory law.

sale and leaseback A transaction in which an owner sells his or her improved property and, as part of the same transaction, signs a long-term lease to remain in possession of the premises.

sales comparison approach The process of estimating the value of a property by examining and comparing actual sales of comparable properties.

salesperson A person who performs real estate activities while employed by or associated with a licensed real estate broker.

SARA *See* Superfund Amendments and Reauthorization Act.

satisfaction of mortgage A document acknowledging the payment of a mortgage debt.

secondary mortgage market A market for the purchase and sale of existing mortgages, designed to provide greater liquidity for mortgages; also called the *secondary money market*. Mortgages are first originated in the *primary mortgage market*.

section A portion of township under the rectangular (government) survey system. A township is divided into 36 sections, numbered one through 36. A section is a square with mile-long sides and an area of one square mile, or 640 acres.

security agreement *See* Uniform Commercial Code.

security deposit A payment by a tenant, held by the landlord during the lease term and kept (wholly or partially) on default or destruction of the premises by the tenant.

separate property Under community property law, property owned solely by either spouse before the marriage, acquired by gift or inheritance after the marriage or purchased with separate funds after the marriage.

servient tenement Land on which an easement exists in favor of an adjacent property (called a *dominant estate*); also called a servient estate. *See* dominant tenement.

setback The amount of space local zoning regulations require between a lot line and a building line.

severalty Ownership of real property by one person only, also called *sole ownership*.

severance Changing an item of real estate to personal property by detaching it from the land; for example, cutting down a tree.

sharecropping In an agricultural lease, the agreement between the landowner and the tenant farmer to split the crop or the profit from its sale, actually sharing the crop.

shared-appreciation mortgage (SAM) A mortgage loan in which the lender, in exchange for a loan with a favorable interest rate, participates in the profits (if any) the borrower receives when the property is eventually sold.

situs The personal preference of people for one area over another, not necessarily based on objective facts and knowledge.

sole ownership *See* severalty.

special agent One who is authorized by a principal to perform a single act or transaction; a real estate broker is usually a special agent authorized to find a ready, willing and able buyer for a particular property.

special assessment A tax or levy customarily imposed against only those specific parcels of real estate that will benefit from a proposed public improvement like a street or sewer.

special warranty deed A deed in which the grantor warrants, or guarantees, the title only against defects arising during the period of his or her tenure and ownership of the property and not against defects existing before that time, generally using the language, "by, through or under the grantor but not otherwise."

specific lien A lien affecting or attaching only to a certain, specific parcel of land or piece of property.

specific performance A legal action to compel a party to carry out the terms of a contract.

square-foot method The appraisal method of estimating building costs by multiplying the number of square feet in the improvements being appraised by the cost per square foot for recently constructed similar improvements.

statute of frauds That part of a state law that requires certain instruments, such as deeds, real estate sales contracts and certain leases, to be in writing to be legally enforceable.

statute of limitations That law pertaining to the period of time within which certain actions must be brought to court.

statutory lien A lien imposed on property by statute—a tax lien, for example—in contrast to an equitable lien, which arises out of common law.

statutory redemption The right of a defaulted property owner to recover the property after its sale by paying the appropriate fees and charges.

steering The illegal practice of channeling home seekers to particular areas, either to maintain the homogeneity of an area or to change the character of an area, which limits their choices of where they can live.

stigmatized property A property that has acquired an undesirable reputation due to an event that occurred on or near it, such as violent crime, gang-related activity, illness or personal tragedy. Some states restrict the disclosure of information about stigmatized properties.

straight-line method A method of calculating depreciation for tax purposes, computed by dividing the adjusted basis of a property by the estimated number of years of remaining useful life.

straight (term) loan A loan in which only interest is paid during the term of the loan, with the entire principal amount due with the final interest payment.

subagent One who is employed by a person already acting as an agent. Typically a reference to a salesperson licensed under a broker (agent) who is employed under the terms of a listing agreement.

subdivider One who buys undeveloped land, divides it into smaller, usable lots and sells the lots to potential users.

subdivision A tract of land divided by the owner, known as the *subdivider,* into blocks, building lots and streets according to a recorded subdivision plat, which must comply with local ordinances and regulations.

subdivision and development ordinances Municipal ordinances that establish requirements for subdivisions and development.

subdivision plat *See* plat map.

sublease *See* subletting.

subletting The leasing of premises by a lessee to a third party for part of the lessee's remaining term. *See also* assignment.

subordination Relegation to a lesser position, usually in respect to a right or security.

subordination agreement A written agreement between holders of liens on a property that changes the priority of mortgage, judgment and other liens under certain circumstances.

subrogation The substitution of one creditor for another, with the substituted person succeeding to the legal rights and claims of the original claimant. Subrogation is used by title insurers to acquire from the injured party rights to sue in order to recover any claims they have paid.

substitution An appraisal principle that states that the maximum value of a property tends to be set by the cost of purchasing an equally desirable and valuable substitute property, assuming that no costly delay is encountered in making the substitution.

subsurface rights Ownership rights in a parcel of real estate to the water, minerals, gas, oil and so forth that lie beneath the surface of the property.

suit for possession A court suit initiated by a landlord to evict a tenant from leased premises after the tenant has breached one of the terms of the lease or has held possession of the property after the lease's expiration.

suit to quiet title A court action intended to establish or settle the title to a particular property, especially when there is a cloud on the title.

Superfund Popular name of the hazardous-waste cleanup fund established by the Comprehensive Environmental Response, Compensation and Liability Act (CERCLA).

Superfund Amendments and Reauthorization Act (SARA) An amendatory statute that contains stronger cleanup standards for contaminated sites, increased funding for Superfund and clarifications of lender liability and innocent landowner immunity. *See* Comprehensive Environmental Response, Compensation and Liability Act (CERCLA).

supply The amount of goods available in the market to be sold at a given price. The term is often coupled with *demand.*

supply and demand The appraisal principle that follows the interrelationship of the supply of and demand for real estate. As appraising is based on economic concepts, this principle recognizes that real property is subject to the influences of the marketplace just as is any other commodity.

surety bond An agreement by an insurance or bonding company to be responsible for certain possible defaults, debts or obligations contracted for by an insured party; in essence, a policy insuring one's personal and/or financial integrity. In the real estate business a surety bond is generally used to ensure that a particular project will be completed at a certain date or that a contract will be performed as stated.

surface rights Ownership rights in a parcel of real estate that are limited to the surface of the property and do not include the air above it *(air rights)* or the minerals below the surface *(subsurface rights).*

survey The process by which boundaries are measured and land areas are determined; the on-site measurement of lot lines, dimensions and position of a house on a lot, including the determination of any existing encroachments or easements.

syndicate A combination of people or firms formed to accomplish a business venture of mutual interest by pooling resources. In a *real estate investment syndicate* the parties own and/or develop property, with the main profit generally arising from the sale of the property.

tacking Adding or combining successive periods of continuous occupation of real property by adverse possessors. This concept enables someone who has not been in possession for the entire statutory period to establish a claim of adverse possession.

taxation The process by which a government or municipal quasi-public body raises monies to fund its operation.

tax credit An amount by which tax owed is reduced directly.

tax deed An instrument, similar to a certificate of sale, given to a purchaser at a tax sale. *See also* certificate of sale.

tax lien A charge against property, created by operation of law. Tax liens and assessments take priority over all other liens.

tax sale A court-ordered sale of real property to raise money to cover delinquent taxes.

tenancy by the entirety The joint ownership, recognized in some states, of property acquired by husband and wife during marriage. Upon the death of one spouse, the survivor becomes the owner of the property.

tenancy in common A form of co-ownership by which each owner holds an undivided interest in real property as if he or she were sole owner. Each individual owner has the right to partition. Unlike joint tenants, tenants in common have right of inheritance.

tenant One who holds or possesses lands or tenements by any kind of right or title.

tenant improvements Alterations to the interior of a building to meet the functional demands of the tenant.

testate Having made and left a valid will.

testator A person who has made a valid will. A woman often is referred to as a *testatrix,* although testator can be used for either gender.

tier (township strip) A strip of land six miles wide, extending east and west and numbered north and south according to its distance from the base line in the rectangular (government) survey system of legal description.

time is of the essence A phrase in a contract that requires the performance of a certain act within a stated period of time.

time-share A form of ownership interest that may include an estate interest in property and which allows use of the property for a fixed or variable time period.

title (1) The right to or ownership of land. (2) The evidence of ownership of land.

title insurance A policy insuring the owner or mortgagee against loss by reason of defects in the title to a parcel of real estate, other than encumbrances, defects and matters specifically excluded by the policy.

title search The examination of public records relating to real estate to determine the current state of the ownership.

title theory Some states interpret a mortgage to mean that the lender is the owner of mortgaged land. Upon full payment of the mortgage debt, the borrower becomes the landowner.

Torrens system A method of evidencing title by registration with the proper public authority, generally called the *registrar;* named for its founder, Sir Robert Torrens.

township The principal unit of the rectangular (government) survey system. A township is a square with six-mile sides and an area of 36 square miles.

township strips *See* tier.

trade fixture An article installed by a tenant under the terms of a lease and removable by the tenant before the lease expires.

transfer tax Tax stamps required to be affixed to a deed by state and/or local law.

transaction broker *See* nonagent.

transaction coordinator *See* nonagent.

trust A fiduciary arrangement whereby property is conveyed to a person or institution, called a *trustee,* to be held and administered on behalf of another person, called a *beneficiary.* The one who conveys the trust is called the *trustor.*

trust account *See* escrow account.

trust deed An instrument used to create a mortgage lien by which the borrower conveys title to a trustee, who holds it as security for the benefit of the note holder (the lender); also called a *deed of trust.*

trust deed lien A lien on the property of a trustor that secures a deed of trust loan.

trustee The holder of bare legal title in a deed of trust loan transaction.

trustee's deed A deed executed by a trustee conveying land held in a trust.

trustor A borrower in a deed of trust loan transaction.

undivided interest *See* tenancy in common.

unenforceable contract A contract that has all the elements of a valid contract, yet neither party can sue the other to force performance of it. For example, an unsigned contract is generally unenforceable.

Uniform Commercial Code A codification of commercial law, adopted in most states, that attempts to make uniform all laws relating to commercial transactions, including chattel mortgages and bulk transfers.

Security interests in chattels are created by an instrument known as a *security agreement*. To give notice of the security interest, a *financing statement* must be recorded. Article 6 of the Code regulates *bulk transfers*—the sale of a business as a whole, including all fixtures, chattels and merchandise.

unilateral contract A one-sided contract wherein one party makes a promise so as to induce a second party to do something. The second party is not legally bound to perform; however, if the second party does comply, the first party is obligated to keep the promise.

unit-in-place method The appraisal method of estimating building costs by calculating the costs of all of the physical components in the structure, with the cost of each item including its proper installation, connection, etc.; also called the *segregated cost method.*

unit of ownership The four unities that are traditionally needed to create a joint tenancy—unity of title, time, interest and possession.

usury Charging interest at a higher rate than the maximum rate established by state law.

valid contract A contract that complies with all the essentials of a contract and is binding and enforceable on all parties to it.

VA loan A mortgage loan on approved property made to a qualified veteran by an authorized lender and guaranteed by the Department of Veterans Affairs in order to limit the lender's possible loss.

value The power of a good or service to command other goods in exchange for the present worth of future rights to its income or amenities.

variance Permission obtained from zoning authorities to build a structure or conduct a use that is expressly prohibited by the current zoning laws; an exception from the zoning ordinances.

vendee A buyer, usually under the terms of a land contract.

vendor A seller, usually under the terms of a land contract.

voidable contract A contract that seems to be valid on the surface but may be rejected or disaffirmed by one or both of the parties.

void contract A contract that has no legal force or effect because it does not meet the essential elements of a contract.

voluntary alienation *See* alienation.

voluntary lien A lien placed on property with the knowledge and consent of the property owner.

waste An improper use or an abuse of a property by a possessor who holds less than fee ownership, such as a tenant, life tenant, mortgagor or vendee. Such waste ordinarily impairs the value of the land or the interest of the person holding the title or the reversionary rights.

will A written document, properly witnessed, providing for the transfer of title to property owned by the deceased, called the *testator.*

workers' compensation acts Laws that require an employer to obtain insurance coverage to protect his or her employees who are injured in the course of their employment.

wraparound loan A method of refinancing in which the new mortgage is placed in a secondary, or subordinate, position; the new mortgage includes both the unpaid principal balance of the first mortgage and whatever additional sums are advanced by the lender. In essence, it is an additional mortgage in which another lender refinances a borrower by lending an amount over the existing first mortgage amount without disturbing the existence of the first mortgage.

zoning ordinance An exercise of police power by a municipality to regulate and control the character and use of property.

$950 - Rent
$100 - cable/phone
$100 - cell
$220 - daycare
$60 - water
$140 - elec
$300 - food&hh
$80 - gas
$2000

80 Student loan
200 savings/month

2280

1150
2
2200
+ 300
2500

5K
2K
$7K

$2000 - car
$1000 ins
$1.500 couch/tables

4500

1000 savings

5500

1500 left to
$950 1st mo rent

$550 left to purchase
w/h items needed/food